The Altruistic Imagination

Long March, Short Spring: The Student Uprisings at Home and Abroad
(with Barbara Ehrenreich)

The American Health Empire: Power, Profits and Politics
(with Barbara Ehrenreich)

The Cultural Crisis of Modern Medicine
(edited)

The Altruistic Imagination

A HISTORY OF SOCIAL WORK AND

SOCIAL POLICY IN THE UNITED STATES

John H. Ehrenreich

Cornell University Press

ITHACA AND LONDON

First published 1985 by Cornell University Press

Printed in the United States of America

Library of Congress Cataloging in Publication Data

Ehrenreich, John, 1943–
The altruistic imagination.

Bibliography: p.
Includes index.
1. Social service—United Sates—History.   2. United States—Social
policy—History.   I. Title.
HV91.E38   1985   361.3'0973   84-45807
ISBN 0-8014-1764-3 (alk. paper)

Cornell University Press strives to use environmentally responsible suppliers and
materials to the fullest extent possible in the publishing of its books. Such materials
include vegetable-based, low-VOC inks and acid-free papers that are recycled, totally
chlorine-free, or partly composed of nonwood fibers.

Cloth printing   10   9   8

For Sharon

Contents

A house divided against itself cannot stand.
Abraham Lincoln, 1858

Two souls, alas! are lodged within my breast.
Which struggle there for undivided reign . . .
Johann Wolfgang von Goethe, 1808
(trans. Anna Swanwick)

Preface

Social policy and social work are central to the functioning of modern American society. Merely to list the concerns of social *policy* is to underscore its importance: poverty, economic insecurity, and their consequences; inequality and discrimination (by race and sex but also by age, physical handicap, and other conditions); education, both in the broad sense of socialization of the young into the dominant social values and in the narrower sense of transmission of specific ideas, skills, and facts; deviance, ranging from crime and delinquency to individual mental illness, maladjustment, difficulty in coping with stress; health and health care; family structure, norms of behavior within the family, and sexual mores; and more.

Social *work*'s importance, most obviously, is as the occupation that administers or delivers many of these services or policies. But such a formulation minimizes the significance of social work. Social work serves as a key mediator between virtually all other professions and their clients and between a wide variety of bureaucratic institutions and the people they serve. It is a major transmitter of ideology, with respect to such concerns as child rearing, sexual behavior, and deviance. As mediators, "humanizers," administrators, advocates, watchdogs, and therapists, social workers intrude into the central life concerns of all social classes.

Social work and social policy are, of course, intimately associated. To mention Jane Addams is to evoke the social reforms of the Progressive Era; to name Harry Hopkins is to enter upon a discussion of the New Deal and the creation of the modern welfare state.

9

Lyndon Johnson's War on Poverty, whatever its impact on the poor, was virtually a jobs program for social workers; and a large fraction of contemporary social work jobs are directly or indirectly created, or financed, by government action.

But the relation between social work and social policy is neither clear nor untroubled. In the early years of this century, prominent caseworkers such as Mary Richmond and prominent social reformers such as Simon Patten debated the relative merits of what Richmond called the "retail" and "wholesale" methods of social reform (i.e., casework and social policy).[1] In the thirties, with millions out of work and the demand for massive governmental relief policies growing, Miriam Van Waters, president of the National Conference of Social Work, wrote: "A program cannot make men moral, religious, or happy. The springs of action are in the internal nature of man. Hence the uselessness of programs, especially those that depend upon state action or force."[2] And in 1978, George Gilder, the guru of Reaganite social and economic policy, wrote: "To get a grip on the problems of poverty, one should also forget the idea of overcoming inequality by redistribution. . . . The only dependable route from poverty is always work, family, and faith."[3] Again and again the tension between social policy and social work, between social reform and individual change, between explaining human misery in terms of the social environment and explaining it in terms of individual character flaws, has reappeared.

Browsing in almost any recent issue of the major social work and social policy journals reveals some contemporary forms of this tension. From the perspective of the social worker, for instance, consider the editorial, written by Anne Minahan, in the May 1980 issue of *Social Work*, the journal of the National Association of Social Workers.[4] Minahan asks, "What is clinical work when it is performed by a clinical social worker?" To some social workers, the answer to that question may be obvious, and its relevance to broader issues of social policy may seem nonexistent. But Minahan herself goes on to note that there are practically as many answers to her question as there are clinical social workers. Raising a series of issues on which she sees clinical social workers as sharply divided, Minahan asks: "Is the environment merely a backdrop or stage set that affects individual emotions, cognition, and behavior, and thus should be understood by the social worker but not viewed as a legitimate target for change? . . . Should the social worker always focus on

10

unconscious drives and fantasies of the client? [Or] should a social worker focus on the conscious coping behavior of people and their aspirations and life choices?" In partial answer to her own questions, Minahan lists a number of environmental concerns impinging on the individual that make a simple, individual-change–oriented response untenable: "inflation, reduction in spending for social programs, unemployment of youth, huge service bureaucracies, energy crises, high interest, loss of money for the aged and people on public assistance, anxiety about the draft, fear of war, and uncertainty about the future." All this, I might add, was what Minahan suggested clinical social workers had to worry about in their work with individual clients eight months *before* Ronald Reagan took office.

In another article in the same issue of *Social Work,* Eda Goldstein raises what appears superficially to be a very different question.[5] What, Goldstein asks, is the "knowledge base" of clinical social work? But she quickly acknowledges:

> Historically the social work profession has reflected a dual commitment. Efforts have on one hand been directed toward enhancing the functioning of individuals and on the other have been focused on promoting a better society and environments that are more responsive to human needs. . . . The behavioral sciences in general, psychodynamic theories in particular, and strategies for individual change constituted one pole, while the social sciences, theories of social change, and strategies for social action represented the second. A worker's familiarity with one knowledge base signaled ignorance of the relevant facts and theories of the other.

Quoting social work administrator Max Silverstein, she suggests that this tension can be resolved by understanding that "the locus of social work practice is neither in the 'inner psychological' nor in the 'outer reality' but in the crucial life space where inner and outer confront each other."

This book is concerned with the struggle of social workers and social policy planners to locate that "space where inner and outer confront each other." How have social workers and social policy makers understood (or not understood) that space, and why? What constitutes the conflicts and linkages between inner psychological space and outer social reality, between the historic domains of "casework" and those of "social policy"? Why have the various approaches to this problem created so much controversy, generated such unbridgeable gaps within social work and between case-workers and policy planners? Why has it been so hard to find middle positions, to design social programs or modes of individual intervention that speak to that point of inner and outer "confrontation"?

My starting point is in the observation that this problem is as old as social work and social policy themselves. The history of social work and of social policy is one long account of pendulum swings between the two poles—between a focus on individual treatment and a focus on social reform. Very crudely, in the last decades of the nineteenth century, the 1920s, the 1940s and 1950s, and the present time, the more individual orientation has predominated (and along with it, despair as to the possibility of reform and disdain for social action). Conversely, in the years before World War I, the 1930s, and the 1960s, community action and social reform dominated the attention of social workers and planners, and casework fell into a degree of disrepute.

This sequence of alternation has several major implications for our understanding of social work and social policy. First, clearly, there is no one "right" answer. One generation's certainty has been the next generation's foolishness and blindness. And in the following generation, positions again reverse. The question we must ask, then, is not "Which position is right?" but rather "Why does each position appear so persuasive at different historical moments?"

Second, the alternation between dominant perspectives suggests that the problem of the relationship between individual and social-environmental etiologies and solutions is not simply an objectively existing problem, out there in the world for social analysts to ponder and investigate. Rather, I would suggest that the conflict is built into the nature of social policy and social work practice; it is built into the act of trying to change individual or social realities rather than into the structure of reality itself. The clinician, focusing on the individual, is forced to identify real-world problems that are causally related to the client's intrapsychic problems, problems that must be solved to effect change in the individual. Conversely, the most optimistic policy maker and reformer is quickly forced to confront the difficulties and complexities of mobilizing people for change—even for changes that, viewed "objectively," are in their own individual best interests. And so even the practitioner most oriented to change is

12

forced to recognize the need for social reform, and the most energetic activist or policy planner is forced to deal with individuals, the imperfect human material on which reforms rest. The oscillations in social work attitudes that create the individual-change–social-change pendulum can be analyzed only in terms of this practical tension.

③ Third, the crude timetable suggested earlier for the alternation of positions parallels, of course, broader political, social, and ideological currents. The Progressive Era, the 1930s, and the 1960s were all periods of massive social unrest, in which broad-based movements for social change accelerated large-scale expansions of the role of government. Conversely, the interim periods have been characterized by the repression and decline of social movements, retreat into political apathy and acquiescence, and, to a degree, the rolling back of earlier reforms. The history of social work and social policy is in a sense "overdetermined." We can explain its oscillations within a framework of a history of social work and social policy alone, but at the same time, we can explain them as nothing more than one reflection of a larger history. And still again, the larger history, in significant measure, was influenced by the development of social work and social policy.

Bertha Reynolds, associate director of the Smith College School for Social Work in the late twenties and thirties, a leading psychiatric social worker of the period but also a radical political activist, wrote: "The philosophy of social work cannot be separated from the prevailing philosophy of a nation, as to how it values people and what importance it sets upon their welfare. . . . Practice is always shaped by the needs of the times, the problems they present, the fears they generate, the solutions that appeal, and the knowledge and skill available."[6] I would suggest that it is the character of social work and social policy—endeavors focused on the intersection between the individual and the social, and constantly pulled between these two poles—that makes them sensitive to the broader social currents.

In the following chapters the history of social policy and social work is organized more or less chronologically, but threaded through the chronological account are a series of continuing themes.

First, social work and social policy function within a specific political, social, and cultural context. Their history has been shaped by three interacting variables: the rise and fall of massive social movements, creating fluctuating pressures for social reform; the ongoing concern of social workers to enhance their professional status and power in the face of changing economic, political, and institutional circumstances; and finally, the changing needs of American business to rationalize and regulate its markets, work force, and political environment.

Second, the nature of social reform bears investigation. Throughout its history, social reform has had multiple motives. Ostensibly aimed at the amelioration of social need, it has often served the needs of businesses and professional groups more effectively than it has those groups for whom it was supposedly designed. True, amelioration has been granted, but grudgingly and only under intense pressure.

Third, social work, too, has had multiple faces. Engaged in providing desperately needed services to individuals, families, groups, and communities, social workers are, at the same time, agents of social control. This dual role intrudes into the most intimate recesses of the social worker–client relationship, itself a close alliance threatened with tensions and confounded by class, race, ethnic, and gender issues.

Fourth, social work, perhaps more than any other major profession, has been obsessed with professional status. What, it has asked, is the appropriate "knowledge base" for professional social workers? What is the proper division of labor and authority among social work, psychiatry, psychology, and other helping professions? What are the proper boundaries between social worker and client? How can social work increase its prestige and its material conditions of work? Behind these questions lurk more basic issues about the nature of professions in modern industrial societies.

Fifth, the relationship between individual change and social change demands attention. Social workers and social reformers have at different times embraced different theories. Some have focused on the deviant individual, others on the defective culture (for example, the "culture of poverty"), and yet others on the larger economic, political, and social structure, the "social environment." Correspondingly, some have focused their energies on changing individuals, others on changing society. Only rarely have social workers and social reformers thought systematically about the relation between the two forms of change.

Finally, although the orientation of this book is historical, its ultimate aim is to illuminate the central issues facing social work and social policy today. In the mid-eighties, both social work and social policy appear to be at a crossroads in their history. Social work appears less unified as a profession, less certain of its direction than at any time since the 1920s. The social policy initiatives of the last half century face a vigorous and, for the moment at least, successful counterattack; the traditional forces for reform are in disarray. American political coalitions are in flux; the international economy is in crisis; and personal and cultural norms and behaviors are in transition.

Thirty years ago, in the early days of McCarthyism, Bertha Reynolds wrote that social workers were faced with "a choice between contradictory forces in our society: those which are moving toward the welfare of the people, as the people's own concern and responsibility, and those which destroy human life in preventable misery and war, and relieve poverty only grudgingly to keep the privileged position they hold."[7]

Her words continue to resonate.

This book grew out of a course in the history of American social work and social policy which I have taught at the Smith College School for Social Work since 1980. To my students in that course I owe an enormous debt. They have inspired, encouraged, criticized, probed, and contributed their own rich experience. Thanks also are due Cathy Riessman (who brought me to Smith in the first place) and Margaret Cerullo, both of whom provided insightful feedback on the lectures in the course, and Jill Kerr Conway, who delivered a regular and insightful guest lecture in the course.

I also have incurred a number of specific intellectual debts. The history of American social policy and of social work cannot be understood outside the context of the social forces and movements for social justice that have shaped modern American history. My understanding of those forces and movements has been heavily influenced by my colleagues in the American Studies Program at the College at Old Westbury (New York). I am especially grateful to my fellow teachers in the team-taught American history course "The American People": over the years these have included Ros Baxandall, Liz Ewen, Eddy Gouraige, Paul Lauter, John McDermott, Naomi Rosenthal, Laura Schwartz, Elaine Scott, and Steve Talbot. Laura Schwartz and my father, Joseph Ehrenreich, read chapters and provided useful substantive and editorial advice.

Much of the central thesis of Chapter 1, on the Progressive Era, was worked out several years ago in collaboration with Barbara Ehrenreich, who has kindly permitted me to reprint, in somewhat modified form, portions of our joint work. For my understanding of the mental hygiene movement of the teens and twenties, I am indebted to Christine Shea's masterful doctoral dissertation, "The Ideology of Mental Health and the Emergence of the Therapeutic Liberal State," and to a number of valuable discussions with her about it. I have also been heavily influenced by the ideas of Richard Cloward and Frances Fox Piven on social movements and the function of the welfare system.

Karen Kuester Rossler and Melanie Fletcher-Howell expertly typed the manuscript.

In writing a book, one also incurs debts that are less easily specified. To my parents, Joseph Ehrenreich and the late Freda Ehrenreich, and to their extraordinary, close, and enduring circle of teacher and social worker friends, I owe the understanding, far deeper than I could have obtained from intellectual effort alone, that a passion for social justice and involvement in social action can coexist with and inform human service work directed at individuals. I owe them an intellectual, emotional, and moral debt too deep and complex to express in words.

My children, Rosa and Benjy Ehrenreich, were patient, good-humored, and encouraging, despite my frequent immersion in the pains and hassles of producing a book. I owe them thanks, as well, for keeping before me a vivid and personal vision of the kind of just and humane society that I dream of for them, a society that social work at its best has dared to advocate.

Finally, Sharon McQuaide read and reread every chapter, offering me a wealth of insights as well as editorial comments. She has provided a model of a humane, socially informed social work practice. More personally, her steadfast enthusiasm and support and love made it possible for me to write this book.

JOHN H. EHRENREICH

Northampton, Massachusetts

16

The Altruistic Imagination

1

The Origins of
American Social Policy

Modern American social policy and the social work profession as we know it today were born in the Progressive Era, the two decades or so immediately preceding World War I.[1] To understand social policy and social work by examining them in their contemporary, "mature" form would require a difficult task of excavation. We would have to unravel their "true" natures from their self-descriptions and aspirations, to get under their surfaces to identify the functions they serve, the social forces they represent, the logic of their structure. To go back in time, however, to a period when the very idea of "social policy," the very concept of "social work" had not yet been developed, when no names had yet been applied to link disparate ideas, occupations, and social purposes, is to simplify our task radically. For in the formative period, the fears and hopes that created social policy and engendered social work were openly stated, clearly revealed.

At a distance of almost a century, we tend to romanticize the turn-of-the-century years. They were the "gay nineties," the years of "Daisy, Daisy, give me your answer, do," of Teddy Roosevelt charging up San Juan Hill to the cheers of small-town America, of children shouting "Get a horse" to the first intrepid motorists. But, in fact, the decades from 1877 to World War I were a time of deep economic, social, and political crisis in American society. Social work and social policy first emerged as a more-or-less conscious effort to deal with that crisis, to stabilize American industrial society. To understand that effort, we must first examine the turn-of-the-century crisis in some detail.

The half century following the Civil War was the great period of industrialization in the United States. From a predominantly agricultural, rural land, of no great importance in the world, the United States became the world's leading industrial power. A few statistics tell the story well enough for our purposes: the 37,000 miles of railroad track of 1865 multiplied sevenfold, to 253,000 miles, 39 percent of the entire world's total, by 1914. Energy production—a good measure of both industrialization and urbanization—soared: coal from 15 million tons in 1860 to 514 million tons in 1914, oil from 74 million barrels over the period 1857–75 to 266 million barrels in 1914 alone. In 1859, just before the Civil War, slightly more than 1 million industrial workers produced industrial goods worth about $2 billion and more than 60 percent of the U.S. labor force was still engaged in agriculture. By 1914 seven times as many workers labored in industry, producing twelve times as many goods as half a century earlier, and the proportions of agricultural and nonagricultural workers were reversed: 69 percent of the work force had *non*agricultural jobs.[2]

Industrial growth itself is not important, however. The importance of industrialization lies, rather, in the impact that it had on society—on social institutions, on people's lives, on people's consciousness. And to see this impact, it is important to reemphasize the rapidity of the changes: they took place *within the life-span of a single generation.* Consider a few of the most striking changes:

First, industrialization literally transformed the American landscape. A predominantly rural and small-town society at the end of the Civil War, the United States became an urban culture by the 1920s. New York City, already over a million people in 1860, grew to some 5.6 million by 1920. Chicago, a town of about 100,000 just before the Civil War, grew to almost 2 million souls by the end of World War I. The growing cities absorbed the rural populations, literally swallowing up vast areas surrounding them. By 1910, 92 percent of the population of Massachusetts and 79 percent of the population of New York lived in what the Census Bureau defined as "urban areas." The sense of community, the face-to-face interactions between people from all walks of life that had characterized the small town were, for most Americans, a vanished dream.

The vast increases in both the population and the physical size of the cities presented Americans with an entirely new set of problems. There was the problem of transporting people and goods to and within the metropolis, a problem met in the 1890s and early years of this century with the creation and expansion of systems of trolley cars and urban railways (subways, elevated trains). There was a housing crisis: vast slum districts arose as builders threw together flimsy, unsafe housing for the millions of new immigrants to the cities. The tenth ward on New York's Lower East Side, with a population density of more than 700 per acre, was one of the most densely populated places in the history of the earth. One block of houses contained 605 apartments, accommodating 2,871 people; only 40 apartments had hot water, and there were no baths. One out of three people slept in windowless, unventilated rooms, and indoor plumbing was a rarity.

Under such conditions, epidemics were rampant; of every 1,000 urban infants, as many as 160 died before reaching their first birthday—an infant mortality rate not found today in the most underdeveloped of underdeveloped countries. Finally, the early years of this century were not immune from environmental pollution. In New York City in 1900, horses deposited some 2.5 million pounds of excrement and 60,000 gallons of urine in the streets every day, and some 15,000 dead horses were hauled off the city's streets each year![3]

The millions of people filling the turn-of-the-century cities came from rural areas within the United States and, especially during the period 1865–1914, rural areas abroad. About 10 million people arrived in the United States in the twenty-five years immediately following the Civil War, and some 17 million more in the next twenty-five years. Especially after 1880, the immigrants came predominantly from southern and eastern Europe—Italy, Poland, Russia, Greece. The new cities and the booming heavy industries were populated with the foreign-born. By 1915, 58 percent of workers in the iron and steel industry and 69 percent of those in the clothing industry had been born abroad. When unions and other forms of labor struggle emerged, as a consequence they often involved the foreign-born; tensions between the native-born and the foreigners, as well as among various groups of foreigners, shaped the American labor movement. More generally, issues of class and ethnicity were inextricably linked in the United States from the mid-nineteenth century on.

21

The new immigrants were not only poor; they were "different." Their language was not English. They were, typically, Catholic or Jewish, not Protestant like most native-born Americans. They were, for the most part, rural people, and their ideas about work, time, land, money, and family had been shaped by the realities and traditions of agricultural communities. The corresponding values of an urban industrial society seemed quite alien. Conversely, to native-born, small-town Americans, imbued with the Protestant work ethic and other similar values, the immigrants seemed not merely "other" but directly threatening: loud, drunken, sexually uninhibited, violent, and altogether a threat to "decent" values and the structure of the American community.

Nor did the expectations of the immigrants always correspond to the realities they faced. It has been said that the immigrants came expecting to find streets paved with gold—not only were the streets not paved with gold, they were often not paved at all. And what's more, the immigrants were expected to pave them! Some immigrants (most notably, most of the Jews) came to the United States expecting to stay; whole families arrived together, or, husband preceding, the family was fairly quickly reunited. Others came as "birds of passage," hoping to make enough money to bail out or repurchase the family farm or to support the family in the old country through presumably temporarily difficult times. Many of these immigrants did, in fact, return: between 1900 and 1910, 2.1 million Italian immigrants arrived in the United States, but 1.2 million left the United States and returned to Italy. But many others, of course, perhaps contrary to their own expectations, did stay, bringing families over from abroad or creating new families in the United States. In either case, for thousands of immigrants, the United States offered a long period of a predominantly male society (79 percent of Italian immigrants, 70 percent of Poles during the years 1900–10 were male) followed by the problems of reconstructing a family in an environment very different from a traditional peasant village.[4]

Largely absent from the mass migration of rural people to the industrial cities of the northern United States during this period were blacks from the American South. Until shortly before U.S. entry into the war, it was simply more profitable for American business as a whole, North and South, to keep blacks in the South,

22

through laws and terror, as a cheap labor supply for southern agriculture. With the advent of World War I, however, labor shortages, the cutoff of European immigration resulting from unrestricted submarine warfare, and the mechanization of southern agriculture produced a massive wave of north-bound migration. When blacks did come north, in the twenties and thereafter, they experienced many of the same problems of earlier waves of rural migrants (including the characteristic American class/ethnicity mix-up) in addition to the problems of race itself.

The rapid industrial and urban growth of 1865–1900 was accompanied by a rapid concentration of economic and political power. Before the Civil War, not more than a dozen or so Americans could claim to be millionaires. By 1900 there were hundreds if not thousands; some twenty sat in the U.S. Senate alone. One percent of the population owned 47 percent of the assets; and Andrew Carnegie's income was no less than $23 million *a year.* Especially in the 1890s and thereafter, giant monopolistic corporations came to control much of the economy. By 1906 four groups of investors controlled two-thirds of the nation's railroads. One company (U.S. Steel) controlled 62 percent of steel production; another (Standard Oil), 90 percent of oil; and another (International Harvester), 85 percent of agricultural machinery. It was the age of monopoly.[5]

As the new "robber barons" increased their own wealth, there was little concern for the human consequences. "The public be damned," replied William Vanderbilt, when advised that discontinuing a fast mail train in 1883 would adversely affect the public. His father, Commodore Vanderbilt, had put it even more bluntly, a few years earlier, when one of his plans came in conflict with the law: "Law! What do I care about the law? Hain't I got the power?" Judges and legislatures were bought and sold. The Standard Oil Company, opined socialist H. Demarest Lloyd, did everything to the Pennsylvania state legislature except refine it.

At the other pole of society were hardship and poverty. Turn-of-the-century statisticians estimated that a family of four needed about $750–880 a year for mere subsistence. But in Baltimore 40 percent of adult male workers earned less than $300/year; in New York State, average wages for factory workers were $8/week ($416/year, assuming no layoffs), and dock workers averaged $520–624/year. To survive, everyone in the family had to work. Or, alternatively, marriage was delayed—a single man, living frugally in a boardinghouse, could survive and in good times might even save a little.

For those who had work, conditions were harsh. The twelve-hour day remained common; holidays were few, and vacations for blue-collar workers were almost nonexistent. American industry was among the world's most dangerous. On-the-job accidents killed 25,000 workers each year, and 700,000 were disabled, unable to work for four or more weeks. In 1901 alone, one of every 137 engineers, conductors, brakemen, and trainmen on American railroads was killed, along with one of every 161 miners in Colorado. And for workers used to the conditions of farm or artisanal workshop, the workplace was autocratic, impersonal, pressured, and unrewarding of skill, initiative, or creativity.[6]

In the harsh urban industrial world of turn-of-the-century America, childhood ended early. Two million children labored in factories and mines. Said Asa Candler, one of the founders of the Coca-Cola Company: "The most beautiful sight that we see is the child at labor; as early as he may get at labor, the more beautiful, the most useful [sic] does his life get to be."[7]

The efforts of working people to organize to correct these situations were met with violence, court injunctions, and contempt. "The rights and interests of the laboring men," wrote Pennsylvania and Reading Coal Company president George Baer, "will be protected and cared for not by the labor agitators, but by the Christian men to whom God in his infinite wisdom has given control of the property interests of this country."[8]

Much of what I have said, in outline at least, is not unfamiliar. Today we congratulate ourselves on how far removed we are from those days, how much progress we have made. But as the Baer and Candler quotes suggest, *the mere existence of poverty and hardship alone was not enough to move people to a recognition of that hardship, much less to sympathy or action to correct it.* All the hardships I have described existed in 1880 or 1890; yet it was not until the very last years of the nineteenth century and into this century that the so-called Progressive movement arose, seeking to deal with the chaos of the new industrial order. For change to occur, it was necessary for the middle and upper classes to recognize the crisis in the lives of the immigrants and the poor as a crisis for "society," that is, for themselves. Only then were they goaded into action.

By 1900, to the middle class, the crisis of industrializing society was felt. To see why, we have to go back to how the urban poor, the immigrants, the industrial workers, and poor farmers responded to their changing situation. Quite simply, they resisted the oppression and exploitation they felt, in a variety of militant ways, in the face of enormous risks.[9]

From the 1870s on, workers engaged in extremely intense labor struggles. When a nationwide railroad strike erupted in 1877, St. Louis, Chicago, and Pittsburgh experienced massive, deadly battles between strikers and troops. In the wake of the great railroad strike, cities all over the country built armories and strengthened their police forces, and states reorganized the National Guard. In the 1880s the Knights of Labor blossomed, some 700,000 strong by 1886, promising that, in the words of its leaders, "the attitude of the Order to the existing industrial system is necessarily one of war." In the early 1890s came a massive steel strike at Carnegie's Homestead (Pennsylvania) plant; a general strike in New Orleans; near civil war in the eastern Tennessee mining districts; another nationwide railroad strike in support of striking Pullman-car workers; endemic civil strife in the mining districts of Colorado and Idaho. And, at a varying pace, labor unrest continued into the twentieth century: in 1913 the nation's newspapers were filled with photographs of police beating women and children as the children were being put on a train to escape the hardship and violence of a strike of immigrant workers in the Lawrence, Massachusetts, textile mills. In 1914 armed guards at Rockefeller's Colorado Fuel and Iron Company destroyed a tent village of striking miners, killing sixteen (including thirteen women and children).

Along with unionism came the rapid spread of radical ideas. In 1894 only parliamentary trickery prevented the American Federation of Labor convention from adopting a resolution calling for the nationalization of the means of production. In 1901 the Socialist party of the United States was formed. Its presidential candidate, former railroad unionist Eugene Victor Debs, garnered 400,000 votes in 1904 and 900,000 in 1912. By 1912 the Socialists were able to elect 56 mayors, a congressman, and scores of state legislators and city councilmen; and the party published 13 daily newspapers and 298 weeklies. In addition, in 1905 the Industrial Workers of the World, an openly revolutionary union movement, was founded. In the next fifteen years a million or so workers became members, at least for a time, and the "Wobblies," as they were popularly known, organized railroad workers, miners, longshoremen, textile workers, and even janitorial workers and cowboys.

Unrest was not confined to industrial workers. It spread to urban communities, where demands for bilingual schools and other community facilities emerged. New York experienced massive rent strikes; and in New York, Providence, and elsewhere, riots erupted over undue profits and exorbitant prices in the food industry. Farmers, too, shared in the discontent. Squeezed between falling prices for farm products and the monopolies that controlled the prices of seed, fertilizer, and agricultural implements, as well as interest rates and shipping costs, the farmers' alliances and later the People's party (the Populists) arose. Sweeping through large parts of the South, Southwest, and Great Plains in the 1880s and early 1890s, their presidential candidate, James B. Weaver, garnered 10 percent of the vote in 1892, and they elected governors, state legislators, and congressmen. The Populists were decisively defeated in the years following the 1896 elections, by electoral fraud, economic reprisal, violence, and the establishment of the Jim Crow system of legalized segregation in the South, which divided black and white farmers (who had often worked together in the farmers' movement) once and for all. But though the organized movement was dead, its dreams were not forgotten: leading Populist areas were among the centers of Socialist party strength a decade later.

To summarize, the last years of the nineteenth century and the early years of this century were characterized by an enormous amount of what can only be called "class struggle," as poor workers and farmers and city dwellers fought back against their perceived oppressors. A sense of violence and threat hung in the air. And to top it all off, the economy showed signs of faltering. In the mid-1870s, the mid-1880s, and again in 1893–96, serious depressions occurred. Economic recovery at the end of the century was aborted by the Panic of 1907, which was followed by a period of relative stagnation lasting until World War I. As early as the mid-nineties, many observers came to the conclusion that American markets were saturated and that, as a result, American economic expansion had reached its limits, that stagnation loomed. The only way out, many argued, was through enlarged markets and sources of cheap raw materials abroad. "We must have the market [of China] or we shall have a revolution," warned Senator William Frye (soon to become the chairman of the Senate Foreign Relations Committee) on the eve of the Spanish-American war.[10]

The United States at the end of the nineteenth century was a country in crisis. It must be emphasized that in the 1870s and 1880s, when the objective pieces of the crisis already existed, the middle class remained relatively complacent. It was only when mass unrest—the massive and threatening social movements of the poor—arose that awareness of the crisis was forced on the middle class.

In any event, turn-of-the-century America society was a deeply uneasy society. Not a few feared outright revolution. Fear of endemic disorder and unrest, loss of confidence, generalized anxiety, were widespread. Fear of unrest could have led to simple repression, of course, and to some degree that did happen. But what is perhaps as significant as the crisis itself is the recognition by many conservative, sober, sophisticated people that, however much they feared the poor, the rich had to bear much of the blame for the crisis. As Teddy Roosevelt wrote to his successor, President William H. Taft, in 1906:

> I do not at all like the social conditions at present. The dull, purblind folly of the very rich men, their greed and arrogance, and the ways in which they have unduly prospered by the help of the ablest lawyers, and too often through the weakness or shortsightedness of the judges . . . ; these facts, and the corruption in business and politics, have tended to produce a very unhealthy condition of excitement and irritation in the popular mind, which shows itself in part in the enormous increase in the socialistic propaganda.

The constant exposés of corruption and exploitation in the press, he continued, "are all building up a revolutionary feeling."[11]

Roosevelt's fears were shared by many members of the middle class. To this fear, however, large numbers of middle-class Americans added sympathy for the lot of the poor (however mitigated by concern for the property rights of the rich) and anger at what untrammeled capitalism was doing to the small-town America in which they had grown up. This mix of fears, concerns, and angers drove them toward "progressivism," the reforming programs, movements, and ideologies that gave their name to the entire historical period.

But as the mix of fear with anger and concern suggests, progressivism was not to be free of contradictions. Consciously, the middle-class reformers-to-be felt they had to restore justice and morality to an increasingly unjust and immoral society. But they themselves benefited, materially at least, from the industrial system. And although they may have sympathized with the poor, for the most part they did not *like* the poor and certainly did not want to live like, or with, them. So another way of stating their goals is to say that they faced the problem of how to restore and maintain order, how to reestablish social control, and, beyond that, how to stabilize the new industrial order so that it would not be ceaselessly threatened. They had to find ways to modify capitalism but not to overthrow it—rather, to save it. And this goal could bring them into conflict, as well as alliance, with the poor whom they sought to help.

So far we 'have been talking about the crisis confronting turn-of-the-century America. But in addition to the polarization of the rich and the poor, another class transformation was occurring: the decline (relatively, at least) of the "old middle class" of independent-businessmen and professionals and the rise of a "new middle class" of college-educated and usually salaried employees.

Progressivism was the hallmark of this new middle class. If the social reform movements that characterized the Progressive Era can be regarded as mass movements—and I think they can be—then the "masses" involved were *middle-class* masses. The working-class and farmer movements that characterized this period were *causes* of progressivism, part of the *crisis;* they were not progressivism, nor were most of the social reforms of the period a direct response to their demands. Progressivism, in the sense that historians usually use the term, was a middle-class movement occurring in response to this crisis, a *counter* to these movements that threatened to transform American society in more fundamental ways.

Central to an understanding of progressivism, then, is a recognition of the transformation of the middle class that occurred during this period. The middle class, no less than other segments of American society, was deeply affected by the restructuring of the American economic order. It is the rise of, and the structurally determined pressures on, this new middle class that help explain why reform, rather than repression, was the characteristic Progressive Era response to the social crisis.

The traditional middle class in the United States included independent farmers, small-business men, and self-employed professionals. But in the last decades of the nineteenth century, a "new middle class," or a "professional-managerial class," arose: salaried professionals (including teachers and professors, doctors, journalists, and proto-social workers), engineers, managers, administrators, and the like. (Some scholars have argued that the rapidly growing army of clerical and sales workers also belongs in this category. As the twentieth century wore on, however, these latter groups, were transformed into mass occupations, more appropriately categorized as "working class" than as "middle class." But at the turn of the century, they, at least, still saw themselves as part of the middle class. If we include them as part of the turn-of-the-century "new middle class," then from 1870 to 1910, while the entire population of the United States, and the number of people employed in old-middle-class occupations, increased slightly more than twofold, the number of people employed in new-middle-class jobs multiplied eightfold, from about 750,000 to 5.5 million. In 1870 the old middle class had outnumbered the new 2 to 1; by 1910 the proportions were reversed.)[12]

Now recall the broad context within which this new professional-managerial class arose in the last half of the nineteenth century: the repeated depressions and intermittent, violent class warfare between farmers and the growing industrial working class on the one hand and capitalists on the other. The possibilities of long-term economic stagnation and endemic social disorder or, worse, outright insurrection were taken very seriously by all observers, conservative, liberal, and radical alike.

At the same time, however, economic growth and the new concentration and centralization of economic power were opening up new possibilities for responding to the crisis. For the first time there was the possibility (as well as evidently the necessity) for long-term economic and social planning, for the refinement of management and the rationalization of production and consumption. And for the first time there was an economic surplus available, created by modern industry, to support a large number of people to carry out these planning and regulating functions. In the decades around the turn of the century, these possibilities began to be realized. And it is this rationalization and regulation of the society to ward off endemic crisis—a project in which the new professional-managerial class played a key role—that conventionally is called progressivism. In it, as we shall see, new conceptions of social policy and the causes of social injustice arose, and the new profession of social work appeared. (The account that follows is drawn from an analysis developed by Barbara Ehrenreich and myself.)[13]

What were the principal elements of this rationalization and regulation of society? First, in the factories, mines, and railroads, science and its practical offshoot, engineering, were set to work producing not only "progress" in the form of new products but also new productive technologies and processes. The need for skilled workers and the power of those workers who remained were thus reduced by "progress." In many instances, labor was directly replaced by machines. In others, production processes were reorganized, using techniques that the engineer Frederick Winslow Taylor called "scientific management": an effort to reduce labor, insofar as possible, to simple, well-defined, and easily controlled motions, thereby stripping from the workers their knowledge, understanding, and control of their own labor process and concentrating it, instead, in the hands of managers and engineers.[14] The reorganization of production thus had dual ends: it increased efficiency, in the narrow sense of greater production per worker-hour, and it increased control over a labor force that was increasingly hostile and threatening to the imperatives of monopoly capital. These developments drastically altered the terms and conditions of class struggle in the workplace, diminishing the workers' real or potential collective mastery over the work process and undercutting the collective experience of socialized production processes.[15]

Second, the huge economic surplus was increasingly collected and concentrated in private foundations and the public sector and was thus made available for use in regulating and managing civil society. The Rockefeller and Carnegie foundations, each worth hundreds of millions of dollars, as well as slightly smaller (but still huge) foundations such as the Russell Sage Foundation and the Commonwealth Fund appear on the scene in the first two decades of this century. Local governments increased their revenues and expenditures fivefold between 1902 and 1922. Public education was vastly expanded (and made compulsory in many states); public health measures gained sponsorship and the authority of law; charity mechanisms were rationalized and institutionalized, and so forth. These developments brought great benefits, of course. But they also represented a politically motivated penetration of working-class and immigrant community life: public schools imparted not only reading skills but industrially appropriate values and behavior patterns to immigrant children; charity agencies, domestic scientists, and social workers imposed their "American" ideas of proper living habits, family patterns, and behaviors ("right living," they noneuphemistically called it); public health officials literally policed immigrant ghettos.[16]

One slightly extreme but revealing case makes the point: when the Ford Motor Company introduced its celebrated $5-a-day wages (itself tied to the much greater productivity and control of the work force created by the newly developed assembly line), it set up a "Sociology" (social service) Department, whose thirty investigators were to screen applicants and monitor the behavior of employees. Gambling, drinking, and, of course, radicalism and unionism were forbidden; "proper" (i.e., middle-class) diet, recreational habits, living arrangements, family budgets, and morality were taught and encouraged. For the foreign-born, English classes were mandatory, with the text used beginning with the lesson "I am a good American." Symbolizing the school's function was the "graduation" ceremony: walking on stage in the costumes of their native lands, graduates disappeared behind a giant cutout of a "melting pot." After their teachers had stirred the "pot" with long ladles, the graduates reappeared on the opposite side of the pot dressed in proper American attire and waving American flags.[17]

It should go without saying that there were benefits to be gained from all this—such as learning English and learning better health habits. But the losses—in culture, in social solidarity, in control over one's life—should be equally evident.

A third component of progressivism was the creation and manipulation of a national consumer-goods market. Beginning early in the century and accelerating thereafter, items that had been produced in the home or in the neighborhood were replaced by the uniform products of giant corporations. Services that had been an indigenous part of working-class and immigrant culture were edged out by commodified services conceived and designed outside the community. For example, midwifery, which played a vital part in cementing traditional communities, was officially discredited in the early 1900s and replaced by professionally dominated obstetric care. (This was not the inevitable result of the superior technology of the doctors. In fact, as late as 1910, New York midwives achieved lower rates of stillbirths and puerperal sepsis than did physicians, although they were already being forced out.)[18] Traditional forms of group-created leisure activities, from participant sports to family get-togethers, suffered a similar fate at the hands of the new, individually consumed forms of commercial entertainment—records, movies, spectator sports, radio—offered by corporations.

The penetration of working-class life by mass-produced commodities required, and continues to require, a massive job of education—from schools, advertisements, mass media, by teachers, doctors, social workers, domestic scientists, "experts" in everything from child rearing to personal hygiene to interpersonal relationships. As the dependence of American economic prosperity on the domestic consumer-goods market increased, the management of consumption came to be as important as was the management of production.[19] It is no coincidence that Simon Patten, chairman of the Economics Department at the University of Pennsylvania's Wharton School of Business, was both a leading intellectual influence on the social-work educators and administrators of the Progressive Era and the leading proponent of advertising and the "affluent society."

To summarize, then, the crisis created by the rapid industrialization of the United States in the last decades of the nineteenth century required an extensive reorganization of working-class life if capitalism was to survive. But it also allowed such a reorganization and created the mechanisms for it. Aimed simultaneously at social amelioration, social control (the creation of a properly behaved, appropriately docile working class), and the development of a mass consumer market, the reorganization of the working class involved the fragmentation of the labor process at the workplace and the radical isolation of work life from home life and of workplace from home. In the process, indigenous networks of support and mutual aid were disrupted, and central aspects of working-class and immigrant cultures were destroyed and replaced by "mass culture," as defined by the individual, privatized consumption of commodities.[20]

As a result, in broad historical terms, the formation of a unified working class, which might have carried out its nascent challenge to the capitalist order, was aborted. At the same time, of course, a real improvement was experienced in the "standard of living," and faith in the possibilities of reform was renewed. If I have slighted these in my account, such slights should redress the balance, for it is these latter effects that conventional accounts extol, whereas the less savory and negative effects are all but ignored. What is essential, however, is that both aspects—social control and social amelioration—

were central to American social policy from its beginnings. Neither ever existed independently of the other.

Emerging simultaneously with these developments in working-class life were the professional and managerial occupations, including social work. The reorganization of work and the productive process, the emergence of mass institutions of social control, the commodity penetration of working-class communities—did not simply "happen." They required the efforts of more-or-less conscious agents. The transformation of work required engineers and managers of all sorts; the interventions in working-class communities and working-class culture required new culture producers and culture transmitters—social workers, physicians, teachers, journalists, admen, and so on.

It would be wrong, however, to think of this emerging professional-managerial class as being no more than a passive group of recruits for a set of occupational roles conceived of, and required, by capitalists, to think of them as some kind of sinister tools of social control. In this last assertion, I think, lies much of the secret of progressivism. The men and women entering the new professional occupations were drawn, for the most part, from the old, traditional middle class. They were the sons and daughters of businessmen, independent professionals, prosperous farmers—groups that quite properly feared their own extinction in the growing battles between capital and labor. They mourned the passing of the old, small-town society on which traditional American values—*their* values—had been based. The students graduating from college and entering the managerial and professional marketplace between 1880 and 1914 consciously grasped their own situation and the roles they were to play. They understood that their own self-interest (including both their occupational self-interest and their concern for the preservation of their own class values) was bound up in reforming capitalism, and they articulated this far more clearly and persistently than the most farseeing of contemporary capitalists. Their role, as they saw it, was to *mediate* the basic class conflicts of capitalist society and create a newly "rational," stable, efficient, and self-reproducing social order. Thus Edward A. Ross, a key progressive ideologue, wrote in 1907: "Social defense is coming to be a matter for the expert. The rearing of dikes against faithlessness and fraud calls for intelligent social engineering. If in this strait the public does not speedily become far shrewder . . . there is nothing for it but to turn over the defense of society to professionals." Reformer and settlement-house pioneer Jane Addams, wrote a wealthy philanthropist friend, "was really an interpreter between working men and the people who lived in luxury on the other side of the city, and she also gave the people of her neighborhood quite a different idea about the men and women who were ordinarily called 'capitalists.'" Progressivism, noted *New Republic* editor Herbert Croly (himself another key progressive thinker), was "designed to serve as a counterpoise to the threat of working-class revolution."[21]

In addition to the social crisis experienced by their class, middle-class women, such as Jane Addams, Ellen Starr, Julia Lathrop, Florence Kelly, and Mary Van Kleeck, carried the burden of their own, gender-based crisis, the inequality and oppression suffered by women within the family and in the larger society. They were college-educated in a world that offered few practical outlets for their knowledge and skills—women caught in what Jane Addams called the "snare of preparation." They were socially concerned in a world that barred women from participation in the political process, and well prepared for traditional domestic roles in middle-class families, which seemed, to them, empty and oppressive. (Many of them, including Addams, "escaped" by falling into prolonged spells of psychogenic illness.)[22] They had been exposed in college and through church and volunteer work to a sisterhood of collective intellectual and practical activity and to a morality of Christian service.

The same capitalism that had so disrupted the lives of poor workers and farmers had created a personal dilemma for women. "The mere withdrawal of industries from the home has drawn millions of [working-class] women out of the home and left millions [of middle-class women] idle within it," commented editor Walter Lippmann.[23] Full of energy and ability, these women were shut off from practical activity. "They feel a want of harmony between their theory and their lives, a lack of coordination between thought and action," wrote Addams in 1892. Their parents were inconsistent:

> They deliberately expose their daughters to knowledge of the distress in the world; they send them to hear missionary addresses on famines in India and China; they accompany them to lectures on the suffering in Siberia; they agitate together over the forgotten region of East London. In addition to this, from babyhood the altruistic tendencies of

these daughters are persistently cultivated. They are taught to be self-forgetting and self-sacrificing, to consider the good of the whole before the good of the ego. But . . . when all this information and culture shows results, when the daughter comes back from college and begins to recognize her social claim to the "submerged tenth," and to evince her disposition to fulfill it, she is told that she is unjustified, ill-advised in her efforts. . . . We have in America a fast-growing number of cultivated young people who have no recognized outlet for their active faculties. They hear constantly of the great social maladjustment, but no way is provided for them to change it, and their uselessness hangs about them heavily.[24]

To Addams and to thousands of women like her, the skills and values they had obtained had to be projected into worldly activity. Perhaps more than their fathers and brothers, who were directly involved in the exploitation of wage labor, these women were able to see the human problems created for the poor by the onward rush of industry. And, excluded from the political world and from professions such as medicine and law and socialized for the role of wife and mother, they tended to approach social reform in characteristic ways: as feminists (by the turn of the century predominantly, though not exclusively, focusing on gaining the vote for women) and as what historian William O'Neill has termed "social feminists"—women concerned with settlement houses, temperance, reform of mental institutions and tenements, consumer issues, "friendly visiting" (see Chapter 2), and other activities and issues involving disproportionate numbers of women as activists and disproportionate numbers of women and children as targets.[25]

The similarity between such activities and traditional feminine roles was not lost upon these women. Addams herself wrote: "Many women today are failing properly to discharge their duties to their own families and households simply because they fail to see that as society grows more complicated, it is necessary that woman shall extend her sense of responsibility to many things outside of her home, if only in order to preserve the home in its entirety."[26]

To Addams, the call for "social motherhood" was a plea for women to engage in settlement-house work and reform activities. To other women, focusing more on one-to-one assistance to the poor, the same logic applied, however. Thus in 1919, Jessie Taft, one of the first psychiatric social workers and a key figure in the development of social work, argued that the new (and female) profession of psychiatric social work required "a maternal sort of woman. . . . She has to have a genuine liking for people. . . . It won't do for her to be at bottom cynical, carping or critical. She needs a warmth and spontaneity and wholehearted interest. . . . I am inclined to think that she ought to be a settled person, a fairly satisfied person." She needs "strength . . . poise . . . sympathy . . . wisdom . . . patience."[27] In short, she should be the stereotypical wife and mother.

The mix of objective and subjective needs of the new professional-managerial class—the class-based motives of men and the class- and gender-based motives of women—created the specific kinds of reforms and activities the Progressives pursued. We can now summarize those reforms in a more systematic fashion:

First, to create a rational social order, it was necessary to curtail what Teddy Roosevelt had called the "dull, purblind folly" of the rich, that is, the worst excesses of giant corporations had to be regulated. The corporations were not about to regulate themselves. Some corporate leaders—people like Mark Hanna, Andrew Carnegie, and August W. Belmont—did understand that a more moderate stance toward workers and consumers was in the long-run self-interest of the capitalist class. Without it, endemic unrest, if not outright revolution, was inescapable. But no one corporation could carry out such sweeping societal reforms alone, and, in any case, the fear of giving a competitive advantage to other corporations inhibited them. The task of reform, of moderating corporate behavior, had to be carried out on a uniform statewide or nationwide basis or not at all.

In practice, that meant reform had to be undertaken, or supported, by government, that is, it had to take the form of "social policy" in the modern sense. This was precisely the role of Progressive Era governments, at both state and national levels, of governors and senators such as Amos Pinchot of Pennsylvania, Robert La Follette of Wisconsin, and Hiram Johnson of California, and of presidents such as Theodore Roosevelt and Woodrow Wilson. Under these leaders, regulatory agencies, such as the Food and Drug Administration and the Federal Trade Commission, were created, and the Interstate Commerce Commission was strengthened; state laws were passed regulating hours and child labor and female labor; political institutions and processes were reconstituted (for example, the direct election of senators, the direct primary, popular initiative referenda, city manager systems), ostensibly to reduce the possibility of the corruption of government by business but also to reduce the influence of immigrant-based political machines.

The passage of these reforms was not a smooth, conflict-free process. Those who bitterly opposed *any* breach of laissez-faire principles fought every reform to the bitter end. And even among those who believed in an active role for the state, there was widespread disagreement on the forms it should take. On the left, there were the Socialists, such as Eugene Victor Debs, who garnered 900,000 votes for president in 1912 (out of 15 million votes cast) on a platform calling for a government take-over and operation of large-scale industry and very close regulation of those industries remaining in the private sector. Toward the center, Woodrow Wilson argued that government should act to combat monopoly and restore free competition. In Wilson's campaign rhetoric, at least, the interests of big business (though not of private enterprise per se) and those of the common man and woman were incompatible; government had to play a key role in ensuring "justice," that is, the right of all to health, safety, education, economic opportunity, and political participation.

Further to the right, Roosevelt, supported by many business leaders, argued that the rise of the giant corporation was inevitable. The role of government was not to roll back the clock but to harness this development for public welfare. Government should regulate, keep business honest. To many professional-managerial reformers, Roosevelt's position was good enough, allowing for all the specific reforms they desired. In fact, Roosevelt's Progressive party platform of 1912 was drawn in large measure from the report of the Committee on Standards of Living and Labor of the 1912 National Conference of Charities and Corrections (the annual get-together of social workers, social reformers, charity workers, and the like), and, in the words of moderate Socialist party leader William Ghent, "begins . . . with the brazen theft of half the working program of the Socialist Party."[28]

Roosevelt did not stop there, however. He also believed that government should act to rationalize and order the marketplace, so as to advance the interests of the giant corporations and at the same time make the latter's interests harmonize with those of the public. For example, government inspection of the meat-packing industry (following the uproar created by Upton Sinclair's best-selling *The Jungle*) served not only to ensure the public a safer meat supply but to open up European markets to American meat producers—markets from which the low hygienic standards of the industry had previously barred them.[29] Finally, given that the public uproar and disorder of the period made reform of one kind or another seem inevitable, many corporations decided that, at the very minimum, it was in their best interest to participate in the reform process, to help shape the reforms to serve their own interests and minimize their restrictive effects on the corporations themselves.

In the inimitable fashion of American politics, Wilson won the 1912 election and did what Roosevelt had promised. Given the ultimate lack of power of unions, farmers' organizations, Socialists, and those members of the middle class who sympathized with them, a more direct assault on the power of the corporations was impossible. But equally, the outcome testifies to the success of the progressives in creating a broad consensus on a new role for government: laissez-faire (always honored as much in the breach as in the practice) was dead; the unlimited freedom of action of the corporation was dead; the government had been mandated to play an active and positive role in the rationalization of a chaotic society. That this role might be directed at economic rationalizations in the long-run interest of the corporations, rather than unambiguously at the public welfare, should not obscure the magnitude of the change that had taken over government.

One last comment on the new role of government is in order, however. Virtually the entire role of the federal government in the Progressive Era was concerned with the regulation of corporations and aimed at practices affecting other businesses and consumers (i.e., at the problems affecting the middle class as much or more than at those affecting the poor). Regulation with respect to the needs of workers *as workers* (union rights, maximum hour laws, child labor laws, occupational safety laws), when they were instituted at all, appeared primarily at the state and local level and were generally poorly enforced. With the exception of state-level "widows' pensions" (more or less comparable to today's Aid to Families with Dependent Children) in a few states, there were no real gains in welfare legislation. Old-age pensions, unemployment compensation, national health insurance, welfare—what later would be called the welfare state—had to wait another generation, until the New Deal of the 1930s, for even partial realization.

In addition to a new perspective for government, the creation of a

38

rational social order required the direct regulation, or taming, of the working class and the urban poor. This function, as we have already seen, is virtually inseparable from the increased provision of social services, of direct social amelioration. I have already mentioned the roles of social workers, teachers, and the like in teaching "right living," reorganizing community life, reshaping the working-class family. Along with these functions, some settlement houses (e. g., Jane Addams's Hull House) provided meeting rooms for union organizers, organized exhibitions celebrating immigrant traditions, and led campaigns for reforms ranging from the provision of playgrounds and public baths (in an era of no indoor plumbing a significant step) to the democratization of the electoral process and the passage of child labor laws. But other proto-social workers worked the social-control side of the street more intensively. For example, Mabel Kittredge, a leader of the "domestic science" movement, set up "model flats" to teach neighborhood women the importance of such industrial values as regular hours for sleeping and waking and mealtimes, to encourage them to replace religious ikons and traditional home furnishings with modern, store-bought furnishings that were more appropriate in a clutter-free household, and to teach them to provide their children with proper nutrition despite their poverty, rather than struggling against the inevitable. "Let us not be satisfied to force through bills . . . that improve our tenements," she wrote. "At the same time the tenement girl must be receiving her scientific home training so that she, too, can take her part in this great homemaking profession."[30] The poor needed no outsiders to tell them what this meant. As Hannah Breineh, the heroine of Anzia Yezierska's short story "My Own People," cried out: "[The 'friendly visitor'] learns us how to cook cornmeal. By pictures and lectures she shows us how the poor people should live without meat, without milk, without butter, and without eggs. Always its on the tip of my tongue to ask her, 'You learned us to do without so much, why can't you yet learn us how to eat without eating?' "[31]

Other characteristic Progressive Era campaigns—the struggles for temperance and against gambling and for Americanization—were similarly double-edged: sincere efforts at solving social ills whose worst victims were the poor and at the same time conscious or unconscious efforts to control the poor to ensure social stability. Similarly, efforts to imbue working-class people with an interest in, and opportunities to use, middle-class culture—libraries, art museums—were benevolent in intention and in part in effect and at the same time served to disrupt and devalue traditional working-class and immigrant culture. Municipal reform efforts were aimed at breaking the immigrants' allegiance to local political bosses (and hence at the political machines' partial responsiveness to mass concerns) as much as at businessmen's ability to corrupt the machines. And even the women's suffrage movement, a movement that predated progressivism but became intermingled with it, found itself recruiting middle-class male and female supporters with the argument that middle-class women's votes could help overcome the radical tide that was presumably reflected in the voting record of working-class men.

The third characteristic approach of the progressives to stabilizing the social order took the form of creating class-bridging, unifying, harmonizing ideologies. This is best represented in the very idea of the "public" and the "public interest," ideas that gained currency during this period. This had, in fact, a double meaning. In part, the "public" was none other than the new middle class itself, representing itself as the entire society. (Thus the classic progressive tripartite panel, with representatives of "labor," "capital," and "the public": it should be clear that after subtracting labor and capital, the only "public" left is the middle class.) Equally, though, the notion of "the public" was an assertion that society is unitary, classless. "The dependence of the classes on each other is reciprocal," wrote Jane Addams, in the midst of an era of violent class conflict and despite her frequent sympathy for the workers in these struggles. "The things which make men alike are finer and better than the things that keep them apart, and these basic likenesses . . . easily transcend the less essential differences of race, language, creed, and tradition."[32]

Other characteristic progressive ideals, reflecting the occupational and political roles of the new middle class as rationalizers, harmonizers, mediators, and planners, embraced the value-neutrality of knowledge, the beneficence of science, technology, and expertise, and the desirability of efficiency and order in all things. To any social conflict, the progressive response was typically to propose a "commission," with representatives from all sides but dominated by the seamless "public," to study the problem and make "objective," "rational" recommendations—to find a harmonious solution. Because conflict was seen by the new middle class as representing a failure of intelligence, and not as built into the social order, these commissions were expected to identify "one best solution." Above all, the goal was class harmony. As John Spargo, a crusader for children's rights and, for a while, a Socialist party leader, wrote: class hatred is a "monstrous thing . . . to be abhorred by all right-thinking men and women."[33]

But "harmony" to the professional-managerial class was not just the absence of conflict. It embraced positive values as well: a degree of social justice (at least great enough to eliminate the worst sources of social unrest), and, beyond that, rationality and efficiency. It also often implied nationalism, the unity of all classes under the national umbrella. Thus Americanization (assimilation of the foreign-born) and, for most progressives, firm support for American foreign policy as it moved into the age of imperialism were central themes of the progressive impulse. So, too, for some, was nativism—a hearty dislike of the immigrants who were challenging American values and creating the social disorder underlying the progressive movement—as well as outright racism. The proto-social workers—charity workers, settlement-house workers, reformers, a group made up disproportionately of those of the middle class who had more immediately charitable and sympathetic motives and who experienced more intimate contact with the poor, the immigrant, and the black, in daily life as well as in time of crisis—were perhaps less susceptible to nativism and racism than were many others of their class.[34] But their very roles, their function in remolding and controlling the lives of their clients could readily drive them to a reconsideration of their position on nativism and racism.

I should briefly digress, in this context, to emphasize that whereas the social control exercised by social workers was relatively benign—at least they weren't hitting people over the heads as an earlier generation would have done, and they were providing real aid—active, violent repression of dissent did not disappear during the Progressive Era. Violence against strikers was not to become uncommon until World War II. Far more brutal and relevant in the context of racism was the suppression, through lynchings, beatings, and a massive reign of terror, of the black population in the South, ultimately as part of an effort to discourage forever any possibility of unity between poor blacks and poor whites. That is, there remained an iron fist inside progressivism's velvet glove.

I have argued that America in the nineteenth-century and the early twentieth was in a state of crisis, rooted in the process of industrialization. The question confronting America at the turn of the century was how—indeed whether—an industrial, capitalist society could be stabilized. That was the problem the young settlement-house workers, urban reformers, muckrakers, university professors, engineers, reform politicians, and the like took on as their task. They came up with a variety of solutions, most notably with a series of proposals to mitigate the worst features of industrial capitalism and to reorganize working-class life so as to produce a more socially integrated and controllable working class. In these reforms are the origins of the modern welfare state and of both social policy and social work as we know them today.

If this broader task—the re-creation of a stable society—also corresponded to the psychological, occupational, and social needs of the newly emerging class of professionals and managers, it is neither coincidental nor damning. During the Progressive Era, in the context of working-class unrest, the moral vision of the young professionals, their occupational needs, and the desperate need of the poor for social amelioration and reform more or less coincided with, and could be incorporated into, the needs of the capitalists for political-economic rationalization. (There was, as we have seen, conflict between the reformers' solutions and traditional working-class culture and goals as seen from the working class side; there was also conflict between reformers and capitalists, whose short-term interests and long-term visions did not always coincide. This conflict, however, serves only to emphasize the strength of the otherwise happy coincidence of interests.) In the years following World War I, however, that coincidence of motives and needs broke down: the occupational needs of social workers, for example, diverged from concerns for social reform. To this later history we now turn.

2

Casework and the Emergence of Social Work as a Profession

The new constellation of social needs, motives, and opportunities at the end of the nineteenth century produced not only a wave of reforms and a host of new occupations (including those that were to mature into social work) but also a fertile environment for the growth of new understandings of the ground on which social policy rests and in particular a new understanding of poverty. The old Social Darwinist explanations characteristic of the late nineteenth century, which saw individual physical, mental, or moral weaknesses as the source of economic disadvantage, went into eclipse, and the dominant modes of social thought shifted to environmentalist explanations. The poor came to be seen as victims of external forces—unemployment, bad housing, disease, and accidents—which they could not be expected to control through strength of character alone. Concurrently, laissez-faire ideas about government also declined, and the notion that government at all levels should promote social welfare came to be widely accepted.

What needs reemphasis, as preface to any discussion of the decades following World War I, is that the social "crisis" to which progressivism was a response did not consist merely of the *existence* of poverty and other forms of social misery. It consisted more than anything else of the *response of the poor* themselves to poverty and exploitation, that is, to the growing class warfare that characterized industrializing and urbanizing America. Thus the middle class was forced to realize that things had to change if a capitalist, industrial America (and with it the middle class itself) were to survive. That

43

this understanding coincided with other needs of the middle class— to restore a sense of the lost American community and to enjoy meaningful and remunerative occupational roles—and with the desires of corporations to rationalize the economy created progressivism, the first stage of American social policy.

In the decades following World War I, however, all the elements that had coincided earlier in the century changed. As a consequence, social policy and the development of social work came to be governed by a very different coincidence of needs, motives, and possibilities.

Had the intense class conflict in American society during the Progressive Era continued into the twenties, had the social context continued to be one of militant mass movements for social change, for social reform, for social transformation, the position of the new middle class would have remained the same, and it is entirely possible that social policy would have continued to develop along the lines laid out during the Progressive Era. Instead, the various movements previously discussed died down or were repressed or coopted. The environment faced in the twenties by the social workers of the new middle class was not one of acute social crisis. The drive toward state-mediated reforms collapsed, and the members of the professional-managerial class turned instead toward the direct pursuit of their own class and occupational concerns.

During the war itself, these changes were still largely a matter for the future. On the surface at least, progressivism seemed to have triumphed. The need for national mobilization placed a premium on the promotion of class-bridging ideologies and institutions, much like those that emerged in the Progressive Era.

The need to mobilize all segments of the population for the war led, for example, to efforts to bring labor into the national consensus. Instead of crushing strikes with troops, injunctions, and the like, Samuel Gompers, president of the American Federation of Labor, was made a member of the War Labor Board, a board empowered to adjudicate labor disputes and promote labor organization and labor–management cooperation. Partly as a consequence, union membership soared: from 2 million in 1914 to 4 million five years later. Similarly, regulation of industry was stepped up during the war, and measures to regulate the workplace were instituted.

But after the war, these apparent gains quickly faded away. The postwar years saw a tremendous effort—by business and increasingly by government—to roll back the social achievements of the Progressive Era and to restore the historic class relations—that is, a situation in which capital ran the show.

If we look at the period immediately following the war, it appeared that the United States was simply picking up where it had left off five years earlier. The feminist movement, having enlisted millions of recruits during the war years, gained passage of the Nineteenth Amendment, granting women the vote. Labor unrest, after dropping off during the war, resumed.

In 1919 an enormous wave of strikes swept the nation. In Seattle, a general strike of 60,000 workers took over the city for several days, operating public services and determining what should and should not, function. Strikes for the eight-hour day swept the industrial heartland, succeeding in the meat packinghouses but failing in steel, where an epic strike of 365,000 workers was crushed by force. On Memorial Day 1919, in South Chicago, police fired on a peaceful demonstration of strikers, supporters, wives, and children, killing some thirty people, most of whom were shot in the back.[1]

The labor unrest of 1919 seemed especially threatening to businessmen and to "middle America" because only a year and a half earlier, in November 1917, workers and peasants, led by the Bolsheviks, had actually seized state power in Russia. And in the wake of the war, a series of short-lived communist workers' uprisings swept over much of Europe: in Bavaria a Soviet Republic was declared; workers rose in Berlin; Hungary was under Soviet power for weeks before the workers' government was crushed; there was a revolutionary outbreak in Finland. In the United States enormous May Day rallies turned into riots in New York, Boston, and Cleveland. And many recently arrived immigrants who had fled Czarist oppression in Russia were more than sympathetic to the new Bolshevik regimes. A wave of antiradical panic swept the country.

Meanwhile, immigration, interrupted by the war, resumed at prewar rates. Nativism, already a powerful force before the war and strengthened by the wartime drive for national unity—for what Teddy Roosevelt approvingly called "100 per cent Americanism"— took on new life. Before the war, the principal obstacle to the passage of federal prohibitions on immigration had come perhaps from businessmen, concerned lest their supply of cheap labor be interrupted. But mechanization reduced, somewhat, the need for cheap labor. And during the booming production of the war years, with millions of workers away in the armed forces and immigration interrupted by submarine warfare, businessmen learned that cheap labor from rural areas of America filled the void quite handily. With the demand for agricultural labor also reduced by new machinery, the way was open for an enormous migration from farms in the South and West to the industrial cities. In the early 1920s laws restricting immigration from Europe were, in fact, passed, and in the decade that followed, instead of a flood of European immigrants, some 19 million people left U.S. farms for the city. Their numbers included more than a million blacks, and the great ghettos of New York, Chicago, and Philadelphia sprang into being. (Because of loopholes in the immigration laws, the new ghettos in the West were populated by Mexicans.)

As demobilized soldiers returned home—home to face an economy that was shrinking as war production was cut back—competition between workers for jobs grew. The situation rapidly turned ugly, and a wave of vicious nativism and racism swept the country.[2] Italians, especially among the foreign-born, were singled out for lynchings and mob attacks. In California, a popular initiative referendum produced a law barring Japanese from owning land. The Ku Klux Klan experienced a revival, claiming some 4 million members in 1922. As much anti-Catholic and anti-Jewish as anti-black, it was centered in such states as Indiana, Ohio, Arkansas, and Texas rather than in the Deep South. In Alabama, anti-Catholic legislators set up a state commission to inspect convents to make sure that innocent Protestant maidens were not being held against their will. By 1929, as anti-Jewish quotas spread, Jews were barred from more than 90 percent of the general office jobs in New York, and most major universities adhered to strictly applied quotas. Blacks suffered some of the worst attacks. A new wave of lynchings swept the South; seventy-six were reported—surely an underestimate—in 1919 alone. And in the North, where the new waves of black migrants competed with whites for jobs, housing, and recreational facilities, bloody riots broke out: in East St. Louis in 1917, and in twenty-five or so other cities, including Chicago and Washington, in 1919. The riots, in which gangs of whites raided the ghettos, lynching, shooting, beating, and burning, were more akin to the disturbances in Miami in 1980 than to the black uprisings of the sixties. But the sufferings of blacks per se did not disturb white America. Rather, white America was disturbed by the new attitude

46

of black America. In northern cities in 1919, emboldened by their very numbers and remembering their own sacrifices in the war to make the world safe for democracy, blacks fought back. "We return. / We return from fighting. / We return fighting," wrote the scholar, writer, and activist W. E. B. Du Bois. And a variety of social and cultural movements—from the "Harlem Renaissance" of poets, writers, and artists to the Pan-Africanism of Du Bois and the nationalism of the Garvey movement—swept the newly emerging black ghettos. It was this relatively militant black response, more than anti-black violence, that stunned conservative thought.

To sum up, then, the immediate postwar years saw feminist agitation, strikes, urban riots, lynchings, rapid immigration from abroad, increased migration from American farms, and fear of revolution. But if it all sounds like a rerun of the 1890s, the response and the outcome were quite different. Repression and co-optation cooled the movements, and the tensions—or the readily visible tensions at least—subsided.

First, repression: for two or three years following the war, a Red Scare, not unlike the McCarthyite period following World War II, raged.[3] "Criminal syndicalism" laws, making it a felony to *advocate* crimes or violence for purposes of political change, were passed, and used to harass and jail militants and radicals. More ludicrously, twenty-four states passed "red flag" laws: the New York version, for example, threatened six months in jail for anyone showing a red flag "in any public assembly or parade as a symbol or emblem of any organization or association, or in furtherance of any political, social or economic principle, doctrine, or propaganda." Such laws were not ludicrous at the time, however, and around the country some 350 people were jailed. Vigilante groups arose to attack unionists and "reds." A Senate committee (the Overman committee) and several state legislative committees (most notably New York's Lund committee) scrutinized the citizenry for signs of disloyalty. Loyalty oaths were instituted for teachers and other public employees; in New York, hundreds of teachers were fired for suspected disloyalty. The committees staged their own investigatory raids, as did U.S. Attorney General A. Mitchell Palmer, who, on one night alone in early January 1920, rounded up some 4,000 people in thirty-three states, supposedly radical aliens deserving of deportation.

The impact of all this was predictably great. Ideas that had been respectable only a few years earlier were no longer even uttered.

47

Social experimentation and proposals for social reform became dangerous. The very idea of the government being responsible for public welfare was branded "communistic." (The American Medical Association, which as late as 1916 had favored national health insurance, underwent a change of leaders and began denouncing the idea as a surefire road to bolshevism.) And the unions, political organizations, and others against which the drive was aimed were virtually destroyed: their members were jailed, deported, or intimidated; their sources of money dried up as lists of donors were seized by the police; and their publications were seized and banned from the mail.

The Red Scare died down after 1920, replaced by co-optation and prosperity. The twenties, of course, have a reputation as an era of great prosperity. They were the "roaring twenties." the boom before the bust, the "jazz age," the age of flappers and speakeasies and automobiles—all partially true, at least.[4] National income rose 44 percent during the decade; aggregate wages and salaries about the same; and aggregate dividends soared 110 percent. Consumerism flourished. To many, it seemed that poverty, if not already eliminated, was doomed; with eternal prosperity blooming, it was only a matter of years—and not many years—before poverty would be nothing more than an unpleasant memory.

The Depression spoiled the fun, of course. And with a little care, it is easy to see that, aggregate figures notwithstanding, the twenties were not such good times for most of the poor and that the poor did not diminish in number. Workers, farmers, and immigrants were not entirely excluded from the golden bubble, but they didn't quite *participate* in it, either. Wartime farm prosperity collapsed with the postwar revival of worldwide agricultural production; farmers spent most of the decade in a depression. The decade saw a 34 percent growth in the physical output of the manufacturing industry, but with increasingly productive machinery in use, there was no increase in employment. After 1925 the housing boom that had followed the war collapsed, and widespread subemployment and unemployment among construction workers occurred. The principal areas of employment growth during the decade were in services and trade—low-wage industries.

In short, the depression of the thirties began early for farmers and the working class. In 1929, just before the bust, when poverty level income was estimated at $1,000 per year and a family of five needed

$1,800 per year for "minimal health and decency," no less than 42 percent of all U.S. families earned less than $1,500.[5] Some workers, of course, were making it, particularly workers among those immigrant groups that included many artisans, tradespeople, and skilled workers (i.e., people who were already at the top of the working class), such as Jews. But for those less fortunate—Italians, French, Canadians, Poles, Ukranians, and especially blacks and Mexicans—the twenties provided no escape.

Nevertheless, prosperity and the rise of a consumer society did have a major impact on the middle class and on at least part of the working class, and it requires closer discussion. Recall that as early as the 1890s the American economy had shown signs of stagnation because of the apparent saturation of consumer markets. There were two readily apparent ways of solving this problem: expansion of both trade and investment abroad and consumption at home.[6] We will not discuss the former, for it had only an indirect impact on domestic social policy. As for the latter, to state the solution merely raises another problem: how could the consumption of the American people expand, given that most Americans were already spending every cent they earned to ensure bare survival?

The answer, in essence, was to persuade people to save less of their income (if they had any to save), to spend it all, and then to go into debt—that is, to spend more than their income. "The future of business," wrote one trade magazine, lies in "its ability to manufacture customers as well as products."[7] Advertisements and the mass media were used to create the image of a consumer society; and teachers, social workers, and domestic scientists, in propagating the ideas of "right living," did their part.[8]

What was needed, it should be emphasized, was nothing less than a major change in American values. "Industry," recalled Boston merchant Edward Filene some years later, "was perfected to a point which made it absolutely necessary for the masses to spend their money freely and to unlearn their previous habits of thrift."[9] Buy instead of save; consume instead of work; go into debt; live for today, not for tomorrow. Evidently this appeal offered little to the poor, who were already in debt up to their necks; but to the more affluent members of the working class and to the middle class, the appeal was great indeed. By 1926 almost three-quarters of all automobile purchases were on credit; by 1929, 15 percent of all nonfood retail purchases were similarly obtained. And what was financed by credit was a new consumer society: 5 million radios in 1929 (up from 109,000 in 1923); 800,000 refrigerators in 1929 (up from 5,000 in 1921); perfume and cosmetics worth $193 million in 1929 (up from $17 million in 1913). And above all, cars: the one million cars on the road in 1913 gave way to 23 million in 1929.[10]

It is difficult to overstate the magnitude of the change in values the new consumer society required and created. To justify the new spending habits, one had to live for the present and let the future take care of itself. Individualism, once a hallowed American value signifying independence from others, following the beat of one's own drum, was redefined to mean little more than looking out for oneself and expressing one's individual personality through the commodities one chose to buy. A new age of hedonism was upon us.

The social and political impact of these cultural changes cannot be assessed precisely. Some contemporaries saw it simplistically and bluntly: "To those who cannot change their whole lives or occupations, even a new line in a dress is often a relief," wrote one prominent advertising copywriter.[11] But the impact was both deeper and more subtle than this. This is not the place for an in-depth study, but consider just for a moment the impact of the automobile: the car made young people mobile, freeing them, if only for an evening, from the scrutiny and values and authority of parents and community. When the closed car replaced the previously common open models (only 10 percent of the 1919 models had been closed, compared with 83 percent in 1927), the privacy afforded by the car was increased still more. A "house of prostitution on wheels," one Muncie, Indiana, judge called it, noting that of thirty women brought before him for sex-related crimes in no less than nineteen cases the site of the alleged crime was a car.[12]

Equally, the car contributed to the breakup of urban communities. No longer was there any need for workplaces to be located near residential areas. The old city neighborhood, at once a residential community and an occupational community, was destroyed. The age of suburbanization had dawned.

The spread of other commodities had similar effects, in aggregate at least. New appliances and the replacement of the traditional products of home production by commercially produced equivalents undercut "traditional" female roles (themselves created by the first great division of household and commercial labor of the early industrial revolution). To be able to afford the new commercially produced commodities and the mass-media touted American standard of living, growing numbers of women sought paid employment. These changes, along with those previously discussed contributed significantly to the shake-up in traditional intrafamily relationships. Husband–wife roles shifted; parental authority diminished; divorce rates soared.

The other side of mass consumption was, of course, mass production. For our purposes, what is notable about the new mass-production techniques is their devaluation of skill. On the assembly line or tending the machine, what was needed was not skill and experience but youth, stamina, agility, and discipline. Wrote two engineer-analysts in 1915, describing the Ford assembly lines: "The Ford Company has no use for experience, in the ranks, anyway. It desires and prefers machine tool operators who have nothing to unlearn, who have no theories of correct surface speeds for metal cutting, and will simply do what they are told to do, over and over again, from bell time to bell time."[13] A boy of eighteen had become more useful to industry than was his father. Experience and age had lost their value, further undercutting parental authority.

The weakening of parental and community controls or, more positively, the growing pressures to "live" reinforced the new, more hedonistic values. Nowhere is the change more evident than in the area of sexuality. In the 1920s the United States broke out of its Victorian straitjacket. F. Scott Fitzgerald's 1920 heroine of *This Side of Paradise* created a national scandal when she confessed: "I've kissed dozens of men. I suppose I'll kiss dozens more." Sophisticated young men and women went to "petting parties," said by some to have appeared as early as 1916 or so. Increasingly, explicit sex pervaded magazines, newspapers, and movies. In popular music, the romantic violin was edged out by the sensuous saxophone. The writings of Havelock Ellis and Sigmund Freud, interpreted as showing the dangers of sexual repression and the benefits of self-indulgence, became the rage among the avant-garde.[14]

How much these changes directly affected poor people is open to question.[15] What is certain is that they affected the middle class, including social workers and policy makers, and so affected their perceptions of what was possible and desirable, of the nature and even the existence of the social crisis.

One other component of the mass receptiveness to Freud deserves mention: the war itself. The Progressive Era had complete faith in rationality and an abiding belief in progress. But the war was a massive exercise in atavism and irrationality. The massive carnage, the gas attacks and pyrrhic battles of Ardennes and the Somme, the growing suspicion that it was not a war to make the world safe for democracy but a war to enrich the munitions makers and to enlarge empires—all had a massive impact. Pessimism about the power of reason and a renewed belief in the power of people's baser instincts surged. In the United States, these attitudes had to confront an underlying and continuing scientism. In this light, psychoanalysis was the perfect ideology. Not merely was it a way of exploring the irrational, but it presented itself as a *scientific* was of doing so. It dealt with a new issue in an old, acceptable way.

Even more broadly, the war, together with postwar hedonism and the postwar disruption of old family and community structures, undercut the prewar faith in social engineering, in the possibility or even the desirability of organizing society rationally. Conversely, interest in the individual, in emotions, in what *Survey* editor Paul Kellogg somewhat unhappily called the "drama of people's insides," grew. These themes pervaded a broad array of social and cultural phenomena. And so, Freud found a ready audience in the United States.

During the twenties, then, the objectively existing crisis of the poor did not go away. However, as a result of the general prosperity and the decline of overt social unrest, the visibility of the crisis was diminished. Repression had knocked out some social movements. The spread of "welfare capitalism"—company unions, company-sponsored and -controlled benefits, subsidized housing, even employee-relations plans featuring pastel walls, upgraded rest rooms, and softball teams—combined with vicious anti-unionism, knocked out others. Feminism, by 1919 virtually a single-issue movement focused on gaining the vote, collapsed upon achieving this goal. The penetration, disruption, and policing of working-class communities by teachers, social workers, and other "social engineers" and the replacement of autonomous and collectively engaged-in community activities by the privatized consumption of commodities undermined the previously growing collective consciousness of the urban working class. And finally, the new consumer society had found ways of raising people's apparent standards of living without giving them much of a raise. It had created the hope, if not always the reality, of economic improvement through individual effort.

The Emergence of Social Work as a Profession

By 1923 or 1924, from the perspective of the professional-managerial class, the turn-of-the-century crisis seemed to have been weathered. Social peace seemed assured. And in any case, with the overall social and political environment hostile to reform and experimentation, risk-taking seemed neither necessary nor, from a personal viewpoint, desirable.

In the absence of a major working-class movement, even many erstwhile middle-class reformers became disillusioned with the possibilities for far-reaching social reforms and turned instead toward more modest, legislative goals. Others shifted their sights from social change to social service: many of the settlement houses, for instance, once seeing themselves as advocates and fomenters of community self-organization for change, became nothing more than service centers, in which well-trained staff provided a variety of social services for the community. Their staffs, formerly residents in the settlement house, became paid workers, commuting to the slum settlement from more or less distant middle-class neighborhoods. For the professional-managerial class as a whole, the drive to reform society in their own image subsided, leaving the road open for their more immediate and particularistic occupational interests to become the primary focus of their concern.

That is not to say that the professionals had suddenly become autonomous, no longer needed to serve social control *or* social amelioration functions. The capitalism of the 1920s was, as we have seen, creating a new kind of social control task, one centered less on the prevention of mass disorder and more on the perhaps more subtle task of creating new values and socializing people into the new mass-production–mass-consumption way of life. The American personality had to be reshaped to accept the new values of spending and hedonism, while maintaining the social discipline needed by the industrial system.

Finally, the occupational and psychological needs of the professional-managerial class in general, and social workers in particular, were also changing. The professional-managerial class had, by the twenties, carved out occupational niches for itself: professional and managerial jobs were rapidly increasing in number. The class's occupational needs came to focus not on defining occupational slots per se, but on stabilizing them. For one thing, there was the problem of preventing overcompetition. Up until the 1920s, for instance, there were no real fixed qualifications for social work. Anyone could become a social worker; indeed, the volunteer tradition was so strong that, if anything, a premium was placed on the nonprofessional. The same problem faced other professional occupations, too, with slightly varying time frames and intensities. Up until 1910 or so, to take one striking example, almost anyone could become a doctor. Abraham Flexner, in his famous 1911 report on medical education, which played a key role in changing that fact, bemoaned that "any crude boy or jaded clerk" could get into and through the debased proprietary medical schools of the period.

At the same time, the various new middle-class occupations had to find ways of defining themselves with respect to other occupations coveting some of the same social functions and of legitimating themselves with respect to their clients and to the upper-class patrons who alone had the power to grant them monopolistic control over their occupational field. To use the case of medicine again, the doctors had to convince both clients and licensing authorities that they, and not other schools of physicians (osteopaths, homeopaths, "eclectics") or other kinds of healers (e.g., midwives), should be the sole practitioners of medicine and surgery.[16]

The task of convincing upper-class patrons was further complicated by the history of occasional conflict between the professional-managerial class and the upper class, stemming from the perception that the short-term interests, at least, of the capitalists and the professional-managerial class were not fully congruent. After all, it was this new middle class that during the Progressive Era had taken on the task of reforming capitalism in order to save it. To many members of the upper class, social workers and other middle-class social reformers were hard to distinguish from socia*lists*—the enemy!

The solution that emerges from this mixed group of occupational problems is professionalization. Traditional sociological treatments of professionalism argue that a "profession" is an occupation that shows certain characteristics: skills based in a defined and substantial body of knowledge; a prolonged training period; an ethical code employing a "profession" of, or "call" to, service, affective neutrality with respect to clients, collegiality with respect to other professionals, and so on. It is more fruitful, I think, to see professionalism as an occupational strategy, which reflects both occupational needs and characteristic class ideologies, for legitimizing and stabilizing the roles characteristically played by professional-managerial class occupations.[17] These roles, as we have seen, center around the reproduction and control of the social relations of capitalist society. The traits that "characterize" the professions are simply the means of attaining this legitimation and stabilization.

For social workers, we can see the problem more specifically. First, the problem of the clients: casework was rooted in the system of "friendly visitors" developed by charitable organizations in the late nineteenth century. Middle-class women "visited" the homes of the poor to screen them for eligibility for charity and to teach them, largely by moral precept, the "right" ways of living. But by the 1920s, with an increasingly Americanized working class that was increasingly sophisticated in various forms of collective struggle on its own behalf, friendly visits lost their authority—"I'm of a better class, listen to me" no longer sufficed. The poor simply wouldn't listen. But the poor might listen to "I have a whole set of skills in the techniques of living properly; I am an *expert* in matters of child rearing, housekeeping, interpersonal relations."

Of course, the skills offered by social workers, then and now, are rarely "objective." Even in medicine, where doctors' skills would appear to be based on scientific biological "facts," the knowledge base of the profession is hardly objective: medical theories and practice embody a whole series of arguable assumptions about human nature, about the relation of mind to body and of both to the social and physical environment, about doctor–patient relations, about sexuality, about "proper," or "biologically determined," sex roles, about social relations in general—all the issues that recent critiques of medical theory and practice have questioned. This situation is even more evident in professions such as social work and teaching, where human relations themselves are the subject of the apparent expertise: the knowledge base of such professions, far from being objective, embodies a whole set of assumptions, not the least of which is concerned with the "proper" roles for professional and client.

Professionalization was also an effective strategy with respect to the upper class. The roles that social workers, psychologists, teachers, and other human relations professionals want to play are hardly trivial: concerned with the socialization of the young and social control, they want to determine on behalf of society who is fit and who unfit, who is educable and who uneducable, who is educated and who uneducated, who is a proper parent and who an improper one, who is mentally ill and who is healthy, who is institutionalizable and who not, who is eligible for public support through the welfare system and who not. To be delegated by "society" to do all these things, professionals must gain assent (at least permission if not the monopoly right) from those classes that have a disproportionate share of the nation's political and economic power.

The key to gaining such assent (beyond the claims to objectivity, quality control, and so on, claims that are equally easily made and easily dishonored) is an explicit, openly scrutinizable (though difficult to master) body of knowledge, presented as the basis for the would-be profession's authority and autonomy: "*We* should be trusted to play these roles, *we* should have the sole authority to play these roles, because *we* and *only we* have the body of knowledge that enables us to do it. (Moreover, once you have decided to let us do it, you should stay out of our hair, since we, and only we, know what we are doing.)" What is essential is not that those with the power to grant such authority share in an understanding of the knowledge base but that they understand that the knowledge base is at least not inconsistent with their own interests. Once again using medicine as our model, let us examine the reception of theories about the transmission of disease at the turn of the century. Many physicians understood that low wages, unsafe working conditions, crowded and unsanitary housing, and so on were at least as potent "explanations" of disease as was germ theory. State legislatures, however, heavily influenced by industrialists, landlords, and the like, could hardly be expected to grant medical authority to these doctors rather than to those who spoke with scientific expertise about the transmission of germs from individual to individual.

Several unusual characteristics of social work strengthened and shaped its drive to professionalize. First, the problem of raising the status of social work was unusually intense. Social work was concerned with the poor, a group of extremely low social status, evidently a potential source of profit to no one. Given the business values that dominated American culture in the twenties, work with the poor could not be seen as "important." It was, perhaps, a pleasant and safe volunteer activity for the wives of middle- and upperclass men, but it was hardly a "profession," requiring skills and meriting financial recompense. Moreover, social work was, from the start, an activity dominated by women, themselves a low-status social group (although organizational and administrative positions—agency administrators, deans of schools of social work, journal editors, professional association officers—were awarded over-whelmingly to men).[18]

The low status and female composition of social work were, of course, related. Social work was one of the few professions open to women, unlike, say, law or medicine or engineering, precisely because it *was* low status and offered only low pay. Men were not interested in competing for such jobs; women were free to invent it as a profession for themselves if they chose. In any case, service to individuals in need was a traditionally "feminine" activity, easily assumable to a "social motherhood" vision of women's roles. As such, social work seemed to need little "advanced" skill or knowledge; "feminine instinct" alone ought to suffice.

As a consequence, social workers were (and remain to this day) extremely defensive about their professional status and were unusually preoccupied, even obsessed, with the problem of making social work "scientific," of defining a "knowledge base" for the field.

Perhaps even more significant, social work had a unique problem as a would-be profession. Most of its traditional clients were poor, unable to pay for social workers' services. Either social work needed to convince more middle-class (i.e., paying) clients that it had something to offer them, or it had to persuade the middle and upper classes to fund the profession, through either private philanthropy or public programs. Over the course of the years, social work pursued both strategies. We shall return to this effort shortly; for now, note only that the upper classes, if they were to be persuaded that social workers were an appropriate group to be authorized and funded to provide certain services, had to be assured that social workers would limit their endeavors to "helping" the poor cope and not expand into the area of "reforming" society (i.e., to control the upper classes' freedom to exploit the poor). A present-day professional concern of social workers may help elucidate this point: social workers are now seeking the right to be reimbursed for their services to individuals by Medicaid, Medicare, Blue Cross, and other public and private insurance agencies. It should be clear that they are far more likely to be successful in this demand if social work services are defined as individual casework and therapy rather than as community organizing, advocacy, lobbying, and other efforts at social change.

The major phase in the process of professionalization of social work may be said to have begun in 1915, when Abraham Flexner, the Carnegie Foundation staff official who earlier helped medicine to full professionalization, addressed a general session of the National Conference of Charities and Corrections on, "Is Social Work a Profession?"[19] Whatever the expectations of the conference organizers, Flexner's answer was a resounding "no."

Social work, Flexner argued, is not a profession in itself but simply a mediating occupation, coordinating the activities of other professions—doctors, teachers, lawyers, and so on. Social work "is not so much a definite field as an aspect of work in many fields," Flexner argued. It lacks "specificity of aim"; social workers need to be "well-informed, well-balanced, tactful, judicious, sympathetic, resourceful," but no "definite kind or kinds of technical skill are needed." If social work really wanted to transform itself into a profession, he told his dismayed audience, his analysis had several practical implications:

> For example: the social worker is at times perhaps somewhat too self-confident; social work has suffered to some extent from one of the vices associated with journalism, excessive facility in speech and in action. . . . Is it not possible that part of the vast army of reaction is made up of those needlessly terrified by the occasionally reckless—and perhaps somewhat baseless—confidence of the reformer? If so, failure to realize the limitations of social work from the professional point of view is not without practical consequences. . . . I do not want to diminish the vigor of any attack that can be made upon poverty, ignorance, disease, selfishness; but for the moment I am, ignoring all else, looking at the method of the social worker from the merely professional standpoint. Now when social work becomes thoroughly professional in character and scientific in method, it will be perceived that vigor is not synonymous with intelligence.[20]

Flexner's comments caused an uproar among social workers; the social work literature of the next decade is filled with proposals for increasing the professional status of social work which make direct reference to his speech. And Flexner's precept, to be more circumspect, not to antagonize the powerful with reckless calls for their reform did not go unheeded. For example, in the discussions leading to the founding of the American Association of Social Workers in 1921 there are repeated expressions of concern lest the new organization take stands on political issues and so jeopardize the professionalization of social work.[21]

The Emergence of Social Work as a Profession

In 1929, Porter Lee, director of the prestigious New York School of Social Work and president of the (now renamed) National Conference of Social Work, applauded the progress social work had made in professionalizing itself over the decade and a half since Flexner's address. In his widely quoted speech "Social Work: Cause and Function," Lee noted the shift in social work from promoting causes to serving as an ongoing function of "well-organized community life."[22] The shift had "aroused apprehension in many minds," Lee noted, but, in fact, social work could do more to promote the needs of the poor by day-in-day-out services than by grand rhetoric and grander causes. Society would not, in the long run, support causes:

> Social work comes under increasingly critical scrutiny from those who support it. . . . The establishment of social work as a function . . . changes radically the relationship of social workers, both professional and lay, to the public. If I were to put this change into a sentence, I would say that the historic obligation of social workers to the public for leadership had changed to an obligation for leadership supplemented by accountability. In discharging the obligation of accountability we may easily put an unnecessary strain upon the community's acceptance of our leadership by a tendency to claim more than we can perform through a desire to be uncompromisingly cosmic.[23]

We shall see in the next chapter that the impulse to social reform was not so easily quenched as Flexner and Lee believed necessary for social work's professional health. And as a consequence in the decades that followed the same pleas would be heard again and again from those worried about social work's professional standing. For example, in a widely cited 1957 article in *Social Work,* University of California social work professor Ernest Greenwood warned social workers that they "might have to scuttle their social action heritage as a price of achieving the public acceptance accorded a profession."[24] And in 1972, at the end of a decade in which social reform had again come to the fore in social workers' imaginations, Harry Specht, another professor at the University of California, argued that the effect of this activism would be "the deprofessionalization of social work." Although sympathetic to the goals of the activists, Specht warned that "the profession can continue only as long as it assumes the responsibilities and authority of a profession"; he went on to detail all the ways in which the activism of the period undercut the ability of social workers to "proffer help to clients—rich or poor, black or white, oppressed, depressed, repressed, or whatever—within a *framework of ethics and values*" (emphasis in original; Specht seems to mean the "ethics and values" held by social workers and their patrons, since he opposes this to blind "fealty" to the cause of the clients).[25]

To sum up then, the social workers of the twenties increasingly saw the need to professionalize in order to legitimate themselves with respect to clients and to gain the support of state legislatures, foundations, philanthropists, and other sources of prestige, funds, and institutional power. The key to achieving such professionalization, they quickly saw, was an identifiable body of knowledge that focused social worker's practical activities in ways that would be nonthreatening to those patrons.

The solution was psychoanalytic theory. Social work professionalized in the form of the psychiatric social worker or, more generally, the caseworker armed wih psychoanalytic theory.[26] The adoption of psychoanalytic theory as well as other psychiatric theories as the route to professional identity had one obvious problem, however: how would social workers distinguish themselves from other occupational groups oriented to human services, health and mental health, and socialization and social control issues—doctors, nurses, teachers, psychiatrists, psychologists? All of them to some measure, and especially the powerful M.D. psychiatrists, were also absorbing psychoanalytic theory into their professional canons. This problem occasioned much debate in the twenties and thereafter (and to this day); we shall return to it in the next chapter.

What is especially noteworthy about the psychiatric solution to social work's occupational woes is how different it is from the ideals of the Jane Addams generation of social workers, who saw themselves as reformers, as "preventive social workers" rather than as caseworkers. But the Jane Addams tradition was not the only point of departure for social work practice. Let us digress for a moment.

The origins of modern social casework lie in the charities of the nineteenth century.[27] A sense of humanity required that the growing numbers of the poor be saved from outright starvation, even if, as was widely assumed, they had only their own laziness, feeble-mindedness, or moral turpitude to blame for their problems. But pitting humanitarianism against this Social Darwinist understanding led to a dilemma: the continued distribution of alms would merely serve to increase the dependency of the existing poor and increase the numbers of people demanding aid. "The great problem of all charity . . . is how to diminish suffering without increasing, by the very act, the number of paupers," worried Frederick H. Wines, secretary of the Board of Public Charities of the State of Illinois in 1872.[28]

The solution to this dilemma was sought in the so-called scientific charity movement of the 1870s on. The newly organized Charity Organization societies had three main principles of operation: first, they sought to use business methods to rationalize and control the flow of charity. Charity, they tried to persuade the rich, should not take the form of individually doled out alms but of assistance delivered through a formally organized and controllable agency. The activities of these agencies, in turn, had to be carefully coordinated. Otherwise, clients could rip off the system by independently seeking aid from several agencies. Or even worse, a client whose aid had been restricted or cut off by one agency to discourage the development of dependency might obtain aid from another agency and thus undercut the entire purpose of charity.

Second, the activities of the charity agencies should always be focused on the moral uplift of the client. The agency must distinguish between the "worthy" poor (poor through no fault of their own, desperately trying to be independent despite great odds, and willing to conform to all regulations, both bureaucratic and moral, of the charitable agency) and the "unworthy" poor (the drunks, the malingerers, the lazy, the perverse, the malcontents, who given half a chance would rather become dependent on charity than work or otherwise pull themselves up by their own bootstraps). Unemployment, opined the Philadelphia Charity Organization Society's Mary Richmond in 1907, is "prima facie evidence of inefficiency or unwillingness to work."[29] Having identified the worthy poor (the unworthy were simply to be cut off), the goal of charity was to encourage independence, to reform the poor. In practice this meant doling out aid one day's worth at a time, so that the job-seeking activities of the recipient could be scrutinized, and expecting the poor to be properly docile and faithful.

Finally, as mentioned earlier, the central figure in the operation of the new scientific charities was the "friendly visitor"—middle- and upper-class women who volunteered to serve the dual function of social investigator (determining the initial and continuing eligibility of the client) and teacher. By precept and by the simple example of their own civilized and moral selves, the visitors were to impart higher standards and knowledge of how to attain them to their clients. The fundamental service provided by the charities was, in their words, "not alms but a friend."

In the early 1890s a number of charity workers, along with young middle-class college graduates, recoiled at the paternalism and victim-blaming of this approach to charity.[30] Some joined the broad drive for social reform, with consequences we have already seen. Others, pursuing a model already being practiced in England, set up "settlement houses." Young men and especially young women sought out a large house in an urban slum, where they settled, in some cases for a few months, in others for years or a lifetime. Their goals were to provide neither alms nor a friend but a good *neighbor*— to teach, but also to learn, to identify social needs, and to participate in struggles against social injustice. And so Hull House and the Chicago Commons and Greenwich House and Dennison House and dozens of others were set up not as service organizations per se (they became that later) but as opportunities for the classes to get to know one another, to "bring men and women of education into closer relations with the laboring classes for their mutual benefit," as the constitution of New York's University Settlement put it.[31]

The consequences were, in retrospect at least, predictable. The settlement-house workers got to know the poor not just in times of crisis but in happier times as well, not just when dependency threatened but when strength was shown. "We knew not only poverty and crime, but also the intelligence and ability and charm of our neighbors," wrote Greenwich House's Mary Simkhovitch.[32] Women such as Simkhovitch and Jane Addams came to appreciate immigrant traditions and values, to see strengths in the community. Their appreciation was not without ambivalence. But for our purposes now, the point is that in getting to know people and communities it became impossible to continue to see poverty as simply the fault of the poor. The settlement-house workers quickly discarded the worthy-poor–unworthy-poor distinction. They saw that poverty was the lot of thousands of people with energy, intelligence, ambition, and imagination; that you quickly became poor, through no fault of your own, if you lost your job, or your husband was injured at work, or your child was sick, or you had to pay half your income for a rat-infested tenement apartment with no indoor plumbing.

And if this was true, then the road to social amelioration led not to uplifting the poor, not to changing their character, but to changing the environmental conditions that made people poor, sick, and miserable. Minimum wage laws, child labor laws, tenement reform, widows' pensions, factory safety laws, food inspections, the provision of sanitary facilities, parks, libraries, schools—these, and not dealing after the fact with the consequences of their denial, were the proper goals for "social workers." "Poverty is no longer an inevitable condition to be accepted or endured; it is a problem of economic and social life which demands solution," summed up a 1915 manual. Resignation, reflected Walter Lippmann, might have been appropriate in earlier historical times, times of economic scarcity, "but in the midst of plenty, the imagination becomes ambitious, rebellion against misery is at last justified, and dreams have a basis in fact." "Preventive social work," not individual change, became the dominant project of Progressive Era social workers influenced by these developments.[33]

By the early years of this century, then, a polarity had emerged within social work (or, more accurately, among the occupational ancestors of social workers; it was not until the teens that the term "social worker" came into general usage to cover the full range of what we now think of as social work activities). To some, the central roles of social work should be advocacy, community development, reform, an approach that assumed most social and individual ills were, at root, caused by the physical and social environment. To others, individual casework, helping the individual in need through counseling and through provision of direct services, was the core. In this later approach, in some sense the individual client, rather than the environment, was assumed to be the cause of his or her own misfortune, at least in the implicit, nonmorally condemnatory sense that individual change (personality change, improved social or technical skills) was the key to solving the individual's problems.

During the years following the Civil War, the individual-change model (in, as we have seen, its most morally damning form) was in the ascendancy, but during the Progressive Era the environmentalist approach came to the fore. In the early 1890s, settlement-house workers were barely tolerated in the National Conference of Charities and Corrections; but in 1909 Jane Addams was elected president of that body. And, as we have seen, the Progressive Era was above all a time when reformers exuded confidence that environmental reform would solve all the ills of society. Nevertheless,

63

even during the Progressive Era, concern for dealing with the individual in need continued, and techniques for doing so were developed. In this stream of the development of social work, the occupational needs of the as yet unprofessionalized social workers appear evident.

The central figure in this stream was Mary Richmond.[34] As general secretary of first the Baltimore, then the Philadelphia Charity Organization Society, and later as director of the Russell Sage Foundation's Charity Organization Department, Richmond was in an extraordinary position to observe the development of direct services to individuals. To Richmond, it quickly became evident that casework was not merely a matter of goodwill and energy, to be provided by the volunteer friendly visitor, but a skill, to be obtained through disciplined observation, study, and practice. As early as 1897 she called for the formation of a "school of applied philanthropy" to train such workers. (The first such school, the New York School for Applied Philanthropy, which ultimately became the Columbia University School of Social Work, began year-round operations in 1904.) She was equally insistent on the need for a professional organization. To Richmond, social work's slogan had to become: neither alms nor a friend nor a neighbor but "a professional service."

Richmond's most enduring contribution, perhaps, was her pioneering effort to bring order to the practice of casework itself. Bringing together her observations of hundreds of cases in Baltimore, Philadelphia, and New York in her 1917 book *Social Diagnosis*, she sought to provide a system for casework.[35] She called for a process of careful differential social diagnosis of cases: the social caseworker should assiduously collect and interpret "any and all facts as to personal or family history, which, taken together, indicate the nature of a given client's difficulty and the means for [its] solution."

Although Richmond emphasized individual casework rather than sweeping reforms (the "retail" method of social work, as opposed to the reformer's "wholesale" method, as she called it in a celebrated disputation with the Wharton School's Simon Patten), her approach can nevertheless be called "sociological" rather than "psychological."[36] Richmond saw the client as having an objective economic or social problem, which could be understood by a careful interviewing of the client, family members, neighbors, teachers, and employers and by direct and specific investigations of the client's living conditions, neighborhood, workplace, and so on. That is, although the client's problems were experienced individually and had to be solved individually (and here there was some room, at least, for a psychiatric component to treatment—the action of "mind upon mind" as Richmond put it), ultimately they were rooted in environmental conditions and social experience. Consequently, "treatment" involved intervening in the environment to change it or to enable the client to wend his or her way through it as much as it involved changing the client himself or herself.

Richmond's book in one sense marks the beginning of the modern era in casework; however, it virtually simultaneously marks the end of the old era: it is a summing up of the experience and skills of the prepsychiatric generation of social workers. Within two years after its publication, the psychiatric deluge had begun: at the 1919 National Conference, paper after paper describing the new psychiatric approach was presented, "sweeping the convention" in the words of Jessie Taft, one of the principal "sweepers." Let us turn, then, to the development of the psychiatric strain in social casework.

Psychiatric social work is sometimes said to have begun as early as 1905–6 at Massachusetts General Hospital, Manhattan State Hospital, and a few other places where social workers were employed by such psychiatrists as Adolf Meyer, Richard Cabot, and James Putman. But for the most part, these social workers were really simply medical social workers, using the then standard social casework techniques in a psychiatric hospital setting. The true progenitors of psychiatric social work were the mental hygiene movement, the child guidance movement, and the development of veterans' services.

The mental hygiene movement, in a sense the most basic of the three,[37] was sparked by the publication of *The Mind That Found Itself* by Clifford Beers in 1908. Beers, a young Yale graduate, had been hospitalized for three years in various public and private institutions. Upon release, he resolved to expose the atrocious conditions existing in the nation's mental hospitals. His book attracted a great deal of attention, and soon, with funding from the Rockefeller Foundation, the National Committee on Mental Hygiene (NCMH) was formed.

At first the NCMH confined itself to the reform of mental hospitals and institutions for the feebleminded, a classic Progressive Era concern. But under pressure from the Rockefeller Foundation (and against Beers's will), by the late teens and early twenties the NCMH had shifted to much broader concerns, concerns that were also of interest to other large foundations such as the Commonwealth Fund and the Laura Spelman Rockefeller Memorial. The broadly defined mental hygiene movement came to focus on (1) issues of the role of mental hygiene (what today we would call mental health) in education, criminology, and economic dependency; (2) programs of preventive mental health and mental health treatment; (3) research to define the "normal" personality, as a bench mark, and using this concept, to discover ways of ensuring "normality" in most people (through both improved approaches to child rearing and education and the early detection and treatment of "abnormality"); and (4) training a new generation of mental health workers and other professionals to carry out these tasks. This last concern meant, above all, social workers, whose schools, professional associations, and journals were heavily funded by the Russell Sage Foundation, the Commonwealth Fund, and the Laura Spelman Rockefeller Memorial in the early 1920s.

It is beyond my present intention to discuss all aspects of the mental hygiene movement's work and influence. I will merely seek to summarize the development of the normality and abnormality concept and how it filtered into the practice of social work. Earlier in the century, when the notion that the poor and the deviant were morally to blame for their problems was in disrepute and with the development of new approaches to psychological testing (especially IQ testing), a variety of studies had purported to show that most deviance was caused by "feeblemindedness" and other presumably genetically determined psychological problems. For example, studies of prison inmates showed systematically lower IQs among convicted criminals than among the population at large. In the years after World War I, under the sponsorship of the NCMH and other similar groups, new studies were done rebutting the old. At the same time, the new researchers developed an alternate explanation for social deviance. It was due, they said, to "mental disorder"—that is, deviance was a *disease,* which could presumably be prevented, detected, and treated. New diagnostic categories quickly emerged: the "maladjusted" person, the "psychopathic personality," the "borderline patient." The linkage of these notions to the problem of controlling social disorder (or, conversely, to the need to create the personality types needed for consumer capitalism) was clear and explicit. One 1930 article defined the "sociopathic" personality as "all individuals who at any moment are displaying behavior which is futile or antagonistic from the standpoint of the group."[38] And another widely used 1930s text, William Sadler's *Theory and Practice of Psychiatry*, listed among its personality disorders and maladjusted people such types as "paupers . . . prostitutes . . . misfits . . . criminals . . . drug users . . . extraordinarily backward and bashful individuals . . . the general run of gypsies . . . volitional old maids . . . many unskilled laborers . . . dreamers and artistic types . . . deep thinkers—including many writers and novelists . . . moral reformers . . .radicals and agitators . . . chronic grouches . . . peace-loving pacifists . . . [and] . . . the over-studious."[39]

These ideas—clearly relevant both to the control of industrial unrest and to those who might dissent with respect to the new consumer and mass producer personalities needed by 1920s capitalism—were explicit themes of mental hygiene activists. Neuropathologist E. E. Southard, director of Boston Psychopathic Hospital and one of the principal leaders of the mental hygiene movement, noted a 1920 strike in which "according to the records, every one of the strikers had something wrong with them from a nervous or mental standpoint." He wrote article after article, in psychiatric and industrial relations journals, proposing the usefulness of a new kind of industrial social work to detect and treat such malcontents before they created open labor strife. (Although his focus was on the worker malcontents, in good professional-managerial class fashion he felt compelled to note that some strikes, at least, were caused by "mental disease or character defect" among employment managers, executives, and owners.)[40]

Some specific constructs of the 1920s mental hygiene movement seem ludicrous, in retrospect, but their traces, in contemporary ideas of the "normal" personality, have endured. And the social control content and intent of these concepts, now obscured in the thousands of pages of scholarly studies based on them, are evident in their inception. The central argument of the mental hygiene movement researchers went like this:[41] (a) Personality traits in the individual are shaped by the environment. (b) But "environment" is not to be interpreted as the larger social structure, as the Jane Addams generation of reformers would have had it, nor even as the individual's school, job, and neighborhood, as the Mary Richmond generation of caseworkers would have had it. Rather, the key environmental factors in shaping personality are emotional relationships *in the home* (not at school, at work, in the market place). (c) The critical emotional factors in the home have to do with child rearing, and in particular with the child's learning how to deal with frustration, deprivation, and external authority. Thus toilet training, feeding schedules, and similar concerns become the focus of attention. (d) Various modes of child rearing will produce accordingly different adult personalities. In particular, elaborate studies of the child-rearing patterns typical of the different social classes "revealed" that the child rearing of the upper classes produced dilettantish adults, suitable for sports and partying but little else; the tightly scheduled and controlling patterns of the middle class produced entrepreneurial types, full of energy and individuality but without the "other directed" (to use David Riesman's later word) characteristics needed for teamwork in the large corporate and public bureaucracies; and the permissive (though coupled with corporal punishment) mode of the working class produced acceptably docile and nonindividualistic adult workers who had an unfortunate tendency to sudden outbreaks of rage. That is, the mental hygiene researchers located the dynamics of American social structure not in social institutions but in individual personality, mediated by socially stratified modes of parenting. E. E. Southard and Mary C. Jarrett were explicit: a "psychopathic interpretation of history must replace the economic interpretation; history . . . can best be interpreted by the technique which starts from the outset to observe the minor variations, the differences and the contrasts, rather than the similarities and the analogies that so fill the mind of the observer of averages."[42] (e) Finally, if all this is true, the key to maintaining social order and appropriate economic behavior, at all levels of the social and economic system, lay in new and improved modes of child rearing, now labeled as "normal" or "adequate" parenting. Thus the Yale Psycho-Clinic's Arnold Gesell (whose account of the normal stages of child development became one of the bibles of post–World War II mothers), in a 1924 article on the significance of the newly developed nursery schools, hoped that "the playgrounds of the nursery will give a glimpse of what social living can be and demonstrate that while the art of peaceful cooperation is difficult to learn, it is not impossible."[43] If Gesell was right, American civilization would be built on the playgrounds of the nursery school, not the playing fields of Eton. And Laurence Frank, the official at the Laura Spelman Rockefeller Memorial who directed that foundation's massive interest in the mental hygiene movement, suggested that the personality of a child who had received proper parenting would display "the characteristic submissiveness to authority and acceptance of limitations of income and possessions . . . largely because the underlying feeling tone toward life, derived from breast feeding and mothering will prevent any strong resentments and will foster an attitude of cheerful acceptance."[44]

These ideas were transmitted to the public through popular books and articles. (Dr. Benjamin Spock's *Baby and Child Care,* published in 1946, represented the fullest expression of the positive child-rearing prescriptions of the mental hygiene movement.) But the theories were carried most persuasively and pervasively via the intermediaries of teachers, doctors, and social workers. The Laura Spelman Rockefeller Memorial set up a program in "parent education"; the Commonwealth Fund financed a Program for the Prevention of Delinquency; and the U.S. government established a network of psychiatric services for veterans, including a chain of veterans' hospitals.

Veterans' services fit readily into the developing psychiatric approach. The war had posed new problems for social workers, psychologists, and psychiatrists. Recruiting for the army involved new programs for testing and then training soldiers. Even more important were the problems of rehabilitation of the wounded and those suffering from "battle fatigue." The latter were especially intriguing to mental health workers. The poor or the deviant were no longer the only appropriate subjects of the mental hygiene forces. Here were perfectly normal, working or middle class men who under the stress of battle had developed puzzling mental symptoms. To deal with the problem, the army set up a special corps. The National Committee on Mental Hygiene and the Boston State Hospital volunteered to establish an eight-week intensive training program to prepare social workers to deal with these problems. The program, held the summer of 1918 at Smith College, was a great success and soon became institutionalized as the Smith College School for Social Work. Other social work schools quickly introduced psychiatric training into their programs, as well. Immediately after the war, the government began providing psychiatric services for veterans, first through a network of local and state facilities and then through federal veterans' hospitals. During the twenties the Veterans Bureau was to become the largest employer of the new breed of psychiatric social worker.

The Commonwealth Fund's Program for the Prevention of Delinquency embraced the entire mental hygiene field. There were programs to educate and train social workers and nurses and doctors in the new ideas and techniques; programs to fund research on the causes and prevention of delinquency; the establishment of an experimental system of "visiting teachers" (school social workers, whose tasks included working with teachers to identify potential delinquents early and then to work with child, parents, and school to abort that feared development; in so doing, the social worker provided an entrée into the schools of mental hygiene ideas and ideas of "normal" child development and behavior); programs of direct public education; and a system of demonstration "child guidance clinics" in which psychiatrists, psychologists, and social workers worked as a team to treat disturbed children and their families (referred by courts, schools, doctors, social service agencies, or families themselves). Several components of the program were self-sustaining. The child guidance clinics were literally demonstrations: after a couple of years in a particular city, the demonstration team packed their tents and moved on, leaving behind an ongoing, self-financing center. Boards of education, it was expected, would sustain the visiting teacher programs. And the training programs would induct an entire generation of social workers, teachers, and psychiatrists into the psychiatric era.

The Laura Spelman Rockefeller Memorial's Parent Education Program, equally broad in scope, sought to rationalize child rearing, to improve the "management" of the child both at home and in the school. Between 1923 and 1929 the LSR Memorial (which later became part of the Rockfeller Foundation) poured some $7 million into research institutes to investigate children's behavior and development, into laboratory schools to provide research material and training experiences for social workers, nurses, teachers, and parent educators, into conferences of "experts" in the field, into fellowships and other support for training professional workers in the field, and into demonstration projects. In alliance with the American Association of University Women, the program set up thousands of "child study" (i. e., discussion) groups for middle-class mothers. For the presumably less verbal and less literate poor, there were "mothercraft" classes, directed by social workers, nurses, nutritionists, and home economists. *Parents' Magazine* carried the message to a still larger audience. What made the LSR Memorial programs especially effective was the foundation's conscious decision to use the funds to influence existing agencies, that is, to seek to redirect existing programs rather than to establish new, competing ones.

The Commonwealth Fund, Laura Spelman Rockefeller Memorial, and veterans' programs (along with other important programs sponsored by the Russell Sage Foundation and a number of other foundations) had an enormous impact. Involving large numbers of professionals, the programs pioneered new understandings of human personality and new techniques of social intervention with individuals and transformed training schools in ways that would influence future generations of professionals as well. For our present concerns, above all, they were the key mechanisms for the introduction into social work of the teachings of Sigmund Freud.

Why were social workers so responsive to psychiatric ideas? The most obvious answer, and one frequently given, is that they "worked." That is, the caseworker, armed with psychiatric insights and methods, could intervene more effectively to help clients resolve their problems.[45] Whatever the validity of this assertion in reference to the present time, there is little evidence to support it from the twenties, the period when psychiatric ideas were adopted wholesale by the social work profession. Maurice Karpf's 1931 study of social workers' actual practice showed more evidence of "common sense concepts and judgements" than of use of scientific knowledge and techniques.[46] To a handful of the most sophisticated social workers, the psychiatry of the twenties may have offered a keener *diagnostic* tool than they previously had had (although the crudely value-laden diagnostic categories discussed above would lead one to doubt even that). But there was widespread agreement, even among the leaders of the move into psychiatric social work, that psychiatry offered little by way of practical use in casework treatment. "When we come right down to the real essentials of *treatment*, we know almost nothing," complained the New York School of Social Work's Porter Lee in 1930 (emphasis mine). Psychiatrist Lawson G. Lowery, the director of the influential Institute for Children's Guidance in New York concurred, lamenting that "I think most of us would agree that whereas there are many people in this country who can write a most satisfying and elevating textbook on the causes of behavior disorders, there isn't any person, as far as I know, who is really qualified to write a textbook on treatment." Social worker Charlotte Towle made the distinction even clearer: "Social diagnosis has attained an adequacy which has not yet been realized in treatment."[47]

But if the psychiatry of the twenties could not assist caseworkers in dealing with their client's concerns, it was not useless to them. Bertha C. Reynolds, associate director of the Smith College School for Social Work, observed that during this period most social workers saw in psychiatry a more effective means of manipulating their clients, of more easily gaining their cooperation.[48] It was not until the 1930s, following the publication of Virginia Robinson's *A Changing Psychology for Social work,* that the shift to a more client-centered psychotherapy took place. M. J. Karpf, a prominent voice among those social workers who argued that more fruitful sources of insight were available through sociology than through psychology, was even more cynical, suggesting in 1925 that the value of psychology to the social worker had nothing to do with meeting a *client's* needs. Rather, it served the *social worker's* need for a sense of certainty: "Psychology offers something positive: it tells [the social worker] what to do even if it is only to institutionalize the subject. . . . It is a great help if only because it eases the all too great tension of the social worker who is conscious of her many failures and few successes by declaring the failures as lacking the mental equipment to become successes."[49]

Psychiatry appealed to social workers on a more personal level, as well. The Freudian ideas permeating American culture in the twenties were immensely attractive to the urban, middle class, including social workers. More specifically, by the 1920s there was a growing understanding that the complex emotional reactions of the social worker to the client—frustration, sympathy, strong feelings of like or dislike—had a major impact on the interaction with the client. To be effective, in the counseling situation, social workers needed to master these reactions. Consequently, as potential recipients of psychiatric services and as providers of such services, social workers were responsive to psychoanalytic ideas on both a personal and a professional level. Bertha Reynolds, a member of the first class at the Smith training institute, later recalled:

No subject was more debated among psychiatric social workers in the 1920s than the question of whether a psychoanalysis was necessary for professional success. That it was an advantage was rather generally conceded, and for a period of years, New York City, which was almost the only place to obtain an analysis, was overloaded with social workers whose job performance was made unpredictable by the emotional storms they were riding in their personal therapy.[50]

Thus, the applicability and appeal of psychoanalysis to caseworkers themselves no doubt helped pave the way for its adoption as both a tool and a professionalizing strategy. By the late 1920s, psychoanalytic theory had gained wide acceptance among leading social workers as the route social work must take if social work was to achieve full professional status.

That psychiatry did not yet offer much practical value was no serious bar to its use as a basis for professionalization.[51] Medicine itself, the very prototype of a modern profession, had had a similar history. Although the nineteenth century had seen great advances in anatomy, physiology, biochemistry, and, above all, microbiology and the development of the germ theory, little of this knowledge had been turned into therapeutically useful form by the early years of the century. "I think it was about the year 1910 or 1912," wrote medical historian L. J. Henderson, "when it became possible to say of the U.S. that a random patient, with a random disease, consulting a physician chosen at random, stood better than a fifty-fifty chance of benefitting from the encounter." Yet by 1912, "regular" physicians, claiming a legitimacy based on their mastery of the new scientific medicine, had swept the field of their competition. Licensing laws had become universal; midwives and competing schools of physicians were being suppressed; and, with the aid of Abraham Flexner's famous 1911 report on medical education, "nonscientific" medical schools (as well as most medical schools admitting blacks or women) were well on their way to elimination.[52]

The adoption of the psychiatric approach transformed the relation of social work to broader currents of social policy and, in the long run, was to deepen the split between the environmentalist and individual approaches to the field. Most obviously, psychiatric social work is an interior approach. In 1917 Mary Richmond still saw the social environment as objectively existing and primary; she called for adjustments *"between* man and his environment" (my emphasis) even though her focus was on individual change rather than on broad social change.[53] But to the new psychiatric social work, what was important was not "objective reality" but how the client perceived that reality, the "capacity of the individual to organize his own social activity in *any* given environment," as the report of the Milford Conference of social work leaders put it.[54] "When one considers that environment is to a a large extent expressed through personality, it becomes apparent that lack of adjustment to one's environment is largely a lack of satisfying relationships to other persons. Hence attitudes become important focal points of treatment," wrote Porter Lee and Marion Kenworthy, a psychiatrist who was medical director of the Commonwealth Fund's Bureau of Children's Guidance.[55] Mary Jarrett of the Boston Psychopathic Hospital, an organizer of the Smith College program in 1918 and a close associate of E. E. Southard, reexamined the cases described by Mary Richmond in *Social Diagnosis* a few years earlier. Richmond had misunderstood the cases, she proclaimed. Fully 50 percent "clearly" involved psychiatric problems, not social problems, and another 15 percent were "probably psychiatric in nature."[56] In 1940, the end of the greatest depression in American history, with the unemployment rate still above 15 percent, Gordon Hamilton (whose text, *Theory and Practice of Social Casework,* became the bible for the psychiatric social work generation of the forties) complained that some social workers are "unable to or unwilling to see poverty except as a purely economic event, without acknowledging the possible existence of childhood dependency wishes which, if they do not actually cause, may certainly prolong dependency."[57]

A radical retreat from environmentalism, and its replacement with a theory emphasizing client culpability, thus accompanied the birth of psychiatric social work as a profession. But the blame was placed not, as in the 1880s, on the client's lack of moral standards but on the client's personality disorder. It was, a matter of St. Sigmund rather than of St. Peter. But as social-work historian Chambers noted, it was certainly not a matter of St. Karl.

Psychiatric theory per se does not demand such a retreat, I should emphasize. Psychoanalyst Nathan Ackerman, studying unemployed miners in western Pennsylvania in 1937, attributed their mental health status (disastrous in his account) to their economic and social condition.

> I studied twenty-five families in which the father, the sole breadwinner in the mining community, had been without work for between two and five years. The miners, long habituated to unemployment, idled away their empty hours on the street corner or in the neighborhood saloon.

They felt defeated and degraded. . . . Humiliated by their failure as providers, they stayed away from home; they felt shamed before their wives. The wives and mothers, harassed by insecurity and want from day to day, irritably rejected their husbands; they punished them by refusing sexual relations. The man who could no longer bring home his pay envelope was no longer the head of the family. . . . Mother and son then usurped the leadership position in the family. Among these unemployed miners there were guilty depressions, hypochondriacal fears, psychosomatic crises, sexual disorders, and crippled self esteem.[58]

The split between environmental and psychiatric explanations of individual and social problems did not occur simply along political lines, with more radical or liberal social workers remaining true to environmentalism. Hamilton was politically liberal, and Bertha Reynolds, associate director of the psychiatrically oriented Smith College School for Social Work, was a major figure in the radical social work movements of the thirties. Regardless of the individual political beliefs of its proponents, however, psychiatric theory in the hands of social workers such as Hamilton did signal a withdrawal from environmental explanation and, with it, from social reform. "A program cannot make men moral, religious, or happy," proclaimed Miriam Van Waters, president of the National Conference of Social Work in the early days of the Depression, with the breadlines growing day by day. "The springs of action are in the internal nature of man. Hence the uselessness of programs, particularly those that depend upon state action of force."[59] It should scarcely be necessary to emphasize how attractive this position was to the upper class and how adaptive it was for an occupation seeking recognition by that upper class as a full-fledged profession.

The psychiatric orientation led as well to a change in the characteristic clientele of social workers. By turning toward the inner life, social work escaped its previously almost exclusive concern with the problems of the poor. "The deepest human misery, the inner problems, are common to rich and poor alike," wrote Jessie Taft of the Pennsylvania School for Social Work in 1928.[60] Casework, observed Cleveland social work administrator Edward D. Lynde, is of "universal value"; it appeals to the "average man."[61] The psychiatric perspective, unlike the sociological viewpoint, included the problems of all, rich and poor alike (recall the earlier citation from Harry Specht: "rich or poor, black or white, oppressed, depressed, repressed, or whatever"). The implications of this position are enormous: those clients who are amenable and responsive to analysis, who have time, money, and an appropriately verbal/introspective personality become the most desirable clients. And that, of course, means middle-class clients, not the poor. Social work shifted massively toward a concern with the middle class. Even in the twenties, the shift was evident. The clinic at the New York Bureau of Children's Guidance, for instance, reported that 32 percent of their clients were "affluent" or "comfortable." (Studies of social work agencies in the 1950s and 1960s showed even higher figures, with from 65 percent to 75 percent of the clients identified as "upper," "middle," or "lower middle" class.)[62] By 1927 some social workers were exploring the possibility of the private practice of social work, justified explicitly as a means of breaking the linkage of social work to the poor and instead, in Robert W. Kelso's words, "reaching upward more and more into the stratum of the well-to-do and the wealthy."[63] In short, social work, or one branch of it, was freeing itself from its historic focus on poverty, discrimination, economic dependency, social injustice—that is, from the core concerns of social policy. "Thus the relationship [between social worker and client] has been removed from a class or economic basis to an objective professional basis," wrote Charlotte Towle. "This change would seem to facilitate identification on a more constructive level."[64]

Thus, during the 1920s social work moved toward a psychiatric understanding of individual problems and away from efforts at reform and an identification with the poor. This movement coincided with the broader retreat of society itself from reform and with social work's growing need for occupational stabilization, for professionalization. And the new focus on personality coincided as well with the new needs of capitalism for ensuring social peace and creating personalities congruent with the consumer society in the making. A new constellation of occupational needs, personal needs, and social needs had come to dominate the development of social work and social policy.

Put slightly differently, the social work attitudes of the 1920s regarding social policy shifted decisively away from broad social reform, state intervention, and an emphasis on social responsibility and toward individual treatment and a deemphasis of class issues. These new patterns soon came to dominate the profession. Indeed, in the 1930s and again in the 1960s, when broad movements for social reform reemerged, social workers were reproached by re-formers for their lack of response. Individual social workers played a role in these reform movements, as consultants and sometimes as activists. But unlike the Progressive Era, when social work was al-most synonymous with the reform movements themselves, in these later periods social work's role was more subdued. For better or for worse, professionalization had had a price.

3

The Construction of
the Welfare State

By 1929, on the eve of the Great Depression, social work was approaching full professional status, surrounded with the standard paraphernalia of a modern profession: professional organizations, schools, journals, codes of ethics, and so on. More than 4,600 social workers belonged to the forty-three chapters of the American Association of Social Workers (founded in 1921); almost as many, in aggregate, belonged to three more specialized social work organizations, the American Association of Hospital Social Workers (founded 1919), the American Association of School Social Workers (founded 1919), and the American Association of Psychiatric Social Workers (founded 1926).[1] (These groups, along with several others, merged into the present-day National Association of Social Workers in 1955.) A growing number of workers had completed formal training programs; by 1929 twenty-five master's degree programs had been established, and the social work schools themselves had formed a professional organization, the American Association of Professional Schools of Social Work.[2] To keep abreast of professional news and developments and new techniques, social workers read such journals as *The Compass* (published by the American Association of Social Workers and later renamed *Social Work*), *The Family* (published by the Family Welfare Association of America, the federation of social agencies in the family field, and later renamed *Social Casework*), and *The Survey* (published until the 1950s by the Russell Sage Foundation and focused more on social developments and policy concerns). Codes of ethics had been widely discussed and adopted by various state and local social work societies. Bills providing for the licensing or credentialing of social workers had been introduced in several state legislatures, including those of California and New York.[3] Perhaps the surest sign of social work's growing credibility was the formation of Community Chests, common fund-raising and distributing organizations, by social work administrators and local philanthropic elites. These groups eliminated wasteful duplication of effort and competition in soliciting philanthropic contributions. By controlling the allocation of the money raised, they ensured that financial support would be distributed to only those agencies whose policies and programs were acceptable to the local elite. The "more dependent a settlement house was on a community chest, the more conservative it was on social issues," concluded a later researcher.[4]

Despite its possession of all the outer signs of a profession, however, social work's professional status was not yet secure. For one thing, the knowledge and skills on which the claim to professional status rested remained a bit vague. It was widely agreed that social work's "knowledge base" consisted primarily of the theories and techniques of casework (rather than community organizing) and that these, in turn, must be primarily rooted in psychological (rather than sociological) understandings. Psychology had triumphed in the social work school curricula, in the funding proposals submitted by social work agencies, in the proceedings of the annual national conferences, in the practice of the rapidly expanding network of social-worker-staffed mental health agencies.[5] But large caseloads and inadequate training denied the luxury of differential psychological diagnoses, much less of careful psychological examinations and treatment, to most caseworkers. In any case, at least until the 1930 publication of Virginia Robinson's *A Changing Psychology in Social Work*, most contemporary observers noted that psychology was used more as a tool to enhance the social worker's ability to manipulate clients and gain their compliance with the social worker's advice than as a technique for helping clients understand their own problems.[6]

Equally serious, social work remained divided internally: was social work one profession or several? The old division between caseworkers, on the one hand, and settlement-house workers, group workers, and social reformers, on the other, still remained (although in muted form, for the caseworkers had become dominant). To this was added divergent tendencies within casework: casework itself, whatever its methods, was carried out in a variety of very different circumstances. Was the casework carried out by a social worker in a family agency controlled by social workers the same thing as casework carried out in a psychiatric clinic or in a doctor-dominated hospital or in a teacher-dominated school system?[7]

The answer, a resounding "yes," came from the social work administrators and agency board members who met at the Milford [Pennsylvania] Conferences of the mid and late twenties. While the conferees acknowledged, in their influential 1928 report, that "at the present time the practice of casework is more precise than the formulations of philosophy, knowledge, methods, and experience," they nevertheless insisted: "Social casework is a definite entity. It has a field increasingly well-defined, it has all of the aspects of the beginnings of a science in its practice, and it has conscious professional standards for its practitioners. . . . The outstanding fact is that the problems of social casework and the equipment of the social case worker *are fundamentally the same for all fields.*" (Emphasis added.)

Still, the executives and board members recognized that the theoretical weakness of social work practice was the weakest link in the occupation's claim to full professional status. Social casework, they noted, is "potentially both scientific in character and professional in its practice. Scientific and professional, however, are terms which can at the present time justifiably be applied to social case work chiefly because of its potentialities." Intensified research into the concepts, problems, and methods of casework was, therefore, the highest priority of the profession.[8]

The problematic knowledge base of social work gave rise to still other concerns: how to distinguish social workers from other professions (for example, psychiatrists, psychologists, psychiatric nurses), and how to prevent social work from being absorbed, or controlled, by psychiatrists (as, in large measure, nurses had been by doctors).[9] "The marks by which a professional service is distinguished from other professional services are its field, its objectives, its vocational resources, and its characteristic methods of work," noted the Milford Conference report.[10] Thus social work faced a dilemma: it had seized on psychology as the means of providing a "scientific" and socially irreproachable base for its claim to professional status, yet it was precisely the old and now often rejected *social* emphasis that distinguished social workers from other mental health practitioners.

Social work was able to articulate a set of distinguishing marks that were fuzzy, at best: in the child guidance clinics, for instance, psychiatrists worked with the child, social workers with the family, and psychologists tested and designed remedial programs. In other settings the psychiatrist worked with seriously ill patients (psychotics), and the social worker worked with clients suffering from milder problems of "adjustment." The Milford Conference threw up its hands in despair: "At the present stage of [social work's] development, no definition of social case work can distinguish it sufficiently from other professional fields."[11]

Others were less pessimistic, if no more able to define the distinguishing features of social work. Psychiatrist Lawson Lowery, a major figure in the development of child guidance centers, argued that social work and psychiatry were complementary professions: "It is not contended that either is necessarily the leader, but rather that, for certain types of problems, they constitute a unit working together for the benefit of the client, each not only supplying special techniques, but contributing to a pooled or common technique as well."[12] Social worker Ernest Boulder Harper, reflecting the views published by many others in his field, concurred: "Case work and psychiatry are mutually independent but cooperative techniques, and nothing approaching the 'doctor–nurse' attitude will be allowed to develop by farsighted practitioners."[13] Despite the apparent confidence of these assertions, however, the problematic identity of social work was to continue to plague the profession in the following decades.

The continued low status and even lower pay of social workers was also a matter for growing concern. Although volunteerism had been all but eliminated by the late twenties, social work salaries had stagnated since before World War I.[14] Some observers attributed this to the continuing predominance of women in the field: the 1930 U.S. Census revealed that almost 80 percent of "social and welfare" workers were women. Because of the prevalence of women in the field, it was said, community leaders found it difficult to take social work seriously; therefore, recruiting more men into the field should be a priority.[15] But others suggested that the causality ran the other way: men shunned social work *because of* its low status and low pay. These, in turn, were the result of social work's almost exclusive preoccupation with poor (i.e., low-status and nonpaying) clients. "Social service has as strong an appeal as the Wednesday night prayer meeting," lamented Beulah Weldon of the Henry Street Settlement House. Shifting toward a more middle-class clientele, then, however much violence this might do to the historic roots of social work, represented a road to professional status. For example, Robert W. Kelso, the executive secretary of the Boston Council of Social Agencies, suggested in 1928 that "social service is not limited to poverty and dependency. It applies to the whole of society." The development of private practice in social work, he noted, both reflected this reality and would advance the status of the profession.[16]

Despite these obstacles to professionalization, the greatest obstacle, the historic identification of social work with social reform and radicalism, seemed to have been overcome by the late twenties. *The Survey*'s accounts of the annual meetings of the National Conference of Social Work trace the shift from the "deep interest in radical movements" of 1917 to the "spiritual lethargy" of 1926.[17] As early as 1919, responding to early efforts to form a national organization of social workers, a number of prominent social work figures objected to suggested bylaws that would permit the proposed organization to take stands on controversial issues. The same year, Roger Baldwin was refused reelection to the National Conference's Divisional Committee on Industrial and Educational Problems because of his World War I pacifism. In 1923, on a rule from the chair, Julia Lathrop's resolutions on peace, prohibition, child labor laws, and minimum wage laws were refused consideration.[18]

Among the self-styled professional social workers, caseworkers, not reformers, dominated. The professional concerns summarized earlier focused almost entirely on caseworkers, to the exclusion of social workers engaged in other forms of practice. In Boston two-thirds of the AASW membership were caseworkers; in the New York area, caseworkers outnumbered settlement-house, group, and recreation workers by 3 to 1.[19] Many social worker-reformers of the older generation decried the trend. "The social diagnostician who places all of the blame for maladjustment upon the individual and none upon the social order must in the end become servile to those whose interests are vested in that order. He must, in short, become a tool of the power groups," wrote group-work pioneer Eduard Lindemann in 1924.[20] And Jane Addams, preeminent among the earlier generation of reformers, warned at the 1926 NCSW meeting at Cleveland against the "danger" of looking at social work "too steadily from the business point of view," subjecting it "to tests which are totally irrelevant to its purposes." Social workers "share a certain desire to conform and be safe," she warned; the profession was "living on accumulated capital in spiritual and ethical affairs." The new leaders in social work, she continued, "are the psychiatric social workers. They are the newest and most popular group among us and perhaps we can ask a favor from them: that in time they go beyond this individual analysis and give us a little social psychiatric work." Describing the inability of individual casework to deal with the manifold social problems she observed in prohibition-era Chicago, she bade her farewell to the field she had served so long, observing: "I am saying this not as a social worker, but as an old woman who is perplexed."[21]

The retreat of social work from social reform, of course, mirrored the larger collapse of the social movements of the Progressive Era. Although small groups of reformers continued to investigate and to write model legislation to establish social security systems, child labor laws, and so on, their efforts had no practical consequence in the political desert of the twenties.[22] Instead, the twenties were a period of rollback and retreat: In 1922–23, the Supreme Court declared unconstitutional the federal regulation of child labor and federal minimum wage laws. Although scattered state laws protecting workers remained on the books, in the face of an employer backlash, enforcement of these laws came to a virtual halt. Even in the face of the social disaster of the early years of the Great Depression, government policy toward the unemployed, the poverty-stricken, and the working poor remained, at best, one of benign neglect (and at worst, one of active repression).

Social work leaders, once on the cutting edge of reform but now abjuring reform in favor of professional acceptability, did little better. Concerned, in *Survey* editor Paul Kellogg's words, with "the drama of people's insides rather than the pageantry of their group contacts and common needs," and ignoring the tide of reports from rank-and-file social workers on the growing hardship and increasing unemployment already evident by 1928 and 1929, social work leaders remained silent. Casework journals such as *The Family* literally took no notice of the Depression until early 1931, fifteen months after the stock market crash. And under pressure from the elites who controlled their funding, even many settlement-house leaders opposed New Deal efforts at relief and reform.[23]

83

Thus the professionalization of social work emerged, not coincidentally, during a period when social reform and social policy were in eclipse. Social work was able to escape its earlier identification with reform and so begin the transition from occupation into profession, in part, at least, because the larger social currents were running against the reform elements within the occupation. The story of the professionalization of social work, insofar as it is the story of the triumph of casework over reform, is as much a tale of the *weakness* of the reform element as it is of the strength of the caseworkers. The weakness of the caseworkers' knowledge base, the inability of caseworkers to differentiate themselves clearly from other mental health professionals, the failure to upgrade the status and financial compensation of social workers—all were, in a sense, untested.

And so, when social reform movements reappeared during the Depression, it is not surprising that the precarious professional consensus among social workers quickly collapsed. Observers such as Paul Kellogg, seeing a quick deflation of the disdain of the caseworker for social conditions, heralded "a new equilibrium between individual and group concerns. You found case working agencies canvassing the economic background of their activities, industrial workers inviting the psychiatrists to come in and explore the psychological and emotional factors entering into the workaday world around them."[24]

But Kellogg's perception of a "new equilibrium" proved premature. The massive social programs of the New Deal "solved" the profession's earlier concerns with recruitment by drawing tens of thousands of new, untrained, and "unprofessional" workers into the social welfare field. And the new programs themselves transformed the social welfare system and the functions of social work and introduced a new era in the relation between social workers, social agencies, and the state. The young profession of social work was faced with its first great crisis.

To trace the development of this crisis, however, we must first trace the history of the Depression itself, of the social movements that arose in response to it, and of the emergence of the modern American welfare state.

At a distance of half a century, the Great Depression of the thirties has faded into mythology. Its leading political figures loom larger than in life, its massive social movements have been reduced to a barely visible chorus in the background, and its hardships and hopes have been romanticized. To recapture it for analysis, we have to go back for a moment to the America of the 1920s.

In the twenties, a period of great prosperity, national income and corporate profits boomed, consumerism flourished, and the mass media celebrated the whole affair. But the media image of the "roaring twenties" is only partially accurate. For a large fraction of the American population, the twenties were not "roaring" at all; they were, in Irving Bernstein's well-chosen phrase, "the lean years." Farm income lagged; housing construction was depressed from 1925 on; millions of workers faced seasonal unemployment. The spread of new, low-wage industries and occupations (social work among them!) masked the stagnation of employment levels in the higher wage industries. With unions on the defensive in the face of a massive corporate attack, wages remained low. The economic tendencies of the decade are best summed up by the changes in the distribution of wealth: whereas overall disposable per capita income rose 9 percent during the decade, income received by the best-paid 1 percent of the population rose 75 percent. In 1919 the richest 5 percent of the American people had earned 24 percent of the nation's total personal income; by 1929 the top 5 percent earned 34 percent of the income. Whereas a small minority lived out the roaring twenties myth, half the American population lived at economic levels below that needed for minimum health and decency.[25]

The growing maldistribution of wealth and income was to prove the Achilles' heel of the boom. Although American production was expanding dramatically, the incomes of the millions of people who produced the steel, the electricity, the cars, the radios, the perfumes, were not sufficient to permit them to buy what they had produced. As the decade wore on, the capacity of American industry to produce raced ahead of the ability of American consumers to buy. Only the enormous expansion of consumer credit, which enabled millions to live beyond their income, and the growth of the export market (also financed on credit) permitted industry to sell its products and the boom to keep booming. When debt became so deep that more credit could not be extended, consumers stopped buying, companies stopped producing goods that couldn't be sold, and the workers who would have produced those goods were laid off. This reduced consumer income still more; and in short order, the whole economy collapsed like the house of cards it was.

85

There had been depressions before 1929–41 and there have been depressions since, but none has rivaled the Great Depression of the thirties. By 1933 manufacturing production had dropped 40 percent below its 1929 level. The gross national product was down 25 percent, and average weekly wages (for those lucky enough to have a job) were down 35 percent. Aggregate corporate profits, which had hit a record $8.7 billion in 1929, dropped to *minus* $2.7 billion in 1933. The nation's banking system collapsed entirely in the winter of 1932–33, as some 4,000 banks closed their doors. Most important of all in terms of most people's daily lives, unemployment rose to 13 million in 1933—an official nationwide unemployment rate of 25 percent (in Detroit it reached 41 percent!). And even this astronomical figure does not tell the whole story, for millions of people had simply given up looking for jobs and were no longer counted. The unemployment rate would not drop below 15 percent until 1941. (By contrast, the highest unemployment rate of the four decades following World War II was 10.8 percent in late 1982.)[26]

To make matters still worse, the systems that today provide a modicum of relief from the worst impact of unemployment did not exist. There was no unemployment compensation, no Social Security for the elderly, no food stamps, no Medicaid—and virtually nothing by way of public "relief." There were simply no public mechanisms to buffer the economic catastrophe, and private charity, inadequate to meet the needs of the poor even in good times, was totally overwhelmed. Thousands took to selling apples or depending on handouts; thousands more took to the road, a new generation of "hoboes." Shantytowns of cardboard and tin sheeting ("Hoovervilles," the residents called them, in bitter mockery of the do-nothing president) sprang up in parks and on the outskirts of big cities. Millions sank into hopelessness and misery.

Now the mere existence of poverty and human suffering has never been sufficient cause for the enactment of massive social reforms. With ups and downs in degree, massive poverty and misery have been constants in American history. As we have already seen, the reforms of the Progressive Era were initiated by a breakdown of social control mechanisms and a massive threat to public order. When the threat subsided in the post–World War I years, the interest of the middle class in reforms also diminished. The thirties provided a replay of this theme.

The early years of the Depression were filled with complacency.

"Prosperity is just around the corner," opined President Herbert Hoover. "The fundamental business of this country, that is production and distribution of commodities, is on a sound and prosperous basis."[27] For two years, Hoover temporized, vetoed legislation to provide aid for the poor, and argued that private agencies could handle the crisis. Not until December 1931 did he propose a loan program to help businesses get back on their feet and another system of loans to state governments to help them finance relief activities aimed at individuals. And, in fact, by the time the loan money started flowing to the states, Hoover was out of office. The poor were left to their own devices.

Neither were major existing organizations of the poor able to provide help. The unions, in particular, all but abandoned the effort. For one thing, they were small and weak. In the face of vigorous employer union-busting, they had actually declined in aggregate membership from 5 million in 1920 to fewer than 3 million in 1923 (out of about 40 million wage and salaried workers). For another, with a few exceptions, the unions of 1930 represented only skilled, white, male, and generally native-born workers, a group with a long history of antagonism to the unskilled and semiskilled immigrants, women, and minorities who made up the bulk of the American poor and working class. "We don't want to charter [locals of] the riff-raff or good for nothings," proclaimed Teamsters' president Dan Tobin. And finally, the union leadership itself was conservative, more supportive of ideas of class harmony and cooperation than of government intervention in the economy. The American Federation of Labor quickly moved to support President Hoover's 1930 call for a union–management no-strike/no-wage-cut/share-the-work agreement. In practice, it was a one-sided bargain: wages and hours were cut, but unions did not strike, and the number of workers on strike declined precipitously from 1929 to 1932.[28]

It was, then, not from the organized but from the unorganized— and especially from among the unemployed themselves—that the first massive response to the Depression came. Partially spontaneously, partially organized by the then tiny Communist party, a movement of the unemployed arose.[29] In March 1930 more than a million people demonstrated in the streets of dozens of cities, demanding relief. Rioting broke out in Cleveland, Philadelphia, Chicago, Los Angeles, and Detroit. A series of petition drives—at least three gathering more than a million signatures each—

demanded government action. Several thousand World War I veterans marched on Washington, demanding that a "bonus" promised them for 1945 be paid immediately, when it was needed. Local Unemployed Councils sprang up all over the country to fight against evictions, to protest cutbacks in what little public welfare there was, and to demand a massive program of relief.

Militant and often disorderly, the actions of the unemployed movement often met a violent response from officials. In New York, Chicago, and other cities, crowds gathered when families were evicted, moving the furniture back into an apartment as fast as the sheriff's men moved it out onto the streets. A survey of five New York relief agencies reported 196 group disruptions of their activities in one month alone. Social workers who sided with the demonstrators were often fired. In Washington, President Hoover called out the army (commanded by General Douglas MacArthur) to rout the Bonus Marchers. Nationwide, some 2 million people were involved in unemployed movement actions; thousands were jailed or hurt; fourteen were killed.

The unemployed movement succeeded in many of its immediate aims. Thousands of evictions were averted (the New York City Unemployment Council alone claimed to have prevented 77,000 evictions between 1930 and 1934). Local cutbacks in relief programs were reversed, and states and cities were forced to expand the programs instead. In New York, the 1898 law forbidding public "outdoor" relief (as opposed to "indoor" relief—i.e., the poorhouse) was first subverted—the police took over the task of distributing privately raised charity funds—and then overturned. Nationwide, between 1929 and 1932, public relief expenditures expanded eightfold—though relief still amounted to the equivalent of less than $30 per unemployed person per year. More fundamentally, the issue of relief was forced to the top of the national agenda.

Faced with growing disorder and with the growing role of the radicals who were leading it, the dangers of inaction became increasingly evident. Equally, many politicians and reformers were impressed with the potential effectiveness of reforms in heading off trouble. Frances Perkins, a former resident of Hull House and soon to be Franklin Delano Roosevelt's secretary of labor, went to Europe in 1931 at the request of New York State Governor Roosevelt and reported back that unemployment insurance there had blocked "desperation and disorder." In 1933 Congressman (and later New

York City mayor) Fiorello LaGuardia proclaimed: "We are either going to have child labor laws, old age pensions, and unemployment insurance in this country, or we are going to have chaos and disorder and something worse. There is something peculiar about human beings. They just simply refuse to go hungry. And you can't preach loyalty on an empty stomach."[30] Perhaps Franklin Roosevelt himself put it most succinctly: Warned by a friend on taking office that if he succeeded he would be remembered as the nation's greatest president, but if he failed, as the worst, he replied: "If I fail, I shall be the last."[31] And so, when FDR came into office in March 1933, a new wave of social reforms, the "New Deal," began.

The early New Deal (the "Hundred Days") focused not on fundamental reforms but on providing relief and stimulating recovery. For relief there was the Federal Emergency Relief Administration (FERA), headed by social worker Harry Hopkins, and the Civilian Conservation Corps (CCC). The FERA provided billions of dollars of direct grants to states to subsidize relief systems (replacing Hoover's more limited loan program). The CCC set hundreds of thousands of young people to work at activities such as building parks and dams, planting trees to halt soil erosion, and fighting forest fires.

For recovery, there was the National Recovery Administration (NRA), the Agricultural Adjustment Administration (AAA), and a series of acts regulating the banking and securities industry. The NRA in effect temporarily suspended the nation's antitrust laws. It authorized companies to meet to establish "codes" to regulate production levels, wages, and prices for their industry and so ultimately to bring supply and demand back into kilter. Although the act required participation of both large and small companies as well as consumers and representatives of workers in the industry in drawing up the codes, in fact it quickly became a tool of the biggest companies.

The AAA, the agricultural counterpart of the NRA, provided for a system of production and acreage controls to reduce the nation's output of agricultural products. Prices would then presumably rise and farms would be restored to profitability. Again, it was mainly the big farmers who benefited: they had the political clout to secure for themselves the largest acreage allocations (and sometimes reduced their acreage by evicting their small-farmer tenants). They also could afford to compensate for their reduced acreage by investing in more productive equipment. And finally, since the benefits offered by the system took the form of higher farm prices (rather than, for example, income subsidies), with their larger absolute levels of production it was the big farmer who reaped the profits.

The relief measures of the early New Deal reflect the concerns of the then-current wave of social unrest. In the recovery program, innovative though it was, we can see Roosevelt's conviction that with a temporary boost from the government the economy would recover. The Roosevelt of the early New Deal shared with his predecessors the belief that the economic system of the United States was fundamentally sound. True, it needed assistance in getting back on the track but it did not need fundamental restructuring. Thus, the early New Deal provided for *emergency* relief measures; it did not set up a permanent welfare system or a system of social insurance against the perils of unemployment, disability, sickness, or old age. And it developed short-term mechanisms to help restore the balance between supply and demand; it did not propose direct government efforts to reorganize the economy or an ongoing program of governmental stimulation of aggregate demand. In the face of the banking crisis, to take just one example, Roosevelt could have nationalized the banking system "without a word of protest," said New Mexico senator Bronson Cutting. Instead, he opted for a program of reopening banks under federal supervision followed by a modest program of regulation. "Capitalism was saved in eight days," Roosevelt adviser Raymond Moley later recalled.[32]

Still, the early New Deal did represent a major break with the social policies of both the twenties and the Progressive Era. For the first time the federal government was embracing a direct role in financing and organizing relief for the destitute in time of economic crisis. For the first time governmental powers were mobilized to promote recovery from a depression. (They had previously been used to promote production, but only in wartime.) And finally, the early Roosevelt actions signaled a new governmental attitude toward big business. Breaking with the Progressive Era rhetoric of his political ancestor Woodrow Wilson and embracing that of his distant relative Theodore Roosevelt, Franklin Roosevelt and his advisers embraced the giant corporation. "We are no longer afraid of bigness," wrote presidential adviser Rex Tugwell. "We are resolved to recognize openly that competition in most of its forms is wasteful and costly; that larger combinations must in any modern society prevail." What was needed, then, were not attacks on bigness but a new role for government as "planner, arbiter, balancer." Government was to take an active role in assessing and coordinating the sometimes-conflicting needs of producers and consumers, employers and employees and in establishing the large-scale organization needed to implement these purposes.[33] Thus the National Recovery Act asserted the need to promote "the organization of industry for the purpose of cooperative action" and to "induce and maintain united action of labor and management under adequate governmental sanctions and supervision."

The first New Deal, then, though bold, represented a fundamentally conservative social policy. The Roosevelt of later mythology is the champion of the "forgotten man," the architect of the welfare state, the friend of labor, the embodiment of modern liberalism. But up to 1935, at least, the reality was far different. If anything, despite the occasional outbursts of rhetoric, the early Roosevelt administration was pro big business. By 1935, with the NRA about to expire, a poll of big-business executives showed that they approved of the NRA by 3 to 1. Meanwhile, a similar survey of small-business men revealed disapproval by the same ratio.[34] Organized labor was even more critical. "Labor Breaks with New Deal" headlined the *New York Times* for February 3, 1935. Labor leaders, the article explained, were "almost in despair of making headway toward union recognition in the face of powerful industrial interests and an unsympathetic administration."[35]

Had the economy improved, or had the level of social disorder subsided, perhaps the story of the New Deal could be ended here— a story of the significant expansion of government's role in economic emergencies and a shift in attitude toward big business but not an epoch-making tale of the restructuring of American economic, social, and political institutions and the creation of the welfare state. But by 1934 the level of social misery was still growing. And social unrest, far from diminishing, increased in intensity and took on more threatening forms.

The Depression hit bottom in early 1933 and then a recovery, of sorts, occurred. By 1937 the gross national product had climbed to the 1929 level. But unemployment, though down sharply from its 1933 peak, remained extraordinarily high—still above 14 percent. As businesses resumed production, they had put their most efficient plants back into operation first, leaving the older, less efficient equipment in mothballs. And many of the less efficient companies

91

had gone under for good. The excess manufacturing capacity of 1929 had been reduced by eliminating the least efficient part of the nation's industrial apparatus. The result: in 1937 American industry could produce the same quantity of goods and services as in 1929 using several million fewer workers.

Recalling our discussion of the ultimate causes of the Depression, the obvious question is: how could several million fewer wage earners purchase as many goods and services as several million more had been unable to do in 1929? The answer is: they couldn't. Government spending, not consumer spending, made recovery possible. In retrospect, this is obvious, but in 1936–37, Roosevelt, seeing business activity recovering, retreated to conventional "balance the budget" wisdom. A variety of government programs were cut back, and the "recovery" was aborted. By early 1938 manufacturing production had fallen almost 25 percent over the previous year and the unemployment rate was back up to 19 percent. In the end, government spending—for war preparation, not for relief, public works, and the like—created the mass purchasing power needed to end the Depression once and for all. Only in 1941, with the war buildup well under way, did unemployment finally drop below 10 percent.

The American economy had changed permanently. All previous depressions had ended on their own, although often only after enormous suffering. The Depression of the 1930s did not end on its own. Only government spending could re-create and sustain prosperity. Indeed, in one sense, the economy *never* recovered from the Great Depression: the relatively low unemployment rates of recent years (in contrast to the 15 to 25 percent rates of the thirties, the 6 to 10 percent rates of the seventies and eighties are "low") are made possible only by, first, massive government spending, which creates employment, and, second, the government-financed programs that keep millions of adults out of the labor force altogether.

The millions of people absorbed by public schools, colleges, the armed forces, medical and mental institutions, and penal institutions are not counted as unemployed, but neither are they employed. In fact, since the late 1920s the American economy has never been able to provide anything close to full employment on its own. True "full employment" has always carried with it the threat of massive "overproduction" (i.e., of production of far more goods than consumers, with their limited incomes, could possibly buy). Consequently, America has been in a permanent potential economic

crisis since 1929, and the government has had to assume a permanent role in dealing with it.[36]

In any event, with the Depression hanging on, mass social unrest
continued to spread. As early as 1933 wildcat strikes broke out in the
auto, steel, rubber, and textile industries. In the coalfields organizers
for John L. Lewis's United Mine Workers fanned out, telling the
miners that section 7a of the National Recovery Act—which proclaimed that workers have the right to "organize into unions of their
own choosing"—meant that "the President wants you to join the
union"; United Mine Workers' membership soared from 60,000 to
300,000. In 1934, as industrial unrest increased, general strikes broke
out in Toledo, Minneapolis, and San Francisco; a nationwide textile
strike led to martial law in Georgia. In 1934 alone some forty workers were killed in strike-related violence, and in eighteen months in
late 1933 and 1934 troops were called out in sixteen states.

The growing strike activity was accompanied by a growing radicalization of the labor movement. In San Francisco communists
played a major role in the longshoremen's strike; in Minneapolis the
"Trotskyite" Socialist Workers party led the way; and in Toledo it
was independent radical socialists led by A. J. Muste. At the same
time, the employer counterattack grew. By 1936, according to a Senate investigation, the Republic Steel Corporation's arsenal included
552 pistols, 64 rifles, 245 shotguns, 143 gas guns, and 2,707 gas
grenades. From 1934 to 1936, General Motors spent almost a million
dollars spying on union activities among its employees. In 1934 a
big-business executive approached an army general with a proposal
to finance a 500,000-man private army to stage a coup. Class warfare
raged, on a scale unseen since the 1890s.[37]

To John L. Lewis and a number of other labor leaders, the rising
role of the far left and the failure of the conservative American
Federation of Labor, tied to its skilled, white, native-born membership, to take the lead in seeking to organize the growing chaos was
deeply disturbing. As International Typographers president Charles
P. Howard said:

> The workers of this country are going to organize, and if they are not
> permitted to organize under the banner of the American Federation of
> Labor, they are going to organize under some other leadership I
> submit to you that it would be a far more serious problem for our
> government, for the people of this country, and for the American Fed-

eration of Labor itself than if our organizational policies should be so molded that we can organize them and bring them under the leadership of this organization.[38]

By October 1935 Howard, Lewis, and several other labor leaders had set up the Committee on Industrial Organization (CIO; later, after breaking completely from the AFL, it was renamed the *Congress* of Industrial Organizations) to organize industrial workers.

The CIO organizing drive rapidly picked up steam. Bitter strikes, many of them involving "sit-downs" (what a later generation would call "sit-ins"), spread like wildfire. In December 1936 in New York City alone there were sit-downs of shirtmakers, seamen, subway workers, hotel workers, glaziers, WPA artists, and domestic servants; in Philadelphia, among battery workers, hosiery workers, dressmakers, shipbuilders, and prisoners in prison workshops. To the tune of enormous disorder (and several hundred deaths), some 6 million workers organized themselves into unions in three years.

By 1935, in addition to the massive disorder in the streets and mills, Roosevelt faced a growing political challenge. In the November 1934 elections, an overwhelmingly Democratic Congress, including many congressmen well to FDR's left, was elected. The "New Deal coalition" of urban workers and ethnic and racial minorities had emerged, and soon the newly developing unions would become the organizational backbone of the Democratic party.

To Roosevelt and to American politicians ever since, this signified that members of the working class (more accurately, white male workers) had become direct participants in politics—often voting nearly as a bloc. Thus the nature of reform politics was transformed. In the Progressive Era, social reforms aimed at ameliorating the lot of the poor had come from "above." They represented middle-class sympathy for the lot of the poor and middle- and upper-class fears of the massive disorder that would be the result of failing to initiate reform. But from 1934 on, the poor themselves came to play a central and direct role in gaining the reforms they needed.

The growing power of the poor and working class was reflected not only in government but also in the affairs of voluntary agencies. Before 1930 it was rare to find a union official or other working-class leader on the governing board of social service agencies, but by 1939 it was the rule rather than the exception.

Meanwhile, to Roosevelt's left, new political threats emerged. In

California there was socialist Upton Sinclair's candidacy for governor on the EPIC (End Poverty In California) ticket. In Minnesota, Governor Floyd Olson declared "I am not a liberal. . . . I am a radical" and demanded the creation of a "cooperative commonwealth." In neighboring Wisconsin, Governor Philip La Follette and Senator Robert La Follette, Jr., sought to build a "real leftist party" to end the "insanity and cruelty" of capitalism.[39] Dr. Francis Townsend, a retired California physician, proposed the Townsend Recovery Plan—a universal $200-a-month pension for all those over age sixty, to be financed by a national sales tax. By 1935 Townsend supporters had gathered 25 million signatures in support of their plan and enrolled some 3 million people in Townsend Clubs. And most immediately threatening of all, there was Huey Long of Louisiana, a reform governor, who in January 1934 founded a political organization with the simple slogan "Share the wealth!" Within a year there were 27,000 Share the Wealth clubs across the nation with a mailing list of more than 7 million names. Long threatened to challenge Roosevelt for the presidency in 1936, and polls suggested that he might draw from 3 million to 4 million votes away from the president—possibly enough to tip the election. The threat was ended by Long's assassination in September 1935, but not before Roosevelt became well aware of the need to "steal Long's thunder."[40]

Finally, in early 1935 the Supreme Court dealt a death blow to the two central acts of the early New Deal, declaring both the NRA and the AAA unconstitutional. With the principal sources of Roosevelt's business support destroyed, with massive unrest in the streets, with FDR threatened by more radical figures at the polls, with the economy going nowhere, the New Deal was in a shambles. Roosevelt responded by moving sharply to the left, proposing the "Second New Deal" of 1935–37.

The Second New Deal represented a far more dramatic shift in American social policy than had the first, for now Roosevelt moved to create the "welfare state." For starters, there was the National Labor Relations Act (the Wagner Act), initially opposed by Roosevelt but at the last minute warmly embraced. Reiterating the National Recovery Act's declaration of the right of workers to join unions, the Wagner Act put teeth in the policy: it declared illegal a laundry list of anti-union activities on the part of employers; it provided a procedure (government-supervised elections) by which unions could gain recognition; and it established a new government agency, the National Labor Relations Board, to enforce the law. Second, there was the Social Security Act. This provided not only for pensions for the elderly but for unemployment compensation and for a permanent system of federal aid to states to provide "welfare" for certain categories of poor people (notably dependent children). Next, the Works Progress Administration (WPA) provided a massive work relief program, employing, by 1936, one-third of all unemployed Americans. Other new laws provided for tax reform and for the strengthening of federal regulatory authority over banks and public utilities. A Housing Act financed slum clearance and low-rent housing projects. And finally, the Fair Labor Standards Act established a national minimum wage, the forty-hour workweek, and national child labor laws.

It was at this point, 1935–37, that the New Deal became a decisively new approach to social policy. We have already seen how, early in the New Deal, the government had accepted the responsibility for economic recovery and temporary relief for the poor, shifting away in the process from any remaining notion of restoration of a premonopoly past. Instead, it encouraged the large-scale organization of labor and consumers as well as business. And we have seen the growing political power of the poor and the working class, embodied above all in the alliance between the Democratic party and organized labor. To these, the Second New Deal added a number of new elements.

First, government can—and must if social disorder and economic collapse are to be avoided—take permanent responsibility for managing the economy. From the 1930s through the 1970s this responsibility centered around the need to keep unemployment levels reasonably low; under President Ronald Reagan in the 1980s it shifted to a focus on the control of inflation. But since Roosevelt, liberal and conservative presidents alike have used the power of government to manipulate the economy in various ways: the use of fiscal and monetary policy to control the overall rates of savings, investment, and consumption; the design of specific programs to encourage the growth of particular components of the economy; and the creation of mechanisms to keep significant numbers of people out of the labor market.

The governmental role in controlling the economy extends beyond this (and far beyond the Progressive Era conception of merely regulating the excesses of individual corporations), however. New Deal social policy embraced the need for government to restructure the economy itself if necessary. New Deal legislation focused on the labor market: the Wagner Act and its postwar revisions brought order to labor–management relations by regulating the process by which unions are organized and recognized and by setting boundaries and standards for labor–management negotiations. The Fair Labor Standards Act reached directly into the workplace, regulating wages and hours. Unemployment compensation helped maintain a stable work force in the face of temporary economic fluctuations. Later legislation, such as the Occupational Health and Safety acts of the seventies, are essentially extensions of this approach.

The New Deal also introduced a new, and now permanent, role for the government in providing for economic security and well-being. The government took on a permanent role in helping maintain the incomes of nonworkers (relief for the poor, Social Security for the aged). And workmen's compensation, unemployment compensation, wage and hour legislation, housing legislation, vocational training programs, and the like expanded the governmental welfare role still further, to the non-poor and the working poor. The only major area omitted was health care, blocked by the determined opposition of the American Medical Association. It was not until the passage of the Medicare and Medicaid amendments to the Social Security Act in the mid-sixties and the Occupational Health and Safety Act of the early seventies that this omission was partially rectified.

As we have seen, Progressive Era social policy, insofar as it was not mere economic rationalization in the interests of big business itself, had centered on protecting consumers and businesses against the worst excesses of monopoly. For the most part, efforts at more positive types of social intervention to protect individual health, welfare, and economic security were defeated (with some exceptions at the state and local level). Now, with the growing power of the working class, organized as workers in unions and as voters in the Democratic party, a social policy pattern more like that of European countries, with their powerful Social Democratic parties and their broad social insurance systems, emerged.

Finally, the New Deal instituted an enormous and permanent strengthening of government, and especially of the executive branch, manifested, for example, in Roosevelt's 1939 Executive Order establishing the Executive Office of the President (an office that now includes the powerful Office of Management and Budget, the

National Security Council, the Council of Economic Advisers, the Central Intelligence Agency, and a host of presidential assistants). The historic domination of the legislative process by Congress shifted to a pattern in which, most commonly, the executive branch took the initiative in proposing legislation. The Cabinet departments, responsible for a broad array of new programs, expanded dramatically; the number of civilian employees of the federal government doubled during the Depression years. Although many of the New Deal acts retained an emphasis on state and local government administration (as was the case, for example, with unemployment compensation and welfare under the Social Security Act), overall the federal government's power was vastly extended.

The change in perspective was summed up, just after World War II, by Thomas P. Jenkin, the counsel for the National Association of Manufacturers:

> Regulation has passed from the negative stage of merely preventing improper conduct, to the positive stage of directing and controlling the character and form of business activity. The concept that the function of government was to prevent exploitation by virtue of superior power has been replaced by the concept that it is the duty of government to provide security against all of the major hazards of life—against unemployment, accident, illness, old age, and death.[41]

It is easy to quibble with this account: it understates the interpenetration of business and government and the power of business over government. And as we have seen, the New Deal was more a matter of necessity than of altruism; that is, to protect the overall social order, the government was forced as well to protect the less-privileged members of that order. Still, as a crude description of the new approach to social policy, it is not inaccurate.

The story of the New Deal would not be complete, however, without a recognition of its limitations as well as its legacy. First, there were enormous "gaps" in the newly created "welfare state." Health care was excluded altogether, unemployment benefits were paid only for a relatively short period of time, and the problem of permanent disability was neglected. Throughout, benefit levels were very low (and were based on past earnings rather than on present needs). And millions of people were excluded from the protection of the new laws, which covered only regular workers in private industry and commerce. Protection for many of those most in need—farm laborers, seasonal and migrant workers, part-time workers, domestic servants, and workers' dependents—was denied. Although subsequent legislation closed many of these gaps, a number still remain.

Of more fundamental importance, the permanent social programs of the New Deal were designed to aid the working (or *temporarily* unemployed) poor, not large numbers of *permanently* unemployed people. For the former, unions and minimum-wage and maximum-hour laws would raise incomes and improve working conditions. Unemployment compensation would tide them over relatively short periods of unemployment; and Social Security pensions would take care of them in their old age. The major relief programs—the Federal Emergency Relief Administration, the Civilian Conservation Corps, the Works Progress Administration—were temporary measures, intended to deal with the massive but presumably short-lived unemployment of the Depression years. Roosevelt and his advisers assumed that the return of prosperity would make them unnecessary. The only ongoing relief program set up under Roosevelt was a title in the Social Security Act which provided federal matching funds to states to help them finance relief for specified categories of the poor—mothers with dependent children, the crippled, the aged, and the blind. But all of these were relatively small, residual categories, added to the Social Security Act of 1935 almost as afterthoughts. That is, the New Deal planners expected that economic growth, not handouts, would solve the problems of the one-third of the nation that was "ill housed, ill clad, ill nourished."

In fact, history dashed their hopes. During the three decades following World War II the economy was relatively stagnant. Even in years of "prosperity," unemployment never fell below 3 percent (except for two years during the Korean War and another two during the Vietnam War); in most years it was much higher. Several million people had become "long-term" unemployed. Beyond that, agricultural modernization drove millions of people from the nation's farms and into cities where low-wage jobs were increasingly scarce. A new urban underclass emerged. With middle-class people and businesses fleeing to the suburbs, the fiscal ability of the cities to deal with the problems of the poor was eroded. And shifts in family patterns turned the category "mother with dependent children" from a relatively small category largely made up of widows into a huge group of long-term "female-headed" families.

As a consequence, a large pool of more or less permanently unemployed and unemployable poor people developed. The primitive, residual relief system of the Social Security Act, with its particularistic categories and limited funding, was forced to play a role for which it had not been designed. The poverty crisis of the sixties, to which we shall turn in a later chapter, reflected in large part this failure of the New Deal's welfare state.

Ultimately, the inadequacies of New Deal social policies were rooted in their blindness to the actual structure of American society and the American economy and the unwillingness of the architects of the policies to make fundamental changes. The New Deal provided broad programs of economic stimulation and broadly available economic benefits. In the context of the actually existing enormous disparities in wealth and power, these crudely targeted programs inevitably benefited most those of wealth and power who needed help the least. In agriculture, for example, white farmers with large farms reaped the benefits of farm subsidies, whereas poor black and white tenants and sharecroppers were forced off the land entirely.

Similarly, programs aimed at industrial and commercial workers, in a society in which the overwhelming majority of blacks were locked into agricultural poverty, inevitably provided a disproportionate share of benefits to whites, thus helping to sustain and increase racial disparities. The New Deal was, in fact, less than color-blind: the CCC had a racial quota limiting black participation; the NRA administration approved industry codes containing discriminatory pay rates; TVA model towns were segregated; New Deal work programs followed discriminatory hiring practices; government agencies themselves maintained segregated office facilities; and Roosevelt, beholden to an electoral coalition that included the southern planter aristocracy, refused to support federal anti-lynching legislation much less to commit himself to a broad civil rights program or to economic programs targeted at the unique problems of blacks. Only insofar as blacks left the farm and found employment as mainstream urban commercial or industrial workers did they share in the benefits of the new welfare state.[42] And with the postwar economic stagnation, even that opportunity was barred to a large fraction of blacks.

Finally, the new welfare state assumed a "traditional" nuclear family structure and "traditional" female roles. Focusing on ensuring an adequate family wage, it failed to provide for variant family structures. At the same time, the structure of the permanent welfare programs (i.e., Aid for Families with Dependent Children) assumed that a family with an able-bodied male present did not need support. This actually created a *disincentive* for maintaining stable families: a woman with children could do better on welfare and without a husband than with an unemployed husband and without welfare benefits. And so it increased the percentage of the poverty population that was poorly covered by the new welfare state.

The New Deal, in establishing the "welfare state" pattern of social policy, set the standard for American social policy for the following quarter century. Subsequent administrations tinkered, filled gaps, added to, or cut back, benefits. But conceptually, nothing was added until the Johnson administration's War on Poverty. Meanwhile, the limits of New Deal policy became more and more evident as new social problems, created in part by the New Deal policies themselves and recalcitrant to treatment by those policies, moved to center stage.

4

The Crisis in Social Work, 1929–1945

At the outbreak of the Great Depression, the leaders of the social work profession were unprepared to deal with the crisis. In their preoccupation with treating individual woes, it was as if the "social" had disappeared from their profession's name. Despite soaring unemployment rates, many social workers could still see only individual sources of economic discomfort. In words reminiscent of her Charity Organization movement colleagues of a half century earlier, one midwestern agency executive wrote: "Most poverty and financial dependency can be traced to wrong physical habits and mental attitudes. The work of a social worker is to find out these cases and help overcome them."[1] Even as the crisis mounted, the American Association of Social Workers' journal, *The Compass*, editorialized that social workers should "stick to our knitting,"[2] and AASW leaders proceeded to amend the bylaws to make entrance to membership more difficult for future social workers.[3]

But the sheer magnitude of the economic calamity soon overwhelmed even the most complacent. Caseloads soared; agency resources were drained; and with traditional sources of philanthropy jumping out of Wall Street windows, a financial crisis loomed in many agencies. Salaries were slashed, working conditions deteriorated, and the ability of social work to serve its clients, worthy or unworthy, was called into question.

More and more social workers were led, hesitantly, to question the old "truths" of the profession. In November 1930 a committee of the Family Society of Philadelphia set out to investigate whether there were any "considerable number of families in need through no fault of their own, or have a few examples of this blinded us to the fact that the vast majority of men out of work are borderline workers, their families always in and out of the agency's offices and in the best of times barely able to scrape along?" (They quickly discovered that the only need was financial assistance for more than half the cases they examined and that many others had only minor personality problems.)[4]

The victim-blaming attitude did not die easily. As late as 1937 Grace Coyle described hearing "social reform" used as a "disparaging" term and hearing it "implied in some authoritative quarters that to engage in it is an evidence of emotional maladjustment."[5] But more common was a growing attitude of questioning and self-criticism. Social workers had to bear part of the blame for the Depression, Rabbi Abba Hillel Silver told the 1932 National Conference of Social Work, "for we did not throw ourselves into the struggle for a radical reconstruction of our economic society as zealously as we gave ourselves to the perfection of our technique."[6] June Purcell Guild commented: "If social workers who know why the poor are poor [i.e., low wages, unemployment] are content to prate of 'adjusting' personalities when there is no longer any hope that there will ever be enough work to go around, what difference does it make whether social work lives or not?"[7]

Along with the self-criticisms went a new commitment to social reform and social action. "The fashion of crusading has gone out and social work has not yet invented the brilliant combination of social reform, social education, and social engineering which we all hope for," lamented Gordon Hamilton in 1931. The need was urgent, she continued, for "the present economic world is not fit to live in."[8] Social work organizations responded very cautiously to the new mood. But slowly respond, they did. By fall 1931 the Social Workers Conference on Federal Action called for a federal relief program; by early 1933 the AASW's conference on National Economic Objectives for Social Work called not only for social and economic planning and federal responsibility for guaranteeing a minimum standard of living, but for social workers to take part in reform efforts. Even the elite Milford Conference, reconvened in 1932–33, noted that, despite its proclamation only four years earlier that the progress of social work professionalism must be based on growing knowledge and more effective casework techniques, "the future of social work is bound up with the coming of a sounder social order."[9] Social work, exulted Leroy A. Ramsdell, executive secretary of the Hartford Council of Social Agencies, "has had enough of patching up. Social work has had too much relief. Henceforth, the central purpose of social work is going to be the development of a social order in which every honest and industrious citizen will be forever freed from the menacing shadow of economic insecurity."[10]

By 1933–34, the social work establishment had moved enthusiastically into the camp of the New Deal. Among the social workers and settlement-house veterans to take on official responsibilities were Henry Morgenthau, Jr., Adolph A. Berle, Frances Perkins, Harry Hopkins, Grace Abbott, Paul Kellogg, and Eduard Lindemann. The 1934 annual meetings of the AASW endorsed a letter to President Roosevelt expressing both support for the programs of the preceding year—especially unemployment relief, the Civilian Conservation Corps, and the programs of employment through public works—and concern about the impending shift to work relief programs and cutbacks in public works.[11] Although some social workers still saw the New Deal programs as a step in the wrong direction, the majority firmly supported them.

Social work criticisms of the New Deal thenceforth were to come not from a right wing, critical of reform altogether, but from a left wing, demanding far more and far deeper changes. The divisions appeared full-blown at the dramatic May 1934 annual meeting of the National Conference of Social Work in Kansas City. "Intellectually controversial, emotional, explosive," it "brought professional social workers to the crossroads of social if not political philosophy," reported *The Survey*.[12] Roosevelt administration officials such as Rex Tugwell, Harry Hopkins, and Eduard Lindemann were greeted warmly, and Monsignor Robert F. Keegan, the conference's presidential nominee for 1935–36, echoed support for the administration's programs. But the big event was Mary Van Kleeck's assault on the New Deal from the left.

On May 22, with "rumors sweeping the hall," 1,500 social workers jammed into a room designed for 500 to hear Van Kleeck's presentation on "Our Illusions Concerning Government."[13] Van Kleeck, the much respected, longtime director of industrial studies for the social-work–oriented Russell Sage Foundation, began by noting that the social workers' organization in the last few years had "committed itself to identification with the present administration, to endorsement of what it supposes its principles to be, and to hope for an adequate program of social work under government auspices." She observed that putting faith in the public sector represented a major shift for social work.

> But the really important question is not whether social work is changing its base from private to governmental sources, but whether this reliance upon government commits social workers to the preservation of the status quo and separates them from their clients, leading them into the position of defense of the politicians in their effort to protect political institutions against the strain put upon them by the failures of industry to maintain employment, and by the industrial policy which seeks to sustain profits at the expense of standards of living.

Is government a neutral force, above the conflicting interests of its constituents, as traditional social work reform programs had assumed, or is government dominated by, and an instrument of, big business, she asked? Analyzing the programs of the early New Deal, she argued that government had gone only as far as it had to to maintain the status quo; it had failed to propose basic economic change and was now planning to cut back on various relief programs. Social workers, she concluded, should seek alliances not with government officials and social work boards of directors but with the growing labor movement and the working class. Workers, she noted, "to be sure, are the clients of social workers, but it is easy to become too professional in one's dealings with clients and to fail to achieve the sense of fellowship which social workers must attain if they are to take part in the struggle for human rights." What was needed was not the NRA, not unemployment relief, but a comprehensive income maintenance program, progressively financed and administered by workers. (In a later speech at the same conference she expanded this to a call for a "collective, worker-controlled society embracing workers and professionals.")[14]

"Never in a long experience of conferences," reported *The Survey's* Gertrude Springer, "has this observer witnessed such a prolonged ovation as followed. . . . To her wearied and discouraged colleagues in social work she brought a new hope and dream when they had ceased to hope and dream. . . . The effect on her hearers was electric. The younger and more volatile rose as to a trumpet call. The soberest were shaken."[15]

William Hodson, president of the conference, himself a government official (New York City's commissioner of public welfare), rose to defend the New Deal.

> Three choices are open to us. The first is to go on in the old way, hoping that chance and good fortune will bring us out of our troubles. The American people have, I think, rejected that choice. The second is to modify the existing economic order in such fundamental ways as will serve the well-being of the people as a whole. This, I think, is the objective of the present national administration. The third is to destroy the present economic and industrial order and to substitute in its place something new and different.

Fearing that "the real danger in too violent a break with the established order is a fascist regime," Hodson called upon social workers to accept the second vision and align themselves with the administration.[16]

The debate dominated the rest of the conference, all but drowning out the traditional discussions of casework techniques, program details, and the like. *The Survey* guessed that the majority of delegates preferred Rex Tugwell's program of a planned and regulated economy within the framework of democratic government to Van Kleeck's more radical vision; and the newly elected president, Katherine F. Lenroot, was an administration official (from the Children's Bureau). But Van Kleeck won many hearts and set the terms of the debate. "There have always been radical sideshows, but this year the radicals had the big tent and the conservatives were in the sideshows."[17]

The debates over the policy and direction of social work in fact reflected not merely differences of opinion but the transformation of social work itself. The New Deal had transferred the financing of social services from the private sector to the public. (In 1929 private sources still provided 25 percent of relief funds, as well as a host of nonrelief services; by 1939 less than 1 percent of these funds were nongovernmental.) The Federal Emergency Relief Administration, the CCC, the WPA, and the Social Security Act, with its categorical relief programs and mandating of state relief agencies, had called into existence thousands of new public agencies at federal, state, and local levels. Social work had changed almost overnight from a "Cinderella that must be satisfied with the leavings" into one of the "primary functions of government," wrote former AASW president Frank Bruno. Social work had become "an acknowledged obligation of every city, hamlet, and village in the land."[18] As the radical social work journal *Social Work Today* put it, social work had become "organic to government."[19]

The new public setting for social work created an entirely new environment for the profession. The implications of being dependent on the government for funding were widely discussed, as were the new kinds of accountability that seemed called for. But even subtler questions, reaching to the core of casework, demanded attention.

What, for example, was the relation between the vastly expanded public relief programs and traditional casework? Long before government funding had come to dominate, the question had been debated by social workers. Most caseworkers of the twenties, drawing on analyses going back to the old Charity Organization movement, saw relief not as an end in itself, and certainly not as an unconditionally offered benefit for those in need, but as a tool. They assumed that any client in need of relief needed rehabilitation as well. This, of course, implied individual "treatment" of every relief applicant.

But mass unemployment destroyed the old system. With thousands of clients pouring through the doors, individual attention and counseling was not possible. "From individualization, with understanding, personal service, and adequate relief, attention is shifted to mass production, the cutting of expenses, and consideration of the job as a whole," wrote one contemporary observer. "The psychiatric viewpoint, with its emphasis on personality and human relations, has yielded much ground to the economic and its emphasis on poverty and dependency."[20]

Faced with this objective reality, social workers were forced to acknowledge that, in Gordon Hamilton's words, "the need for relief does not in itself indicate anything whatsoever as to the grounds for casework."[21] Hamilton proposed that a division of labor was in order: public agencies should supply relief funds and only secondarily, and as necessary, casework services. Private agencies should remain the central locus of casework and secondarily (and at government expense) provide relief to their clients. In any event, relief as a tool in treatment must be clearly distinguished from relief as a response to simple economic need.

The transformation of social welfare institutions, which gave rise to such reexaminations of casework practice, was to be a lasting change, one that has continued to reverberate to the present day. Of more immediate importance, however, were the thousands of new social work jobs created by the new agencies and programs. The 1930 Census had counted some 30,500 "social and welfare workers." Within a few months of Roosevelt's inauguration, the Federal Emergency Relief Administration had doubled that number, and more were soon to come.

The new social workers were necessarily drawn from outside the profession. Social work schools were turning out fewer than a thousand trained workers a year. The AASW, the largest of the social work professional organizations, had only 4,657 members in 1930, at the Depression's onset, and had grown to only 8,016 by 1934. The new social work recruits were typically young, unemployed college graduates—teachers, salesmen, engineers, and the like—themselves often employed by public agencies as a form of work relief. They had not been socialized to the profession's norms; they lacked the "whole mystic paraphernalia of professional ethics"; they had not been trained to meet, or hired on the basis of, professional standards; they were not even eligible for membership in the AASW (which in 1933 had raised its entrance requirements from four years' experience in a reputable agency to two years of college, one year of social work school, and two years of additional experience).[22]

To the old-line social workers of the AASW and other professional organizations, the new workers threatened to lower standards of treatment. And even worse, the rapid influx of untrained, unprofessional workers threatened the hard-won gains in professionalization that had been achieved in the previous decade. Thus, in 1935 Rachel Childrey, director of the AASW's Division on Employment Practices and president of the Philadelphia chapter of the association, wrote: "The profession and its standards of performance were seriously threatened . . . by large numbers of persons trained in other fields or without any specialized training, who were employed to do work that was essentially social work."[23] Dorothy C. Kahn, president of the National Conference of Social Work, told the conference's 1935 meeting: "We have seen social work diluted by the introduction into its ranks of vast numbers of inexpereinced and untrained persons. . . . Worse than this is the repeated enunciation of a principle that need rather than qualification shall govern the selection of personnel in this field, and still worse the statement that the administration of relief is not a social job at all and can better be done by other kinds of persons."[24] AASW executive secretary Walter West joined the lamenters: "While the professionalization of social work had at no time [pre-1929] caught up with practice, headway was being made prior to the present emergency. The profession now had an added problem of integrating the newly recruited personnel."[25]

And despite the suggestion of Gordon Hamilton and others that the need for relief did not necessarily imply the need for skilled casework services AASW president Stanley Davies told his membership:

Disastrous as it is that so many millions of people have been forced to accept relief for so long a period, it would be even more disastrous [!] if for an indefinite period to come, the relief of a significant part of the American population, most of whom had been completely self-supporting before the depression, were to be left in the hands of those who have acquired little or no social work knowledge or skill. . . . We are a profession. We have a real sense of solidarity and from this sense of professional solidarity we are strongly motivated to exemplify and to uphold standards of ethics and of performance—to put the interest of those whom we serve before self-interest, and to work together for the realization of the best objectives of social work.[26]

Some social workers saw a possible way out in the training of the new recruits. Professor Helen I. Clark of the University of Wisconsin School of Social Work, a member of the AASW's Recruiting Committee, wrote: "It is necessary and inevitable that public relief departments take on many workers unequipped for social work in the sense that preparation is known to the trained worker. These hundreds of emergency workers should be helped to realize that, except for the specific task for which they were employed, they have no place in the social work picture."[27] If they wanted to continue in the profession, she urged, they must arrange to get training. A number of social work schools, with funds provided by the FERA, did set up emergency training programs, although only a thousand or so FERA workers had received such training by the mid-thirties.

Others, working on a "if you can't beat them, join them" model, proposed that the AASW establish a "provisional" membership category to enable the organization to take into its fold the large number of workers "qualified personally but not professionally. . . . [who] will soon represent a dominant part of the social work personnel with direct client relationships." But this proposal met fierce opposition.[28]

For their part, the new, untrained, nonprofessional social workers in the public agencies returned the old-time professionals' hostility. To the relief workers, the professional caseworkers seemed snobbish. Within the agencies, when conflicts arose between relief workers and administrators, new recruits often found the professional social workers to be pro-administration and anti-labor. The AASW seemed an exclusive club, not an organization that welcomed them and promised to represent their interests.

It was from this group—the young, untrained, new recruits in public agencies—that the first major overt challenge to social work professionalization arose. It was called the rank-and-file movement.[29]

The rank-and-file movement, a loose collection of insurgent social work groups, was prompted by workers' discontent with the existing professional structure of social work. Its earliest precursors were the discussion clubs. Emerging in 1931 in New York, and in the next two years in almost a dozen other cities (including Chicago, Boston, Philadelphia, St. Louis, Kansas City, and Los Angeles), discussion clubs created forums for the analysis of social problems and the role of social workers in the economic crisis. They sponsored public discussion meetings and conferences on such topics as "The Social Worker and the Labor Movement," "The Rights of Labor under the NRA," "Psychiatry and Society," "The Negro and the Crisis," as well as federal relief policy, jobs programs, social insurance proposals, and so on. In a number of cities the discussion groups, not content with discussion alone, became active in support of the unemployed movement and prepared and distributed reports on the administration and functioning of relief programs and welfare agencies.

At the same time the young social workers were showing an increased concern with public policy, they had to deal with deteriorating conditions within the agencies, public and private, in which they worked. As early as the mid-twenties, caseworkers in agencies associated with the Federation of Jewish Philanthropies in New York had formed associations to seek to standardize personnel practices among the agencies and to respond to discontent over salaries and workloads. In 1931 and 1932 the agencies instituted a series of wage cuts, and the associations quickly evolved into unions, representing both caseworkers and nonprofessional staff (clerical workers, custodian workers) in the agencies. Social work professionals had traditionally argued that agency administrators and workers were all "professional social workers," united by their common profession and commonly distinct from the nonprofessional workers in the agencies. But now the administrators were acting like managers anywhere, and the rank-and-file caseworkers saw themselves bearing the brunt of fiscal stringency in just the same way as the nonsocial workers on the agency staff. To many of the caseworkers, it seemed that they should more appropriately identify with the clerical workers and janitors than with their social worker bosses. Similar organizations emerged in Boston, Philadelphia, and Detroit, primarily among caseworkers and staff in Jewish agencies.

But as the Depression wore on, it was in the new public agencies that social work unionism found its real mass base. There the rank-and-file workers, largely drawn from outside the profession, were bound by none of the bonds of professional allegiance to their supervisors. First in the Cook County (Chicago) Department of Public Welfare and then among workers in the Emergency Relief Administration offices, social work unionism flourished. By late 1935 there were unions in New York, Newark, Philadelphia, Pittsburgh, Cleveland, Cincinnati, Minneapolis, St. Paul, Chicago, Baltimore, Washington, St. Louis, Detroit, Milwaukee, Denver, Los Angeles, and Oakland. Many soon came to be affiliated with the national State, County, and Municipal Workers of America or the United, Office and Professional Workers of America (both affiliated with the growing CIO). By 1938 some 14,500 people belonged to social work locals (although not all of this number were social workers; some were other employees of the agencies). By way of comparison, the AASW at the same time counted 10,559 of the estimated 60,000 social workers in the nation as members. Of the unionized workers, 83 percent were employed by public agencies.[30]

The social work unions were primarily protective organizations. They sought to bargain with the agencies (and in some cases, struck) over wages, hours, caseloads, working conditions, benefits, and job security. But they also took positions on policy matters, both within the agencies and within the framework of national political discussions. And, to a degree, they dealt with "professional" issues, too:

for example, they stimulated discussions of worker–client relations and organized schools to upgrade the skills of members and prepare them for civil service exams.

Within some private agencies and in local AASW chapters, too, rank-and-file caseworkers evinced discontent. In several cities "practitioner groups"—arose. These groups reflected disillusion with the AASW's failure to deal with salaries, working conditions, and the like. The AASW was "ineffectual," they charged. Its long-held belief that increased professionalization would lead to growing public recognition of the profession of social work and that that, in turn, would produce higher salaries, they termed an "illusion." The problem, they soon decided, was that the professional organization represented "the program and outlook of the executives in social work. . . . It does not speak to quite such an extent for the mute practitioner member."[31]

Rank-and-file social workers, in both public and private agencies, soon found a "voice" in a literal sense in the journal *Social Work Today*. Published initially by the New York Social Workers' Discussion Club in March 1934, "to meet the need for a frankly critical analysis of social problems and their relation to social work not obtainable through established professional channels,"[32] for the next eight years *Social Work Today* published articles on social work, social welfare policy, the labor movement, social conditions, and world affairs, as well as practical professional concerns.

The New York Social Workers' Discussion Club also organized a conference to bring together representatives of various rank-and-file groups—union, practitioner groups, discussion groups. Representatives from seventeen unions, six discussion groups, and seven other social worker organizations, with a combined membership of 8,200 (compared with the AASW's 8,600), met in Pittsburgh in February 1935. The convention quickly organized a National Coordinating Committee of Rank and File Groups in Social Work to direct future activities and to take over the publication of *Social Work Today*. The committee prepared a platform dealing with personnel practices, professional standards, and national social welfare programs and organized several subsequent national conferences in 1936 and 1937.

Despite the national conferences, the rank-and-file movement never jelled into a sustained national organization. Earlier dreams of a nationwide organization of militant and radical social workers faded; the unions took over local activities aimed at individual agencies; the National Coordinating Committee dissolved in 1937; and *Social Work Today*, now published independently, became the central mechanism for communication and coordination of the scattered groups. But the various groups within this loosely defined "movement" represented a fairly well-defined ideological and practical tendency within social work. The unity of the movement was based, first, in the common history and experience shared by its activist members as public agency workers, drawn from outside the traditional recruiting and training paths of the profession and more or less excluded from the major professional organization, the AASW. They had become social workers in the context of the massive social movements of the thirties, the reemergence of social reform, and the transformation of the institutional structure and social functions of social work. In addition, many of the leading activists, like their counterparts in industry, the arts, and other professions, felt a strong affinity with (if not actual membership in) the Communist party and with a more-or-less Marxist analysis of American society.

The rank-and-filers' analysis of social work reflected these forces. During the first period in the movement's life, they remained far outside the mainstream of professional social work. Rank-and-file writers and activists were deeply critical not only of the professional social workers who dominated the AASW but of professionalism itself. Looking at agency administrators as typical representatives of the "profession," they saw in professionalism a mystification of the real relationships between management and workers within the agencies. Looking at the exclusiveness of the AASW in the face of the rapid expansion in the numbers of social workers, they saw in professionalism a defense of status, not of skills and proficiency. Seeing the many failures of public and private agencies to deal humanely with clients, they saw the agencies themselves and the professionals who ran them as tools of oppression. And feeling oppressed themselves, with their low wages, heavy caseloads, and poor working conditions, they identified more with their clients and other workers than with the profession. There is a "mutuality of interests between industrial, white collar, and professional workers," wrote *Social Work Today*. The social worker is a "white collar proletarian . . . as much a worker as the mill worker or the farm laborer."[33]

The practical implication of this analysis was, first of all, the embracing of unionism, rather than the quest for professional status, as the route to better wages and working conditions, the inclusion of nonprofessional agency workers in the unions, and the exclusion of professional social work managers. Second, the rank-and-file activists sought to turn their allegiance to clients into practical action. When clients, enraged by the lack of resources or inhumane practices of agencies, sought to disrupt the agencies, for instance—a frequent occurrence in the early thirties—the rank-and-file groups attacked the agency administrators for calling the police. More resources, not more police, was the solution, they argued. And they sought to support the clients' cause by leafleting within and outside the agencies and by publicly exposing agency abuses. They even supported the efforts of Baltimore seamen to run their relief agency themselves. The AASW, by contrast, denounced such activities as revealing "over-identification with clients" on the part of the poorly trained social workers.[34]

The rank-and-filers did not deny the need for professional standards. Rather, they argued that the profession's definition of "standards" was inappropriate. If standards were to be defined in terms of clients' needs rather than the needs of social workers for professional status, then those standards would focus not on school-learned expertise and techniques of intervention but on insight and compassion based on experience and identification with the needs and feelings of clients. In any case, current professional ideas about casework were simply irrelevant to the problems faced in actual agencies by caseworkers and their clients. From the workers' standpoint, there was simply no way that clients could be given the kind of individual time and attention casework theory demanded. And, said the rank-and-filers, casework as defined by social work professionals was not even desirable for the clients. Grace Marcus, assistant executive secretary of the AASW, a prominent casework theorist and an antagonist of the rank-and-file movement, summed up the position of the movement (in order to attack it) with unerring acuity: to the rank-and-filers, she said, casework's

> fundamental purpose of adusting the individual to himself, his human relationships, and his environment seems trivial and reactionary. . . . Case work is a sop to the underprivileged, obscures the issues of social justice, imposes on the individual the cruel burden of adapting himself to a psychotic society, and, insofar as it succeeds, constitutes a brake on social action. From this point of view casework is not equal to basic

problems and bears no more relation to social welfare than the art of cosmetics does to health.[35]

What the rank and file proposed to substitute for casework, beyond broad programs of social reform, was less clear. The Pittsburgh convention platform called for a "thorough re-evaluation" of the concept of professional service to reflect "our new understanding of the grouping of forces in society,"[36] but, beyond calling for more training opportunities for new workers in public agencies, the content of that "re-evaluation" was not specified. The rank-and-file caseworker, looking to the new movement for help with the daily problems of work, was not enlightened. *Social Work Today*, complained one such correspondent in 1935, provided no "critical evaluations of technique, or the established social work procedures," no "serious discussions of the role of the caseworker both in the interests of the client and of the status quo." The journal, the writer continued, should "speak for workers . . . who are 'professional' yet definitely aligned with the workers in their struggles."[37]

If the rank-and-file groups were hostile to professional organizations, professional casework aims and techniques, and professionalism itself, the leaders of the profession returned the hostility. "The outstanding fact of this year in social work is the attacks on social workers and their clientele, on professional standards from without and —I regret to say—from within," lamented AASW president Dorothy C. Kahn in 1935.[38] Grace Marcus took on the rank-and-file arguments more systematically, attacking those who "have retreated entirely from any acknowledgment of personal factors in maladjustment into economic dogmas that caricature Marxian theory." Casework, she argued, was an "embryonic professional art" based in a "psychoanalytic understanding of the psyche," which required more disciplined training and more expertise, not less. That casework had limitations, she acknowledged: "The boundaries of casework are narrow. Its immediate practice has to face the ineluctable fact that individual lives have to come to terms with reality, however barbarous and unjust those terms may be. . . . [But] within the restrictions of its functions casework has its unique and indispensable contribution to make to social insight, improvement, and change."[39]

Porter Lee, who only a few years earlier had heralded the shift of social work from "cause" to "function" as the mark of its professional maturity, was more vituperative. He told a 1934 meeting on "competence and leadership" that at present the "most congenial area for discussion among most social workers is not that of professional competence, but it is rather that of the promotion of social change." The following year, returning to his old argument that such actions would undermine the professionalization of social work, he insisted:

> Leadership and advocacy in social action on issues with respect to which one is professionally competent are direct authentic professional activities. . . . There may be social workers who are expert on taxation, on collectivism, on constitutional law, on the proposal to make the production and distribution of milk a public utility—but they did not become expert in these matters as a result of their training and experience as social workers. Unless he [sic] has had other training I do not see how any social worker could assume the role of leader or advocate in these legitimate fields of social action without risk both to these programs and to the status of social work.

The efforts of social workers to promote their own self-interest as workers, or to identify with labor, or to resort to the "unintelligent intrusive methods of radical propaganda," he continued, "[are] embarrassing those service programs for which we are professionally responsible." They were as serious a threat to social workers' efforts "to promote justice and human well-being" as the "equally unintelligent restrictions of conservative donors and boards of directors."[40]

But the rank-and-file challenge to professionalism faded almost as quickly as it had arisen. In late 1935 and early 1936 the movement began to mute its attacks and, in effect, rejoined the profession it had earlier scorned. In part, the shift reflected external events. The New Deal itself had shifted sharply to the left in 1935, and the New Deal programs on which the jobs of most rank-and-filers depended were under sharp attack from the right. The pro–New Deal professional leaders had become potential allies. At the same time, the Communist party softened it attacks on the established order, reflecting the decision of the summer 1935 Seventh Congress of the Communist International to shift from all-out confrontation with capitalism and expectation of imminent revolution to an alliance with progressive elements within capitalism and a "popular front" against fascism. Rank-and-filers who were close to the party followed suit.

But the evolution of the social workers at the core of the rank-and-file movement played an equally significant role. The raw recruits of 1933 had become experienced social welfare workers by 1936. With three years' service under their belts, they had become aware of the need for more knowledge and skills to do their job. They were increasingly sympathetic to the institutional needs of their employers, such as the need to defend budgets against cutbacks. They had begun to perceive a potential or real conflict between endlessly needy clients and agencies that were not only sanctioned and supported by society but also responsible to it financially and programmatically. They had come to have a stake in the very institutions they had earlier denounced and had come to see potential conflicts with their erstwhile allies.

In this new context, the rank-and-file movement shifted its positions and altered the emphasis of its activities. The most obvious shift was a sharp change in attitude toward the government and the overall social order. The early movement had identified fully with Mary Van Kleeck's attack on the New Deal and on reform government in general and her call for radical social change. Now *Social Work Today* moved toward tacit, if critical, support of the New Deal. What was needed, it argued, was a critical evaluation of programs, new programs, and expansion of existing programs. The attack on government was replaced by an attack on the foes of the New Deal.

At the same time, the unions were rapidly becoming the dominant force within the rank-and-file movement. For them, as unions, any proposals to alter public institutions had to be evaluated in terms of their impact on the employees of those institutions. Proposed changes intended to help the poor (the clients of the agencies) that conflicted with staff needs were problematic. Public policy issues still figured prominently in the unions' rhetoric, but in reality, recruiting new members, dealing with grievance, and negotiating contracts had a higher priority.

Major challenges to government social policies had lost urgency. In 1938 the *Social Work Today* editors summed up and reflected the shift in position: noting the close "organic" relationship between social work and the government of the welfare state, they wrote: "Social work is called upon to prove whether it is capable of sustaining and extending the relationship."[41]

During the same period, the "professional" issues, for so long scorned by the movement, assumed new importance. In October

1936 *Social Work Today* began a series of articles on casework problems and techniques. The high point of the relegitimation of casework for the rank-and-filers was Bertha Reynold's 1938 "Rethinking Social Casework."[42] Reynolds had impeccable credentials for the task. A graduate of the first Smith College program in 1918, a major psychiatric social work theorist and practitioner and associate director at Smith from 1925 to 1937, she was also close to the Communist party and had been an early and vigorous champion of the rank-and-file movement. She was respected by both rank-and-file and traditional professionals (although the latter virtually barred her from the practice of her profession in the forties, bowing to McCarthyism).

Casework, Reynolds argued, had its origins in society's "need to place outside of itself those who were not economically successful." Caseworkers were "employed . . . to see that society was not troubled by these individuals and their families." But the emergence of psychiatric methods in the twenties had undermined the class-structure-maintaining function of casework. By eliminating the notion of moral blame for poverty and by making evident the uselessness of coercive methods of social control, psychiatry had "democratized" the casework process. When the New Deal added the "right" of the poor to receive various services and benefits, the function of social work had been democratized still further. And advances in psychiatric theory in the early thirties (e.g., Virginia Robinson's *A Changing Psychology in Social Work*) had led to an even more egalitarian, mutualistic caseworker–client relationship. Finally, with the New Deal, the government had taken over the funding of relief. Because both caseworker and client were interested in the adequate funding of the new agencies, they were drawn together even more firmly and linked in struggle against the antidemocratic forces that would impose inadequate funding, intrusive methods, and victim-blaming attitudes. An intimate alliance had emerged between psychiatric casework and social policy. There was now a "community of interest" between social workers and clients, which sooner or later all social workers would have to recognize.

But if Reynolds's article signaled a reconciliation between the movement and casework, casework practice remained problematic. In principle, rank-and-filers tried to develop a casework model based on the centrality of the environment as a source for individual personality structure. But the precise relation between the individual and society and between the individual and social change remained problematic. Reynolds's plea for collective resistance against reaction by the social worker and the client did not lead toward a solution to these conflicts. Nor was a solution advanced by her assumption that the relationship of the social worker and the client was simply one of alliance rather than of social control.

Radical social workers were not alone, of course, in reflecting on the impact of the Depression and the new institutional and programmatic structure of social work on social work practice. A massive debate within the casework mainstream was developing precisely around this problem, the so-called functional school/ diagnostic school debate, to which I shall return shortly. In practice, more and more rank-and-filers were drawn into this debate, most commonly on the "functional" side.

By 1938 the rank-and-file movement was dealing with both policy issues in a fashion that brought it back into the mainstream of professional social work. But in doing so, it had abandoned its reasons for existence. The rank-and-filers were engaged in a debate that assumed a casework based on psychiatric principles rather than one derived from a radical critique of society. They had dropped their critique of casework-dominated social work, on the one hand, and of the functions of governmental social policy, on the other. Their earlier focus on the social-control functions of casework (and its corollary, the real or potential conflict of interest between caseworker and client) had been dissolved into a belief in the common interests of client and social worker. By 1940 *Social Work Today* noted in a statement of "principles" of the rank-and-file movement that "social work is inherently a constructive pursuit, sensitive to the needs of the individual and committed to the development of a community life geared to the meeting of them. . . . Social work has always been committed to a program of positive education for democratic living." Although casework might remain a process for alleviating problems, rather than for restructuring society, wrote *Social Work Today*, casework nevertheless was "one of the few cases of human decency still left in a brutalized world."[43]

The collapse of the rank-and-file movement's assault on the professional model of social work practice and the structure of the profession did not go unnoticed or unreciprocated by the leaders of the profession. By early 1937, Grace Marcus, whose 1935 defense of casework had been a major theoretical attack on the rank-and-file movement, was a frequent contributor to *Social Work Today* and by 1941 was a member of the National Committee of Social Work Today Cooperators, a support group for the magazine. Porter Lee indicated some sympathy for the movement (and was eulogized by *Social Work Today* on his death in 1939). Early in 1937 Virginia Robinson took note of the change: Initially, she recalled, many of the newcomers to social work were

> scornful of social work and professional workers. *Social Work Today* . . . started off with an attack on everything in social work. It reviled its philosophy as conservative and reactionary; it accused it of capitalist domination. Social action alone was worthwhile and social work as a technical, professional field received scant consideration. [But] as you know if you follow this magazine, its interest has shifted in the past year and there is now some real concern with technical problems.[44]

By the end of the decade, then, the rank-and-file movement had succeeded in unionizing a significant part of social work. (The unions lasted until they were destroyed during the McCarthyite wave of the fifties.) The movement had pushed social work toward a more critical and aggressive stance with respect to public policy issues and had helped restore the social action impulse to the profession. It never represented more than a minority (although a sizable and noisy one) within social work, but its moral and political influence on social workers outweighed its numbers. But equally, by the end of the decade, with social work having moved a small way toward the rank-and-file movement's concerns, the movement had moved a long way back toward the social work mainstream. Its earlier sharp (if rhetorical) critique of professionalism and its skepticism about the benevolence of government had faded. The ability of the movement to generate any unique approaches to the classic dilemmas of social work—social control versus social amelioration, the conflicts between client and social worker, and environmental manipulation and social reform versus individual adjustment and casework—had collapsed. By reentering the mainstream of social work, the movement lost relevance as an alternative to the path of professionalism and any persuasive reason for an independent existence as well. With the approach of World War II, *Social Work Today* became increasingly preoccupied with foreign policy issues. No longer having anything more to offer social workers than did the professional journals and general interest magazines, in 1942 it quietly folded. Social work had survived the most direct challenge to its drive to professionalism.

Most of the social work elite—caseworkers in private agencies, administrators, and social work educators—had never doubted the professional model itself, of course. But the Depression and the New Deal still confronted them with an enormous challenge. Social work had professionalized under the unchallenged domination of the casework model of social work practice. That model had increasingly centered around a psychiatric analysis of individual problems, abjuring the social environment and social structure, and had increasingly concerned itself with the problems of the non-poor. With the advent of the Depression and its massive poverty, its newly energized social programs, its new social work institutions, and its transformed relationship between social workers and government, the twenties' model of professionalism became an anachronism.

First, there was the return of social workers, like it or not, to social reform. The social workers' relation to reform in the thirties was, of course, quite different from that of the Progressive Era, when the reforms had been, in a very immediate sense, the consequence of social movements among the new middle class, which included the proto-social workers themselves. The New Deal reforms, by contrast, were engendered by movements of the poor, the unemployed, and the trade unionists. Social workers were experts, consultants, advisers, and administrators but (except for the militants of the rank-and-file movement) not activists and prime movers of reform.

Beyond that, the rapid expansion of relief programs following Roosevelt's inauguration as president had transformed the relationship between relief and casework. Relief, once doled out at social workers' discretion, had become a right, while casework's previously necessary relationship with relief had been torn asunder. The role of casework—and especially of psychiatric casework—in what had historically been its core social function was no longer clear. With relief a right, and government funds replacing private philanthropy, the twenties' answers to the sources of legitimation of social work (with respect to clients and patrons) no longer clearly applied.

Finally, as we have seen, in the twenties the drive to professionalism had proceeded all but unchallenged within the profession. In the early and mid-thirties, by contrast, the rank-and-file movement represented a noisy, if ultimately ineffective, challenge to the entire model.

By 1937 or 1938, however, the dust was beginning to settle. The New Deal had largely completed its work—no major new programs were to emerge for more than two decades. A large proportion of social workers were by now employed in the new agencies and programs, and the worst of the rank-and-file challenge had been weathered. Social workers turned to a renewed interest in traditional professional concerns: raising the status of the profession, reversing the dilution of professional requirements for employment, resolving disputes as to the nature of social work education, and developing better techniques for social intervention. Linton Swift, in his presidential address to the 1938 AASW convention, told the assembled social workers: "For several years after the beginning of the Depression one might justifiably have thought social action was our major concern, at least in practice. Now, however, we are beginning to reexamine our basic reasons for existence as an Association and the ways in which, jointly or individually, we can most effectively define and achieve professional purposes."[45] (Notice that, to Swift, "professional purposes" were still to be distinguished from "social action," a symbol of the failure of the rank and file's challenge to the old model.)

But the renewed discussion took place in a new social policy environment. Unlike the small social work agencies of the past, the new agencies were large, hierarchical, bureaucratic, publicly funded, and publicly accountable with respect to funds and programs. The would-be profession of the late thirties had to address a set of questions not even imagined by their predecessors: how should social workers relate to these behemoths? How should social workers relate to (and legitimize themselves with respect to) clients who were now legally entitled to their services and to relief? What kinds of techniques were appropriate to the new situations in which social workers were employed? (As a corollary to this question, the old question of social work's relationship to other professions using similar techniques, especially psychiatry, was also reopened.) How could the Depression-born reemphasis on the social environment be integrated with the twenties-born emphasis on individual personality?

As discussed earlier, professionalism is a way of dealing with issues of occupational legitimacy, autonomy, authority, and so on. But those are often not confronted explicitly, but rather are fought out in disguised form, as disputes about the "knowledge base" of the occupation. The theory and methods of a profession can be presented by those both within and outside the profession as "scientific" rather than as self-interested and partisan. In just this vein the renewed discussion within social work took the apparent form of a debate over theory and method: the debate between the "functional" school and the "diagnostic" school of psychiatric case-workers.

We have already traced the triumph of the psychiatric approach over the sociological approach to social casework in the 1920s. It is too easy to read present meanings of words back into the past, however. To social workers in the 1920s, the "psychiatric" approach was, in fact, a mix of ideas drawn from Freud, John Dewey, behaviorist John B. Watson, the "commonsense" psychiatry of Adolf Meyer, the genetically determined psychology of Lewis M. Terman and Robert M. Yerkes, and expertise derived from everyday experience. For most social workers who used the new psychiatric ideas in any practical way, psychiatry was more of an approach to labeling ("diagnosis") and manipulating ("psyching out," gaining "compliance") than it was a source of techniques for "treatment." Most caseworkers in the twenties, like their predecessors of the pre-psychiatric era, sought to diagnose the social problems of the client, decided what should be done to solve them, and then tried to manipulate the client and the social environment to achieve the desired result. The psychiatric theory on which professionalism was based still bore little relation to what most social workers actually did.

At the same time, the old opposition between individual change and social change, although apparently suppressed in the casework model, reappeared in the form of the problematic relationship between the intrapsyche ("personality") and the social environment ("situation"). Social work, after all, was concerned with the adjustment of the individual to his or her situation. Some social workers tried to theorize the "situation," just as Freud and his followers had theorized the psyche.[46]

But the problem remained easier to state than to solve. Person and situation remained separate, the one understood psychiatrically, the other sociologically, with the task of joining them remaining an unsolved problem. Sociology, a method for describing and analyzing social patterns of behavior, may have offered lessons for community organizers and social reformers, but it appeared to offer little to the caseworker seeking to understand an individual personality. Freudian psychiatry—with its emphasis on the unconscious and on instinctual drives and with its psychological determinism based on early childhood experience—seemed to leave little room for societal influences, especially those experienced as an adult. And both sociological and Freudian models seemed to reinforce the manipulative aspect of social work. With their superior sociological understanding, social workers sought to manipulate and remove social obstacles *for* the client. And the Freudian model of treatment seemed to imply that the unconscious motivations of clients were easily understood by workers, who could then act on the clients to change them and thus manipulate their clients' inner life as earlier they manipulated their environment.

The turning point in the use of psychology by social workers was the publication, in 1930, of Virginia Robinson's *A Changing Psychology in Social Work.*[47] Robinson's book crystallized the growing discontent many social workers felt with the old, paternalistic models and proposed a new way to synthesize the individual personality and the social environment. Heavily influenced by the psychiatric theories of Otto Rank, Robinson proposed that casework should focus not on planning for the social welfare of the client, not on the client per se (or the environment per se), but on the *relationship* between the client and the social worker. The client, not the social worker, should be the central actor in the casework drama; the social worker–client relationship was intended to strengthen the client. Robinson attacked even the apparently pro-client phrase "participation of the client" as implying that the social worker had a preformed plan that the client merely entered, no matter how enthusiastically.

Robinson's approach was heavily oriented to the client's emotional adjustment, not to the client's objective social welfare. Concrete services, home visits, and environmental manipulation by the social worker had little place in her model. Rather, the client chose the agency that offered the services he or she wanted; it was the social worker's role to enable the client to make that choice wisely and to use the agency effectively. The agency itself became, to Robinson, a "sample situation" within which the client–social worker relationship was developed and played out. It defined and limited the social worker–client relationship; within it, the client would come to know and test himself or herself, his or her limits and strengths. Even the administration of a simple agency function, then, became "individual therapy through a treatment relationship." (Perhaps because of this placing of agency function at the center of casework, the Pennsylvania School of Social Work, of which Robinson was one of the principal theoretical leaders, had less trouble in adjusting to social work's new role than did many other schools. With the development of federal emergency relief agencies, it quickly moved to train workers for these agencies, whereas other schools and professional groups remained dubious or hostile to the newcomers.)

Many social workers received Robinson's book ecstatically. Bertha Reynolds of Smith College, for example, reviewed it in the Family Service Association journal, *The Family:* "Some books sink into the pool of oblivion with scarcely a ripple. Some, for a brief time, are like molten matter cast up by an erupting volcano. Some are like earthquakes, felt but not comprehended at the time and producing no one knows what changes. One only knows that after their coming nothing is the same again. *A Changing Psychology in Social Work* bears the mark of such a book."[48]

As the decade wore on, the roles of social work agencies were thrown into ever-deeper confusion. Robinson and her colleague at Penn, Jessie Taft, developed their ideas further. But some of the implications of their rejection of Freudian orthodoxy now began to sink in and many social workers had second thoughts. Caseworkers began to split into two "schools": the "functional school" (the followers of Robinson and Taft, a group that included Kenneth Pray, Almena Dawley, Harry Aptekar, Grace Marcus, and Ruth Smalley) and the more orthodox Freudian "diagnostic" (or "organic" or "psychosocial") school (which included Gordon Hamilton, Florence Hollis, Lucille Austin, Fern Lowery, and Annette Garrett, among others). Although the functional school remained a small minority, the debate it provoked has had an enormous influence on social work methods and principles. Continuing for more than fifteen years, the debate quickly grew extraordinarily bitter, even vitriolic. By the late forties, graduates of "functional" schools (e.g., the University of Pennsylvania and the University of North Carolina) had trouble finding jobs in agencies that adhered to the diagnostic school, and vice versa. Bertha Reynolds noted that problems were encountered even in referring clients from functional agency to diagnostic agency and the reverse. Helen Perlman (whose eclectic "problem solving" approach eventually helped bridge the two schools) describes "going to a conference in Atlantic City—I think it was in 1938—where a group of us went into a restaurant and a very bright waiter met us at the door and asked: 'What side of the room do you want to sit on, the diagnostic or the functional?' "[49]

The diagnostic–functional debate has usually been described as a debate over methods and techniques of social casework or over the theoretical base of social work (Freud vs. Rank, his now-heretic former disciple; Taft translated Rank's principal works into English and Rank himself taught for many years at Penn and at the Graduate School for Jewish Social Work in New York). But this description does not explain why the dispute was so bitter, why it lasted so long, or why social work split into only two camps and not more. The debate can be better understood perhaps, in its inception at least, as a struggle over how the newly created welfare state would affect the professional aspirations of social work. It *was* a debate over theory and technique, but *underneath* that debate lay disputes about the nature of people's problems, the relation of men and women to society and to the state, the nature of the new social welfare agencies, and how social work was to deal with these problems. In their writings, Jessie Taft and Virginia Robinson produced a major systematic effort to redefine social work in light of the new social and political realities.

As the technical aspects of the debate have often been recounted, a brief summary will suffice here.[50] The functional school believed in short-term treatment, focusing on the here and now (and specifically on the client in the agency); the diagnostic school tended toward a long-term therapeutic model based on an in-depth investigation of the client's life history. The functional school called for "partializing"—focusing only on the immediate issues presented by the client—whereas the diagnostic school insisted on the necessity of examining and treating the "total personality" of the client, even if the help sought by the client was for a limited, practical problem. The functional school exchewed formal diagnosis and the setting of treatment goals, arguing that these would emerge in the course of the relationship; the diagnostic school, by contrast, insisted on differential diagnosis and a setting of short- and long-term goals. The functional school saw the experience of the client in his or her relationship with the social worker within the specific agency setting and how the client used the agency's functions (hence the name) as the key to personal change; the diagnostic school saw personality transformations—mobilizing the client's ego strengths, resolving inner conflicts, and so on—as central. In the functional setting the client directed the process of change, whereas the worker was responsible only for his or her own part in helping the client release these processes. To the diagnostic school, the social worker was far more central and directive. The functional school stressed the importance of external structure (agency rules, time limits to therapy, agency fees); the diagnostic school believed in a more open-ended and constraint-free process. In the functional setting, clients were to pattern their experiences in their own unique ways and thus develop their own internal norms; treatment in the diagnostic setting was concerned with the adherence of the client to socially accepted norms.

But however great the gap between the approaches of the two schools, these technical issues fail to get at the underlying issues. The case for the functional school was made systematically in three seminal articles: Taft's "The Relation of Function to Process in Social Case Work" (1937) and "The Function of the Personality Course in the Practice Unit" (1942) and Robinson's "The Meaning of Skill" (1942).[51] In these early articles the relation of Taft's and Robinson's theories to the issues raised by the New Deal is clearly revealed.

Decrying the historic swings of the social work pendulum between a focus on the inner self and a focus on the outer world, Taft argued (in her 1937 article) that "either concentration destroys or ignores the reality that lies only in the living relationship between the two."[52] During the twenties, social work had swung toward the inner-self pole, but in the thirties, both the focus of casework and the settings in which it was offered had changed: "The intensely psychiatric, psychological, subjective phase of interest in both client and worker seems to be passing, along with the shift from intensive, indeterminate case work by the private agency to the highly functionalized administration of public money by governmental relief and assistance boards."[53] Even in intensive casework, the exclusive focus on hereditary and intrapsychic and intrafamilial factors was giving way to greater concern with economic and cultural conditions.

127

Yet neither of these shifts from inner to outer, from the more subjective and personal to the more objective and social, holds the solution for a social work that intends to arrive at a technical grasp of its own practice. It is necessary to know and appreciate the economic, the cultural, the immediate social setting of those who constitute our clientele, it is essential to understand and accept tolerantly, but without evasion, the human psychology that is common to worker and client in our culture, but this is only the beginning. There is one area and only one in which outer and inner, worker and client, agency and social need can come together effectively, only one area that offers to social workers the possibility of developing into a profession, and that is the area of the helping process itself.[54]

Social work, Taft continued, had never been able to resolve its professional crisis because of its inability to resolve the duality of inner and outer. For all the talk of developing a "scientific" knowledge base for the field, social work could not be a "science" because it always had to subordinate abstract knowledge (e.g., of personality) to its avowed purpose, helping people. As a result, it had always been more or less "blind, haphazard, well-intentioned, and fumbling." Professionalism lay not in the pretense of being scientific but in the development of a role that can be "taught, learned, and practiced."

Given this critique of the historic road to professionalization, Taft noted that the level of professionalization thus far achieved was astonishing. In explanation, she suggested that such strides had been made because social work had not mattered much in the past, and thus had not been scrutinized very carefully:

That [social work] has succeeded in getting by thus far, despite its slow blundering advance, is due not only to the fact that there was no better way of meeting the human needs it serves, but also to the fortunate circumstance that it has not been a money-making, but a money-spending enterprise, and has served chiefly the poor and ignorant who often had neither the wisdom nor the power to reject a service they could not pay for. But now that the state has gone into an area that social work claims as its own, now that vast administrative and economic problems are involved and huge expenditures of public money at stake, social work will have to meet competition from other groups who want to fill the big jobs, to handle the large sums, and even to grapple with the interesting complexities of the situations now facing us. Unless social work can really bring to bear a skill that outweighs its lack of administrative and business experience, it will not survive the tremendous demands and the public scrutiny involved in meeting the large scale social need of today. There is no escape, therefore, from facing the necessity to establish ourselves firmly, not merely on the basis of social need, but on a foundation of professional skill. . . . In my opinion, we already have that basis if only we can relinquish a little of our too great sense of responsibility for the client and his need, in order to concentrate on a defining of what we can do and a refining of our knowledge and skill in relation to the carrying out of each specific and accepted function.[55]

In the new context, Taft argued, primary emphasis had to be placed on the relationship between client and worker and on the *process* of helping rather than on a static observation of the client in isolation. In particular, "control of the client, either of his needs or of his behavior," was no longer acceptable. Although social workers liked to think of their role as purely benevolent, in reality, the role of the traditional social worker was authoritative and that of the client submissive. The client was left with all the "negative elements," and "negative elements there must be in any reality situation. He is forced to ungrateful, ungracious doubt, to refusal, to hesitation, to escape or evasion, or to a disguised struggle with the very help he sought."[56] Taft also abjured efforts to penetrate every recess of the client's personality: "It is not possible, now or ever, to know a client as he is in himself . . . except as part of a process in which, with one fixed or known quality [i.e., the function, rules, processes, structure of the agency], the other may be defined in terms of what it does."[57] The agency did provide such a fixed point: "We do know of the professional person on his job what we cannot presume to know of him personally, the general direction in which he is going. . . . The caseworker's responsibility . . . real as it is, must first of all be to the agency and its function; only as agency does he meet his client professionally."

Casework, Taft noted, "has been thrown into confusion by its inability to find its place between pure therapy and public relief." The therapy alternative is, in a sense, *too* client oriented: the client is refused nothing by way of a deeper experience of self. But in reality, therapy was not "client oriented" at all when the client, denied tangible aid, that is, specific help with his or her objective, real-world problems, was left alone to find his or her own way in real life. The relief worker, at least, could give tangible aid, although "the power to give, to refuse, to limit the actual means of subsistence for other adult human beings, who have been deprived through no fault of their own of the opportunity to maintain themselves, is a function that cannot be accepted as right or good by any thoughtful person. At best it could only be tolerated as necessary." On the other hand, "if the therapeutic situation is too unreal, public relief may be too real, too actually depriving and controlling for casework, as here defined, to operate to the best advantage. Social casework lay somewhere between these two extremes."

In "The Function of the Personality Course in the Practice Unit," Taft reflected further on the relation between psychiatry and casework:

> The confusions introduced into social work by the post-war psychoanalytic invasion were manifold, but only two results were fundamentally disturbing. First, the authority and definiteness of psychoanalysis as a method of treating emotional problems compelled the facing of a fundamental doubt: Is casework something in itself, or must it become, as far as it is psychological, a modified or diluted form of psychotherapy? Second, whether casework be unique or derivative, does the new psychology apply only to the treatment of the client or must the case worker expose himself directly to its influence in order to utilize it professionally?[58]

In fact, many social workers had answered the second question by seeking personal analyses, and the enthusiasm for psychoanalysis, along with the strictly Freudian approach adopted by social workers, led to a tendency to separate the provision of concrete services and the meeting of specific needs from the meeting of psychological needs. Such a separation

> rules out the administering of actual services as the core of a casework with its own authentic skill and goal and forces the worker to an unwarranted assumption of psychoanalytic diagnostic authority. In other words, the emphasis on psychotherapeutic treatment as a thing-in-itself and the only medium of helping tends to devaluate everything that social work stands for uniquely and concretely in the community. It leaves case work with nothing it can do in its own right, so that its only hope is to obtain the services of a psychiatrist or a highly specialized psychiatric social worker to direct the many case workers who lack special training and first-hand experience of psychoanalysis.[59]

By contrast, the Pennsylvania school, with its Rankian, non-insight-based psychology and its roots in agencies that deemed insight therapy irrelevant, "was never tempted to make therapy of casework, or to desert its effort to train for skill in administering the concrete services of the social agency as intended by the community."

> The intellectual effort of the [Freudian] analytic exploration and interpretation of the material . . . too often felt like the imposition of the worker's will, like pressure or attack [on the client]. The caseworker with Rankian experiences, on the other hand, was not equipped with any conviction as to his right to explore and interpret apart from the reality problem presented in the client's request.[60]

Thus, the Rankian approach and emphasis on the agency lead to limits on the social worker's "invasion" of the client's personality and hence to a distinct role for casework as opposed to psychiatry.[61]

But most social workers were not convinced by Taft's and Robinson's arguments, seeing in the approach of the functional school a threat to the model of professionalization that they had struggled so hard to achieve in the twenties. First, the "diagnostic school" (as the more orthodox, Freud-oriented group came to be known) rejected the functional school's belief that social work was not "scientific" in the usual sense of the word. "Practice" and "process" were not sufficient bases for a profession, they insisted. Social work must base itself in an objectively verifiable, positivistic science of human behavior. For example, Gordon Hamilton, the diagnostic school's most influential spokesperson, argued that "the base of social work is potentially scientific; that the social sciences allied with the physical sciences must increasingly throw light on social needs and social improvement; that the organic and psychogenetic theory of personality is fundamental.[62]

Second, the functional school argued that the essence of social work was contained in the functioning of social *agencies,* functions that were in turn ultimately based in governmental social policy decisions. Even within the agency, the "professional" social worker was, in the end, nothing more than an employee. Consequently, the caseworker was defined as the administrator of the agency's purposes.[63] The more traditional diagnostic school insisted that, despite the rise of the welfare state, the caseworker—skilled and knowledgeable, essentially autonomous in his or her work with clients— must remain the basis of professionalism. Individual casework, not social programs, was the defining characteristic of social work; any efforts at fusing or confusing the two must be rejected. Gordon Hamilton sought to distinguish the schools as, on the one hand, "those who emphasize the objective understanding of social need" and, on the other, "those who emphasize the administration of social services."[64] The essential discipline needed for the first (her own, diagnostic school) was "social study, diagnosis, and treatment." Hamilton acknowledged that only a few years earlier many social workers had focused too exclusively on the client's early experience and personality structure to the exclusion of the present-day social environment. But more recently, she insisted, they had recognized the importance of the immediate practical and interpersonal "situation." (By "situation," Hamilton meant the immediate situation of the client: the particular constellation of family, friends, and neighbors, of job and school and neighborhood. It was not a synonym for the larger patterns of social structure and social forces that shape individuals and impel and limit their personality and behavior.)[65]

Hamilton sharply distinguished herself from the functional school further by insisting on the need for the caseworker to recognize objectively and define the client's needs. This was not to be a task carried out by the client alone, made manifest through the latter's choice of agency to consult. *Diagnosis*, which permits the caseworker to determine what to treat and what not, how to treat it and how not, how to distinguish problems arising from the immediate situation from those arising from the inner personality, was the core of social casework theory and practice. And given this diagnosis, the caseworker had to be free to move flexibly from concrete services to agency procedures and rules to intensive casework therapy. It might appear that Hamilton was simply describing the actual differences in social work carried out in public and private agencies and using the latter as the defining mode for professional practice, but she explicitly denied the existence of any distinction.

Third, Taft and Robinson had sought to define a terrain for social work that differed fundamentally from that of psychiatry. Casework was based in the "administering of actual services," no matter how much psychotherapy was mixed in; they did not treat therapy as an end in itself. By contrast, the diagnostic school was not ready to concede any ground to the psychiatrists in the battle for professional turf. There was, simply, no sharp distinction between caseworker as therapist and psychiatrist: "We have said that there is no essential difference between casework and therapy. The question will follow:

Is there a difference between the psychiatric therapy of the social worker and that of the psychoanalytic therapist? We answer: There is not qualitative difference. . . . The differences are quantitative."[66] Various diagnostic school theorists sought to define those "quantitative" and situational differences more explicitly. For example, Lucille Austin suggested that people suffering from breakdowns in their social relationships tended to seek help from social workers, whereas people with overt neurotic or psychotic symptoms were referred to psychiatrists.[67]

Fourth, recall that the essence of professional status lies in the legitimation of the professional's role (as well as status) to clients. The functional school, basing its definition of casework in agency function, which in turn depended on governmentally determined social policy, sought legitimacy in the explicit state actions that defined the functions of agencies. Under this definition the social worker was no longer autonomous but served, instead, as an agent performing specific functions. The diagnostic school sought to reaffirm the traditional model: the caseworker's authority was legitimized by the caseworker's superior knowledge, and thus it was the caseworker, not the client, who could judge the client's adherence to social norms. Moreover, regardless of whether the client sought help voluntarily or involuntarily, it was the caseworker alone who had the ability and right to define the full extent of the client's problems and subsequent treatment.

This led to several major points of difference between the two schools. The functional school insisted on "partializing" services, that is, the client should receive only those services that he or she sought. For instance: "in administering assistance as a right, the agency is bound not to use the individual's economic helplessness for purposes that have not been generally declared and defined, even though these purposes are presumably inspired by interest in the individual's welfare and welfare of his dependents."[68] The diagnostic school disagreed. "The psychosocial [i.e., diagnostic] approach," wrote Florence Hollis, "has emphasized the need to ascertain the client's need beyond what he presents as his initial problem and has stressed the effort to understand causation."[69] The client, elaborated Lionel C. Lane, "frequently is not in a position to evaluate his problem clearly by virtue of his own closeness to it. We all accept the premise that an essential element of all therapeutic relationships is that the helping person is outside the problem and can therefore see it more clearly."[70] Dorothy Hutchinson suggested, for example, that unmarried mothers are incapable of making their own decisions: "In my opinion the majority of these mothers are unable, if not incapable of making their own independent decisions without skilled case work service. . . . It is true that even without guidance she *will* make a decision but this is one which will be determined by unconscious factors and most always to the detriment of the baby and defeating to herself."[71] What is called for, then, is "totalization." Everything in the client's personality is, potentially at least, up for examination and change at the discretion of the social worker.

In the same vein, to the diagnostic school, it was the social worker, not the client, who was responsible for determining treatment goals. The functionalist position was described by Ruth Smalley, who would later become dean of the Pennsylvania School of Social Work:

> The worker did not attempt to classify a client and select a kind of treatment deemed appropriate for that particular kind of client in order to produce an envisioned end—such as maintenance of the status quo in adjustment, return to a former level of adjustment, or achievement of a different level of adjustment—but rather entered into the relationship with avowed lack of knowledge of how it would all turn out, since that answer had not yet been written. Only client and worker together would discover what the client could do with the help offered. The worker's responsibility was for control of his part in the process not for the achievement of any predetermined end.[72]

But for the diagnostic school's Florence Hollis:

> Goals are a composite of what the client sees and desires for himself and what the worker sees as possible and helpful. . . . It would be irresponsible for the caseworker to participate in moving toward a goal desired by the client if this goal, in the worker's opinion, is either unattainable or harmful to the client or to others. It would also be irresponsible not to attempt to enlist the client's interest in moving toward a goal which the worker considers attainable and in the client's interest, even though at the outset he does not recognize this as desirable or possible.[73]

This, in turn, implies that the diagnostic caseworker is a direct agent of social control, seeking to assure that social norms are observed.

Man with his individual needs lives within an external world of reality
in which he seeks to satisfy these needs. This he can do only as he
learns to adjust to the social and physical laws of this world. He may
fail and need the help of a caseworker either because of a lack of
adjusting power within himself or because he is subjected to unusual
pressures from the environment.[74]

"Change, growth, and adaptation to reality" are what caseworkers
have to offer, wrote Gordon Hamilton.[75]

Finally, the diagnostic school, in the tradition of occupational
groups struggling for professional identity everywhere, tended to
deny that the substance of the debate was concerned with professional issues (legitimacy, roles, turf). Rather, both at the time and in
subsequent histories of the social work profession, the controversy
was described as simply a difference between two schools of
therapy, one based on the theories of Otto Rank, the other on the
theories of Sigmund Freud, or as a dispute regarding techniques of
casework.

The functional school sustained a serious and coherent effort at
dealing with the welfare state and its implications for social work
theory, practice, and professional status. Spurred by the turmoil and
conflict of the Depression years, it sought to rethink radically the
relationship between the social environment and the individual. But
it never convinced more than a small minority of social workers to
adopt its view.

Underlying the functional school's "political" failure was the
threat that its formulations represented to the path toward professionalization taken by social work. Because functionalism itself did
not offer a clear and effective route to professional status, autonomy,
and respect, it failed to meet a major practical and psychological
need of social workers.

But equally important, the strength of the functional school position depended on the social and political mood of the Depression
years. New Deal programs had created the new institutional and
programmatic environment that led to the functional school's challenge. The new programs and the larger cultural impact of the Depression had reopened the issues of the relation of social work to
social control and to the state, the interaction of social and individual forces, and so on. In the context of the breakdown of the old
liberal economy and of widespread social and intellectual ferment, it

was easy to question old ideas of all kinds. It was no coincidence that the activists of the rank-and-file movement (who were generally employed by the new public agencies) leaned sharply toward the provocative, heterodox functional school ideas when they turned to a discussion of "professional" issues toward the end of the decade.

Had the turmoil of the thirties continued into the next decade, or had the government continued to experiment with new approaches to dealing with social problems, perhaps the arguments of the functional school would have gradually become more persuasive to the majority of caseworkers. But, in fact, the Depression was followed by the war, and the war by the great McCarthyite Red Scare. The forties and fifties were characterized not by social ferment and depression but by the collapse of social debate, by prosperity, and by a withdrawal of state energies from innovations in social welfare. The pressure on social work to deal with economic and social realities as well as individual problems declined; the pressure to avoid social issues increased. The focus of the 1920s on individual treatment, interrupted by the Depression of the 1930s, returned to dominance, and with it, social workers in private agencies returned to their roles as the central figures in the profession. In this context, to most caseworkers (of both diagnostic and functional persuasion), the deeper issues raised by the functional school were simply irrelevant. The debate diminished to a more-or-less empirically decidable discussion of practical techniques for caseworkers, which was easily absorbed within the majoritarian "diagnostic" theoretical framework.

Meanwhile, the Freudian theoretical base of the diagnostic school, tailing recent developments in psychoanalytic theory, was also in flux, shifting from its earlier focus on the unconscious and early development to an emphasis on ego functions and the current operations of personality. Writers such as Heinz Hartman, Paul Federn, Melanie Klein, and Anna Freud focused their attention on the *ego*, the moderator between internal drives and external reality, the organizer of perception, and the tester of reality. Erik Erikson extended the concept of psychosocial development to the entire human lifespan. And "Freudian" therapists—psychiatrists and social workers alike—began to focus a large part of their work on strengthening clients' egos rather than on insight, on the analysis and use of the client–therapist relation in the here and now rather than on the recovery of deeply repressed unconscious material. Influenced by such theorists as Margaret Mahler, Rene Spitz, and John Bowlby, therapists focused on issues of separation, often made manifest through the "termination" or ending phase of therapy. A variety of practical considerations (including both client desires and financial constraints) led to a resurgence of interest in briefer courses of therapy. And to a more middle-class clientele, a variety of "existential" issues—loneliness, the sense of mortality, identity, creativity, satisfaction in relationships—became central to therapy, and to explore these issues, a host of new, more expressive techniques emerged.[76]

Although rarely acknowledged, many of the new theoretical concerns and practical techniques bore a strong resemblance to those of Otto Rank, Virginia Robinson, Jessie Taft, and the functional school of social casework. Today they are found not only in social work practice but in psychiatry and a wide range of other modes of psychotherapy and counseling, under various rubrics, including "ego psychology," "gestalt therapy," "existential therapy," and "humanistic therapy."[77]

In most accounts of the roots of modern psychotherapeutic practice, the theories of Otto Rank are seen as a relatively unimportant heresy from the Freudian fold, a sidetrack with few present-day adherents, and the functional school of social casework goes unmentioned.[78] Even within social work, the functional school is seen as a historical oddity, the debate as having no current significance. The great debate was settled long ago, with the diagnostic school (by now terming itself the "psychosocial school") the victor (although it had accepted a number of functional school techniques). And yet, looking at the worlds of psychotherapy and casework today, it is hard not to see Rank and the functional school as having anticipated many of their major themes.[79] Given the vigor and amplitude of the social workers' debates in the late thirties and early forties, it is hard to believe there was not a direct influence on the later theorists, at least in general terms. It is ironic, then, that social work, so desperately anxious to this day about its "knowledge base," has been so quick to dismiss what must count as its most intellectually rigorous and culturally important contribution to the theory and practice of helping emotionally troubled people.

But if social work and a number of other mental health professions have quietly absorbed many of the theories, attitudes, and techniques of Rank, Robinson, Taft, and the functional school, it remains true in a deeper sense that the latter lost the debate within social work. Social work succeeded in ignoring Taft and Robinson's challenge to the underlying basis of social work professionalism and their effort to bring social work into a new relation with the newly developed welfare state. With these efforts overwhelmed, and with the absorption of many functional school techniques into the diagnostic school's practice, the functional–diagnostic dispute lost its reason for existence; by the mid-fifties it had all but disappeared. Social work had weathered the first great challenge to its drive for professionalization. But an even greater challenge was just over the horizon.

5

Social Policy in the
Affluent Society, 1945–1960

The New Deal's zeal for domestic reform dwindled after 1938. The approach of the war drew politicians' attention away from domestic issues. Even more important, rising war orders (and, with the outbreak of war, the transfer of millions of workers, employed and unemployed, into active-duty military service) finally brought unemployment under control. By 1941 unemployment had dropped to 9.9 percent and by 1944 to 1.2 percent, its low point for the entire twentieth century.[1]

During the war years, just as during World War I, the country experienced a surge of national unity. Unions agreed to a no-strike policy to ensure war production. In lieu of wage hikes, the newly created National War Labor Board authorized unions to negotiate for benefits (health insurance, vacations, pensions, and so on), and many unions authorized employers to deduct union dues automatically from workers' paychecks.[2] Under heavy pressure from black leaders, President Roosevelt issued an Executive Order establishing a Fair Employment Practices Commission (although it accomplished little, and other elements of racial segregation, including segregation in the armed forces, were not addressed). On the scale of national and international politics, left and right seemed to have joined together, as the United States joined the Soviet Union in the battle against world fascism.

When the war ended, even though Roosevelt was dead, the New Deal movements, political coalition, and policies seemed set to resume. Strikes erupted nationwide as unionized workers sought to catch up with war-produced inflation. President Harry Truman proposed to complete the major unfinished business of the welfare state by adding a system of national health insurance to the Social Security System. (It was turned down by Congress after several years'' battle.) The 1944 G. I. Bill of Rights directly provided billions of dollars for education, rehabilitation, training, and other benefits to ease the return of veterans to productive employment. Congress also enacted a Housing Act, which promised hundreds of thousands of units of low-income housing. In the Full Employment Act of 1946, the president and Congress committed the U.S. government to intervention in the economy to maintain high levels of employment and established the Council of Economic Advisers to advise on the proper means of doing so.

But liberal and radical dreams of an uninterrupted advance toward social justice were quickly shattered. As in the post–World War I period, repression combined with prosperity to shatter reform movements and thwart the drive for change.

Repression again took the form of a massive Red Scare, which served both to win public support for an anti-Soviet foreign policy (recall that the Soviet Union had been a principal ally of the United States in the war against Nazi Germany) and to silence domestic reform movements.[3] In March 1947, nine days after announcing the "Truman Doctrine" (the decision to intervene in the civil war in Greece, which signaled the unremittingly anti-Communist foreign policy that the United States was to pursue for the next quarter century), President Truman created the Federal Employee Loyalty program to eliminate "subversive" employees from government. Almost simultaneously, the House Un-American Activities Committee launched a series of investigations of Communist infiltration of labor unions, government, the motion picture industry, and the nation's schools. Senators William Jenner, Karl Mundt, Patrick McCarran, and Congressmen Harold Velde and Richard M. Nixon joined the list of investigators, and the list of targets for investigation grew rapidly.

In 1950 Senator Joseph McCarthy proclaimed: "I have in my hands a list of 205 [government employees] that were made known to the Secretary of State as being members of the Communist Party and who nevertheless are still working and shaping policy in the State Department" (a list he never revealed); and Congress passed the Internal Security Act, which authorized the president to declare an "internal security emergency," permitting the detention without trial of suspected dissidents and setting up a system of detention centers to hold those so detained. By 1953, much of the leadership of the U.S. Communist party was in jail or in hiding; two young New York Communists, Ethel and Julius Rosenberg, had been executed (to the accompaniment of a worldwide protest movement, whose numbers included the pope) for allegedly giving the secret of the A-bomb to Russia; and thousands of teachers, social workers, newspapermen, screenwriters, government workers—generally "guilty" of nothing more than having organized unions, having belonged to the Communist party during the wartime alliance of the United States with Russia, having attended a radical meeting, or having supported liberal causes—had lost their jobs for refusing to cooperate with the half dozen or more investigatory committees.

Under pressure from the red-hunters, the labor movement, the principal institutional underpinning for reforms styled in the New Deal image, also caved in. Eleven unions, led by people in, or close to, the Communist party, were expelled from the Congress of Industrial Organizations.[4] The largest of them, the United Electrical Workers (UE), was virtually destroyed by a systematic, eight-year-long campaign. Raided by other unions (the Auto Workers, the Machinists, the Electricians, and the International Union of Electrical Workers, a vehicle created solely for this purpose) and attacked by employers (especially General Electric and Westinghouse), who were eager to rid themselves of a militant union, the Catholic Church (which set up the American Federation of Catholic Trade Unions to combat the UE), and various congressional investigatory committees, the UE's membership dropped from more than 300,000 to fewer than 50,000. With some of the most militant and socially concerned unions destroyed or in disarray, the labor movement's ability and will to effect domestic policy was dramatically weakened.

Although a number of less uproarious investigating committees went on plying their trade well into the sixties, the most visible aspects of the Red Scare faded from view after the Senate censured Senator McCarthy in 1954 (following a series of dramatic, nationally televised investigations of disloyalty in the army). But the damage had been done. Leftist and liberal reform organizations had split, disbanded, or subsided into quiescence. Libraries had removed controversial books from the shelves; bookstores barred the works of Karl Marx. Universities refused even to invite "controversial" speakers to their campuses. New York State required applicants for drivers' licenses to swear their loyalty and their lack of Communist affiliations. To propose a measure to relieve poverty or to combat racism was to risk being called a "communist." And in the atmosphere of the fifties and early sixties, such a charge was serious indeed. Conformity seemed safer. (In one widely-reported experiment, interviewers on the street trying to get people to sign a statement supporting the Bill of Rights in the U.S. Constitution found few who would take the risk!)

The other side of repression was prosperity. Fueled by wartime savings and long-pent-up needs, Americans went on a spending spree in the late forties and early fifties. The GNP rose 250 percent between the end of the war and 1960, and consumerism boomed. By 1960, 88 percent of American households owned electric irons, 56 percent food mixers, 98 percent electrical refrigerators, and 74 percent vacuum cleaners. Television, virtually unknown before 1948, became a multibillion dollar industry that ultimately reshaped the American consciousness. By 1960, 90 percent of American households owned a television set. Above all, the automobile completed its triumph. By 1960 Americans owned some 62 million cars, almost two-thirds of the world total; one out of every six families owned *two* cars.

Once again, in retrospect, it is easy to see the weaknesses in the economy as well as the strengths. By the late fifties the growth rate had slowed down dramatically. Each recession exhibited a progressively higher peak unemployment rate, and even in time of boom, the unemployment rate gradually creeped up. Low-wage jobs in the traditional industrial centers of the Northeast and Midwest were disappearing, lost to mechanization, runaway shops, and the export of unskilled production processes to the Third World. By 1960, new migrants to the old cities of the Northeast and the industrial Midwest faced a job crisis. And certain parts of the country, such as Appalachia and the urban ghettos, did not seem to participate in economic growth at all, regardless of the national growth rate.

Contemporary observers were not entirely blind to these problems, but amid the general prosperity, the problems seemed unimportant and probably transient. Poverty still existed, to be sure, but for millions, steady employment and rising wages had made poverty a thing of the past. *Fortune* magazine in 1960 estimated that fewer than 4 million families remained in poverty and forecast the imminent end of deprivation altogether. Poverty had been reduced to an "afterthought," proclaimed the liberal economist John Kenneth Galbraith in his widely read *The Affluent Society*.[5] Galbraith, far from finding this state of things satisfactory, urged enlarged public investment in schools, health services, housing, and other human needs to deal with the "residual" problem. But his view of poverty, so different from that of the late sixties, reflected the prevailing self-perception of more affluent Americans. It would be with disbelief that Americans would read Michael Harrington's estimate, only four years later, that some 40 million to 50 million Americans, one-quarter of the population, were still poor.[6]

In this atmosphere of faith in exuberant economic expansion and fear of political action for social change, social policy initiatives, in the usual sense of efforts to deal with such problems as poverty and discrimination, were hard to come by. And yet the government did intervene actively in the nation's economic and social structure, to a degree unprecedented before the New Deal had shown the way.

The social policy of the affluent society started with the assumption that no fundamental changes in the welfare state would be made. The Republican Congress of 1947–48 and the Eisenhower administration of 1953–60 did whittle away at some New Deal programs: the National Labor Relations Act was extensively revised (the Taft-Hartley Act of 1947) to weaken labor's power and strengthen that of employers; relatively small programs such as subsidies for school lunches were cut back; and local administrative practices and legislation kept millions off the welfare roles.[7] (A 1960 study showed that only about one-half of the people eligible for welfare had managed to make it onto the roles.)[8] But any lingering conservative dreams that the entire structure of the welfare state might be dismantled were shattered when Senator Barry Goldwater, tagged with the charge that he favored the repeal of the Social Security Act, lost the 1964 presidential election by one of the greatest landslides in American political history.

More positively, the social policy of the late forties and the fifties was built around two central themes: the decentralization of American society and the management and control of the labor force.

Decentralization was promoted through housing and transportation policies. Although these (and especially the latter) are not usually thought of as "social policy," they had major, and to some degree intentional, impacts on the historic concerns of social policy, and so it seems appropriate to label them as such.

As early as the 1930s federal housing acts had been passed by Congress and signed into law. The early legislation ostensibly was designed to produce hundreds of thousands of low-income housing units, but, in fact, little public housing was built: by 1960 fewer than half a million units were available nationwide. The 1949 Housing Act, for instance, authorized the government to build 135,000 public housing units per year, but only 20,000 to 45,000 units per year were built during the following decade. In practice, "urban renewal," as used in the Housing acts, meant tearing down acres of slum housing and replacing it with commercial, industrial, and institutional (hospital, museum, university) construction. No provision was made for the people whose housing, however substandard, was destroyed in the process. From 1949 to 1965 more housing units were destroyed by "urban renewal" than were built under the provisions of the Housing acts. In other words, the Housing acts, far from rebuilding the central city, were used to *reduce* housing opportunities in the cities.[9]

The federal government did subsidize enormous amounts of new home construction, but it was suburban housing for the middle class, not urban housing for the poor. The Veterans Administration and Federal Housing Authority mortgage programs used federal dollars to guarantee mortgages made by private lenders, enabling the latter to charge lower-than-market rates of interest. The mortgages guaranteed by the VA and the FHA were generally not available for building multiple-unit apartment houses or renovating existing housing in the central city, however. They were targeted at new, single-family, owner-occupied homes in the outlying parts of cities and the suburbs. FHA and VA loans also supported loans for housing sold under racial covenants that formally barred their owners from reselling to black families. (This practice was declared illegal by the Supreme Court in 1949, but many private lenders maintained racially discriminatory lending policies without FHA or VA protest.) Thus the net effect of federal housing policies in the postwar years was to strongly and systematically encourage the growth of new suburban areas while ignoring, or contributing to the destruction of, housing in the inner city.

Housing policies in the 1950s promoted the decentralization of

American society. In parallel, the federal government embarked on a massive campaign to subsidize the automobile.[10] As early as the 1920s the government had provided funds for road building. By the 1950s the highway programs had become a torrent of dollars. The Interstate Highway Act of 1956, for instance, provided billions of dollars a year for highway construction. The funds could not be traded in for support for mass transit. By the 1960s federal subsidies for road building ranged from $2.9 billion to $4.3 billion a year, whereas subsidies for urban mass transit ranged from zero to $104 million a year (the latter only at the very end of the decade). The fuel used by cars was also subsidized by the government, via such tax policies as the oil depletion allowance, which provided billions for the oil companies and enabled them to keep the price of gasoline artificially low.

As a consequence of these policies, public mass transit and long-distance passenger railroads stagnated, whereas the automobile and the trucking industry prospered. The 1.3 million miles of surfaced highway of 1940 mushroomed into a network of 3.1 million miles by 1970; the number of automobiles on the road rose from 32 million to 89 million. Meanwhile, the trolley car virtually disappeared, railroad mileage declined sharply, and the number of passengers carried on local mass transit systems dropped by almost two-thirds. By 1970, 69 percent of American workers within central cities got to work by car; in suburban and rural areas the figures were much higher.

Suburbanization and automobilization were, of course, linked. The automobile made the decentralized suburb, with its sprawl of housing developments, shopping centers, and industrial parks, possible. And once housing in an urbanized area was spread across many square miles and located apart from stores, schools, and workplaces, the automobile was no longer a luxury but a necessity. Those too poor to afford a car were at best condemned to ever-longer waits for ever-less-adequate buses and commuter trains; all too often they were barred altogether from access to a large number of the more desirable jobs and residential areas.[11]

Suburbanization and automobilization had major consequences for American political, economic, and social life. First, they created the terrain for the "urban crisis" of the sixties: middle-class homeowners and businesses had fled the central city, just as millions of unskilled blacks and Hispanics were pouring in. When the latter arrived in the city, they found that the jobs had moved to the suburbs along with the city's tax base. The cities were thus unable to finance the array of social services needed by the newcomers.

Second, the suburb and the automobile fragmented the formerly cohesive ethnic, working-class and lower-middle-class urban ghetto. People no longer lived near their parents and grandparents. The suburban mother no longer enjoyed extended family support in child rearing and was ever more socially isolated, a factor that was to make the suburb a breeding ground for feminism in the late sixties. With the work community physically separated from the residential community, except in the most industrially concentrated areas, few neighbors were likely to work at the same place and few fellow workers lived in the same neighborhood. The social cohesion derived from the conjunction of work and residential life that so often in the past had been crucial to social protest movements had been fragmented.

Finally, with cheap housing, made possible by federally subsidized mortgages, and cheap automobiles, underwritten by federal subsidies to roads and fuels, more and more working-class people had a very direct, material stake in the American system. Who would risk their jobs for a cause in the fear-ridden America of the fifties when they had mortgages to pay and car payments to meet? As one Cleveland builder put it, a bit simplistically, "I've never met a homeowner who was a communist."[12] Thus suburbanization and automobilization played major roles in depoliticizing the America of the fifties.

The second major thrust of the social policy of the fifties centered around the problem of maintaining and controlling the labor market. Immediately after the war, government economic planners were terrified by the threat that the Depression would resume. The specter of millions of GIs returning home to face unemployment lines loomed large.

The immediate solutions were straightforward: first, the millions of women who had labored in factories and construction work during the war had to be removed from those jobs and returned to the home, thus opening up employment opportunites for the returning men.[13] A massive campaign to persuade women to embrace domesticity once more filled the media. Suburbanization, the promise of the long-delayed home of your own filled with the new commodities industry was eager to sell, provided the lure. Outright firings provided the impetus when the dazzle of the suburbs was insufficient. Between 1945 and 1947, 2.7 million women were removed from industrial employment. (This displacement proved to be short-lived. Unmarried women needed to support themselves. And married women, finding that the one-income family could not afford consumerist life-styles and rejecting the isolation of suburban life, began returning to the paid labor force before 1950, a tendency that reached a flood level by the late sixties.)

At the same time, at least some of the returning veterans and other potential new entrants into the job market as well had to be persuaded to stay out of the labor force. The major mechanism for doing this was the educational system: Under the "GI bill," millions of returning veterans were assisted in attending college instead of immediately reentering the job market. Whatever the educational benefits, the system worked to spread out the employment shock of the returning vets over a period of several years.

These mechanisms reduced the supply of labor on the job market. The other side of maintaining full employment was to increase the demand for workers—to create jobs by stimulating investment. Political conditions were hardly conducive to programs of public works or other programs of outright creation of public payroll jobs. But the maintenance of a large standing army (never below 2 million men after 1950) and the vast expansion of government civilian employment and government contracts with the private sector for goods and services, largely for military purposes, had the same effect, regardless of the ostensible intentions of such programs. By 1970, according to one estimate, government purchases of goods and services and direct government employment generated more than one-quarter of all jobs in the American economy.[14]

The policies of removing people from the labor force and maintaining high levels of employment at decent wages, both necessary for social stability, paradoxically threatened to create a shortage of low-wage labor (minimum wage and below) however. Traditionally, threat of unemployment had forced people to work at extremely low wages. But unemployment, to the political generation that had survived the Depression, represented an intolerable political threat: mass unrest was the other side of mass unemployment. The solution, discovered more or less accidentally but resulting from a variety of government policies, was the creation of a relatively large pool of low-wage, high-unemployment labor *that could be politically and socially isolated from the rest of the labor force.* Where was such a labor force to be found? The answer was blacks from the American South and immigrants from Central America and the Caribbean.

For our purposes, the case of the American South is especially important. The flow of poor farmers from the South to the industries of the North throughout the early twentieth century was increased dramatically by government policies in the post–World War II years.[15] As we have seen (Chapter 3), New Deal and post–New Deal agricultural policies were a mix of price supports and acreage limitations, a system that benefited those farmers who could increase their productivity dramatically. By so doing, they could *reduce* the acreage they planted while *increasing* the amount of crop they produced for sale at the now-supported price levels. It was, of course, the big farmer who could afford the investment in machinery, fertilizer, and labor needed to achieve these increases in productivity; small farmers simply did not have the capital. Moreover, many small farmers leased their land from large farmers. For the big farmer, the relatively unproductive land farmed by the tenant or sharecropper was the obvious acreage to be taken out of production. Tenants found themselves evicted from their land or, with their small plots and inefficient methods, unable to meet expenses. Meanwhile, the federal government, through research grants, and state governments, through their subsidies of agricultural colleges, underwrote the development of new high-yield seeds, new fertilizers and pesticides, new machinery, and the training of farmers in the application of the new capital-intensive technologies. Again, it was the richer farmers who could afford both to send their sons to "ag" school and to purchase the new technology.

As a positive consequence, fewer and fewer farmers were needed to produce the nation's food and other agricultural needs and the prices of agricultural products remained relatively low. Until the late thirties, more than 20 percent of the American work force was engaged in agricultural activities; by 1970 only 4 percent were so employed. As a negative consequence, however, millions of farmers were forced to leave their farms. From 1940 to 1970 the number of American farms declined by more than half, and the farm population declined by more than 20 million people. Black farmers in the South, particularly tenant farmers, were especially hard hit. Between 1940 and 1969 the number of black-owned or -operated farms declined 87 percent, from 680,000 to 90,000.

The displaced farmers, black and white, poured into the towns and cities of both the North and the South. (The Caribbean and Central American migration to North American cities also was rooted in the process of agricultural "modernization," although the role of U.S. government policies was less direct.) The experience of blacks, in particular, proved to be of immense political significance: before World War II almost four of every five blacks lived in the South (already a shift; at the turn of the century more than 89 percent of American blacks lived in the South), and the black population was overwhelmingly rural. By the end of the 1960s less than 55 percent of the black population lived in the South, and more than 80 percent lived in metropolitan areas, North and South. Many black migrants headed for the big cities of the north: Detroit's black community grew from 16 percent of the city's population in 1950 to 44 percent in 1970; New York's from 10 percent to 21 percent; Philadelphia's from 18 percent to 34 percent. But the black population of southern cities also grew. New Orleans, for example, went from 32 percent black in 1950 to 45 percent in 1970, and the black population in smaller southern towns also swelled.

This massive and rapid migration had many consequences. For many, the move to urban areas was accompanied by great hopes for the future, hopes that were not realizable in the declining cities and stagnant economy of the late fifties and the sixties. Instead of prosperity, the cities offered deteriorated housing, increased segregation, lack of recreational space, lack of services, and, above all, unemployment: limited to the already diminishing low-wage, low-skill job market by lack of skills and discrimination, black unemployment rates soared. In 1940 the black unemployment rate surpassed the white rate by only 20 percent; by 1955 black unemployment rates had reached twice the white level, and they have remained at or above that relative level ever since.

On the other hand, urbanization ended the physical isolation of blacks. Individual southern black families, isolated on lonely farms, dependent on whites for physical safety as well as economic well-being, were totally vulnerable to reprisals should they attempt to resist racial or economic exploitation. But massed in an urban center, the possibility of resistance was greatly increased. Note the divergence of the typical black and typical white experience: blacks went through a process of demographic concentration, whereas whites

149

were being dispersed from the traditional city. The political consequences were correspondingly divergent; for blacks, concentration meant politicization; for whites, dispersion led to depoliticization.

At the same time, migration itself represented a break with the past. Traditional ways of doing things were disrupted. Because younger people were more likely to make the move, family patterns were disrupted and traditional social controls broke down. The urban black population, North and South, was thus a less well-"controlled" and less controllable population than its rural predecessors had been. (As we saw in Chapter 1, this history repeats quite closely that of earlier generations of rural migrants to the American industrial city—the Italians, Poles, Greeks, and others who were the "social control problem" of the Progressive Era.)

For the businessmen who would presumably benefit from the increase availability of cheap labor resulting from these processes, the migration to the cities was thus a mixed blessing. On the one hand, a large pool of cheap labor was now available, labor that was socially and politically isolated from the politically more active white working class. But on the other, the labor pool now available was unsocialized to urban and industrial life, was lacking in traditional patterns of community-based social control, and was increasingly resentful of the dashed aspirations and degraded living conditions that the city represented. It represented a formidable problem of what we have called social control.

To make matters still worse, in much of the South in the 1950s a rigid system of racial segregation still ruled: blacks were unable to travel freely (intracity and intercity buses and trains were segregated as were restaurants and motels); unable to obtain the education or training needed for jobs (schools were segregated; schools for black children, generally far inferior to those for white children, lacked adequate staff, funds, and equipment; and apprenticeship programs open to blacks were all but nonexistent, North and South); and unable to redress their grievances through peaceful means (blacks were virtually barred from voting throughout much of the South). Thus the black population, although it was being freed from the semiservile status predominant on farms, had not yet been turned into an educated, mobile, free labor force suitable for the ever-varying labor-force needs of a modern capitalist society. Nor had the mechanisms for maintaining social order in this population yet been achieved.

Finally, as Frances Fox Piven and Richard A. Cloward have pointed out, the demographic shifts of the black population created a unique political problem for northern politicians.[16] In the South, blacks had not been allowed to vote, for the most part, since the end of the nineteenth century. But in the North, not only could blacks vote, but their growing concentration in large cities amplified their political significance. By 1960, 90 percent of the blacks in the North were concentrated in ten states (California, New York, Pennsylvania, Ohio, New Jersey, Michigan, Illinois, Massachusetts, Indiana, and Missouri). These ten states accounted for 239 electoral votes in presidential elections, almost half the 537 national total. Winning the black vote in these major states was becoming an essential ingredient of winning the presidency. This put the Democratic party in a dilemma: its national coalition, from the days of Al Smith and Franklin Roosevelt on, combined the urban, working-class vote in the big northern states with the white-landowner–dominated, militantly antiblack vote in the South. But now the interests of the two halves of the Democratic coalition were at odds: to woo the black vote in the North, the Democrats would have to take measures that would alienate the white vote in the South; to protect the allegiance of their southern white supporters, they risked losing the black vote in the North. The problem was made even more intractable by the control of the Democratic party machine in the North by big-city mayors and unions, whose electoral base, in turn, was white ethnic voters. To the extent that the latter saw themselves in competition for jobs, housing, and services with blacks, and to the extent that racism made them see "their" tax dollars as being misspent on blacks, the interests of the traditional Democratic machine in the North were also at odds with the needs of the new black population of these cities. The "advantage" of concentrating low-wage jobs among minorities who were politically and socially isolated from the rest of the working class was thus partially offset by the political difficulties it created.

It was out of this complex mixture of needs on the part of blacks, and willingness, if not eagerness, to accept change in the racial system (at least in the South) on the part of northern business interests and national Democratic politicians that the massive social protest movements, civil rights legislation, and later the antipoverty programs of the sixties were born.

In the late fifties, however, massive social movements and massive government social reform programs would still have seemed an unlikely fantasy. The fifties were, in fact, a period of apparent social calm, at least by the standards of the thirties or the sixties. Anti-communism, prosperity, suburbanization, the baby boom, conformity, and caution (and, of course, the cold war abroad and the ever-present threat of nuclear Armageddon), not social unrest and bold new social policies, characterized the decade of the "silent generation" (as *The Nation* called it). Daniel Bell proclaimed it was the "end of ideology"; David Reisman noted, somewhat unhappily, the shift in the American national character from the "inner-directed" rugged individualist to the "other-directed" corporation man; Sloan Wilson's *The Man in the Gray Flannel Suit* and William F. Whyte's *The Organization Man* made the best-seller lists and defined a new social type.

In retrospect, of course, the future was visible: in the massive influx into the universities, the roots of the student movement; in the suburbanized, isolated nuclear family and the growing number of university-trained women, the roots of the feminist wave; in the urbanizing South and the growing northern black ghetto, the sources of the civil rights and black liberation movements. But that is retrospect; at the time, the "peace, prosperity, and progress" that President Eisenhower promised in his 1956 campaign for reelection seemed inevitable, unbreachable, and eternal.

But even at the time, social unrest was beginning to surface. Much of it was expressed as individual deviance rather than as social activism, however. In the mid-fifties young people seemed increasingly out of control. Growing drug use and delinquency, the overt sexuality of rock-and-roll stars such as Elvis Presley (who was photographed only from the waist up when he appeared on Ed Sullivan's popular national television show in 1956), the "beat" cult of Jack Kerouac and Allen Ginsberg, were the nightmares that haunted the American dream of the 1950s.

Most serious was outright delinquency. Between 1940 and 1960 the number of cases disposed of in juvenile courts nationwide rose from 200,000 to 813,000 (from 10.5 to 39.2 cases of delinquency per 100,000 population aged ten to seventeen). Youth gangs "rumbled" in the slums; truancy and vandalism plagued the schools. Delinquency was a long-standing concern of social reformers, of course. (Recall the Commonwealth Fund's influential delinquency prevention program, which gave rise to the child guidance movement of the twenties, for instance.) The level of public concern over delinquency seems to reflect many factors other than the actual level of delinquent activity (which is notoriously hard to quantify accurately, in any case). But whatever the precise reality, in the fifties and early sixties the fear of delinquency resounded in the national consciousness. The novel *Blackboard Jungle* (later made into a movie) became an underground best seller among teenagers; movies such as *Rebel without a Cause,* starring James Dean, and even Broadway musicals such as Leonard Bernstein's *West Side Story* popularized the theme of anomic, rebellious youth, unable to find social outlets for their energies and their grievances, turning to individual delinquency.

Delinquency became a major theme for sociological and psychological study. In earlier years, for the most part, delinquency had been seen as an individual personality disorder, the product of bad genes, inadequate parenting, or inappropriate schooling. But by the end of the fifties, another theory of delinquency arose, one that implicitly at least saw individual deviance as socially determined, just as were more organized social protest movements. The most influential expression of this belief was Richard Cloward and Lloyd Ohlin's *Delinquency and Opportunity.*[17] Cloward and Ohlin, sociologists at the Columbia University School of Social Work, argued that delinquency was rooted in community rather than in individual pathology. The delinquent, they suggested, was not a *deviant* but a *conformist,* conforming to the patterns of a deviant subculture. Whereas middle-class society proclaimed the ideals of financial success, upward mobility, and community leadership, racial discrimination, inadequate schools, and the lack of job opportunities denied millions of young people any opportunity for realizing these ideals by legitimate means. The delinquent subculture could thus be seen as representing an effort to attain the fruits (material and symbolic) of "success" by alternative, "aberrant" means. The source of the trouble, then, was not in the individual delinquent but in the "social systems in which these groups are enmeshed." Ohlin and Cloward's ideas were to provide the ideological underpinning for many of the later strategies of the poverty program of the sixties.

The epidemic of mental illness was also recognized as a growing social problem and increasingly as a sign of underlying social malaise.[18] By 1955 some 558,000 Americans were resident in psychiatric hospitals, and new admissions (both first admissions and readmissions) were running at 200,000 a year. In addition, more than

300,000 other Americans yearly sought help at outpatient psychiatric clinics.

Traditional approaches to mental illness had focused on seeking to cure the "afflicted" individual. But with the numbers of the afflicted growing at a rapid pace, many psychiatrists, social workers, and government officials began looking for ways of preventing mental illness. This search, in turn, led to an effort to identify the *community* sources of individual mental disorder. Robert Felix, director of the National Institute of Mental Health in the early sixties and a key proponent of the new "community mental health movement," described this perspective a few years later:

> Whether one is talking of mental illnesses, typhoid fever, or tuberculosis, the fundamental concept is the same: the community can be nurturing and helpful or it can be toxic and hostile. . . These considerations encompass many aspects of the community. One is concerned with such problems as housing, unemployment, prejudice, and other sources of social and psychological tension in the neighborhood as well as in the home. If one is to carry this concept to its logical conclusion, one would say that a community can be therapeutic or destructive, depending on a variety of elements.[19]

Thus, as had been the case with delinquency, by the beginning of the sixties, individual deviance, in the form of mental illness, was beginning to be seen as a form of social discontent. Just as the control of earlier waves of overt social activism had required social reform, so the control of delinquency and mental illness would require large-scale social intervention.

C. Wright Mills summed up this understanding in his 1959 book *The Sociological Imagination.*[20] True, he admitted, "nowadays men feel that their private lives are a series of traps" and sense that, "within their everyday worlds, they cannot overcome their troubles." But underlying this personal sense of being trapped "are seemingly impersonal changes in the very structure of continent-wide societies."

> The facts of contemporary history are also facts about the success and the failure of individual men and women. When a society is industrialized, a peasant becomes a worker, a feudal lord is liquidated or becomes a businessman. When classes rise or fall, a man is employed or unemployed; when the rate of investment goes up or down, a man takes new heart or goes broke. When wars happen, an insurance salesman becomes a rocket launcher; a store clerk, a radar man, a wife lives

alone; a child grows up without a father. Neither the life of an individual nor the history of a society can be understood without understanding both.

To understand the "personal troubles" of the individual, Mills argued, we must understand the "public issues" of social structure.

From this perspective, our conception of the "silent fifties" is transformed. Although it was, for the most part, a period of quiescence on the part of large-scale social movements, it was not a period of passivity and social quiet.[21] The individually expressed social deviances of the fifties, be it mild (rock and roll, the beats), aggressive (delinquency), or self-destructive (mental illness), have to be seen as social unrest in much the same sense as more traditional social movements. And just as the control of overt social activism in the Progressive Era and the Depression had required large-scale social reform, so the control of delinquency and mental illness would require large-scale social intervention. Individual forms of deviance represented a serious problem, if not an acute social crisis, that demanded the attention of social policy makers.

The fifties and early sixties saw the reemergence of more traditional types of social protest as well. The unions continued to agitate for expansion of traditional welfare-state policies (e.g., improved unemployment benefits; expanded coverage under the minimum-wage laws; and, in alliance with groups of the elderly, health insurance, at least for those over age 65). And, more explosively, the civil rights movement emerged in the South and then moved to the North.

This is not the place for a detailed recounting of the story of the black movement of the fifties and sixties.[22] Suffice it to say that as early as the thirties and forties, and accelerating in the fifties and sixties, black resistance to racism grew. As my earlier analysis suggests, it appeared primarily in the towns and cities, the new centers of the black population. And in response, in the early 1940s national policy makers saw the need to make at least modest concessions to the black community: in 1941 President Roosevelt established a Fair Employment Practices Commission; in 1948 President Truman ordered the desegregation of the armed forces and sent to Congress an (ultimately unsuccessful) civil rights bill. Several large foundations sponsored programs aimed at providing services to the black community. And perhaps most important of all, a series of Supreme

Court decisions whittled away at the system of racial segregation in the South. The turning point came in 1954 when the Supreme Court ruled that segregated school systems were unconstitutional: "separate educational facilities are inherently unequal," ruled the court, ordering desegregation "with all deliberate speed" *(Brown v. Board of Education)*.

The handing down of the ruling was only the beginning, of course. In the face of determined southern opposition, it took a decade of bitter struggles, repeated use of troops, riots, and countless jailings, beatings, and several deaths before the ruling would even begin to be enforced. But the importance of the Brown decision went far beyond the immediate issue of school segregation. It symbolized the end of the era of legal segregation. It announced to blacks and whites alike that national political leaders would no longer tolerate the violent preservation of the Jim Crow system. It was, in a sense, the go-ahead for a massive civil rights movement. One year later Rosa Parks, a black civil rights activist, was arrested for refusing to accept the segregated seating patterns of Montgomery, Alabama, buses. A yearlong, ultimately victorious boycott of the Montgomery bus system, led by Martin Luther King, Jr., began, and the civil rights movement was under way.

The next fifteen years saw a steady pattern of escalation and expansion of protest. At first, in the late fifties, black schoolchildren, trying to enter previously segregated schools under court orders, were confronted with white mobs. Then, in February 1961, students in Greensboro, North Carolina, staged the first sit-in at a segregated lunch counter. The sit-ins spread like a prairie fire: within one year, no less than 25 percent of all black students in the black colleges of the South had participated in at least one sit-in; one in six had been arrested; and the students had demonstrated in more than a hundred cities. In the years that followed, the Freedom Rides, the great demonstrations in Birmingham and a host of other cities, the Selma-to-Montgomery March, the voter registration drives that reached backwater towns all over the South, and, all too often, ugly scenes of anti-black terror and mob violence shook the South.

By 1963 the reverberations of the southern civil rights movement were being felt in the ghettos of the North, as well.[23] There were rent strikes in Harlem and East Harlem, demands for desegregation of schools in Boston and New York, demonstrations at construction sites demanding jobs for black workers in Chicago and New York.

156

Supporters of the sit-ins picketed Woolworth stores and Greyhound terminals in northern cities, and black and white student activists initiated community organizing projects in northern ghettos. In Detroit, New York, and other cities, the Black Muslims were a growing force; Malcolm X, the militant Muslim minister, drew ever-growing crowds. By summer 1964 the first of the northern black "riots" had occurred, in Philadelphia, Cleveland, Harlem, Bedford-Stuyvesant (New York City), Rochester, and several northern New Jersey cities.

By the end of the fifties and the early sixties, then, the nation once again faced a major problem of restoring social order. Individual deviance (delinquency and mental illness),on the one hand, a rising tide of black social activism, both North and South, on the other, were the twin forms of disorder. Looking at the sources of unrest, policy planners readily identified a stagnant overall economy (with certain areas, such as Appalachia and the inner city ghettos, apparently insulated from the benefits of whatever economic growth that did occur); a growing "urban crisis" as city tax revenues fell behind the demand for social services; and a growing black–white disparity in unemployment rates, educational levels, and incomes.

The conservative administrations of President Eisenhower (1953–60) showed little inclination to deal with these problems, however; they simply accumulated, gradually growing in intensity. But when John F. Kennedy was narrowly elected president in 1960, promising to "get the country moving again," the stage was set for the massive social policy initiatives of the sixties.

6

Kennedy, Johnson, and
the Great Society

A systematic and conclusive account of a period so recent as the 1960s and 1970s is not easily written. For one thing, we do not yet have the perspective that only time can bring: It is easy to determine which of the social policies of the Progressive Era or of the New Deal were lasting and significant, which transient or peripheral. But because many of the social policies of the sixties and early seventies—the heightened concerns with poverty, the urban ghetto, racial and sexual discrimination, and the new programs and laws dealing with hunger, health care, reproductive rights, and housing problems— remain matters of intense current political debate, a full history cannot yet be written.

Each period of reform in American history sheds light upon the previous period—its strengths, characteristic approaches, the issues to which it was blind, its limitations. From the perspective of the creation of the welfare state in the 1930s, the limited, regulatory approach of the Progressive Era is clearly seen; from the perspective of the emphasis on racism and hard-core poverty in the 1960s, the inability of the major New Deal welfare programs to address these issues is revealed. But the period of the sixties has not yet had its subsequent period of reform. Our judgment of it, then, must be a preliminary, anticipatory one.

Beyond this, the sixties and seventies are part of my own memories. Academic analysis and personal recollection (with all of its inescapable distortions and emotions) are inextricably mixed. I was a participant in many of the events of the sixties, in a limited way as a civil rights activist and in a more substantial fashion as an antiwar activist and a researcher and writer working with community groups on health issues. Thus my sense of what happened, why things happened, and what was important about them is shaped by my own experiences and observations as well as by subsequent academic research and analysis. Any historian is "biased," of course; one would have to be very suspect of the biases of the writer on social policy who lived through, but was *not* involved in, the ferment of the sixties. But it is well to acknowledge the sources and directions of one's biases, even if they cannot be entirely transcended.

Another problem in writing about social work and social policy in the post–World War II period is the growing disconnection between the two. In the years before the Great Depression, social work and social policy were virtually inseparable. No history of progressivism would be complete without a discussion of the settlement houses, the reform movements led by social workers, and the shift from Social Darwinist to environmentalist understandings of poverty. Equally, the retreat of the reform-oriented middle-class occupations from social concerns into a narrower professionalism is central to defining the social policy of the twenties.

By the thirties, however, the relationship between social work and social policy had become more distant. Social work was certainly powerfully affected by the social policy of the New Deal—the new institutions, new functions for social work, and new sources of funding—and in response to these new programs, the number of social workers mushroomed. The history of social work in the thirties and forties is in large measure a history of how the occupation responded to these new developments. The intensity of the reverse relationship (i.e., the significance of social work for social policy), however, diminished. Individual social workers and others with settlement-house backgrounds certainly were extremely prominent as experts, planners, and administrators. Most social work leaders enthusiastically embraced the New Deal; and New Deal programs, such as the Federal Emergency Relief Administration, were administered by social workers, who also trained many of the newly recruited social workers required by the new programs. But social workers were no longer central to the development of social policy. They were predominantly troops, not officers.

By the 1960s the relationship had become still more diffuse. Social policy continued to be vitally important in shaping social work. But to the planners of the Kennedy-Johnson poverty program, and increasingly to organized client groups as well, social work and social work agencies, far from being major sources of insight and support, seemed to be not part of the solution but part of the problem. In the thirties, the worst that could be said of social work was that it was often irrelevant to social policy. By the sixties, it was all too frequently hostile to social change. And it was the social movements of the sixties, as much as government social policy per se, that had a direct impact on the social work profession.

This changing relationship between social policy and social work (or, to put it more precisely, the growing distance between social work as a profession and its traditional concerns with social change and social reform) has been, of course, a principal theme of this book. It does, however, create a problem: in discussing the Progressive Era and even in discussing the Depression, social work and social policy can be considered an entity (although by the thirties, distinct emphases appear in the account of each, and social work responses to the New Deal have been expanded in a separate chapter). In writing about the sixties and seventies, such an integration is no longer possible. Social policy in the sixties and seventies, and social work in the sixties and seventies, require entirely separate treatments. Consequently, social policy developments, largely without reference to social work, will be the subject of the remainder of this chapter. The impact of the social movements and social policy of the 1960s on social work will be discussed in Chapter 7.

In the early days of the Kennedy administration, social unrest, both in the form of the civil rights movement and in the form of individual deviance and discontent (among both black and white poor), was growing but had not yet emerged as the fully disruptive force that would later compel action. In any case, President Kennedy was not free to respond effectively to it: his electoral margin had been razor thin, and he was dependent on the goodwill of white southern congressmen and big-city, white ethnic-dominated political machines. He was in a weak position to respond to the plight of black America.

And so, for two years, Kennedy temporized on black rights and sought solutions to social problems through a simple application of New Deal–style social policy: macroeconomic manipulation and nonracially targeted welfare measures. If economic growth could be accelerated, he reasoned, unemployment levels would drop. Unemployed young people, black and white, would return to the paid work force. Their immediate economic grievances would be reduced. At the same time, the effect of regular employment itself in structuring workers' lives would provide a basis for restored social control and community stability. The new (or strengthened) social welfare measures would also appeal to a broad constituency. Thus, he could help blacks (and gain their votes) without affronting southern whites or northern white ethnics and without creating conflict with a white ethnic-oriented city hall.

The initial Kennedy economic and welfare program had three major components: First, Kennedy proposed some modest expansions of the welfare state: an extension of unemployment insurance, an increase in the minimum wage, liberalized Social Security benefits, permission for states to provide "welfare" to families with an unemployed parent, and a housing act that would create almost a half million construction jobs. Second, he proposed measures to deal with "structural unemployment" (as the hard-core unemployment that did not respond to overall economic growth was called): a Manpower Development and Training Act to train the unemployed in new skills, Service Amendments to the Social Security Act to provide federal funds for casework and other direct services to long-term unemployed families, and an Area Redevelopment Act to funnel financial and technical aid into areas such as Appalachia, which had unusually high unemployment rates. Finally, he proposed a cut in personal and corporate income taxes to stimulate consumer spending and corporate investment.

But it quickly became apparent that these programs were insufficient. The civil rights movement continued to grow and spread, and poverty and unrest in poor communities remained undiminished.

The civil rights movement gained in intensity year by year. Daily television news programs beamed around the world scenes of blacks being clubbed, beaten, gassed, and set upon by dogs as they peacefully demanded their elementary democratic rights. Disorder was spreading to the North, too; and many of Kennedy's white liberal supporters in the North were providing funds and moral support and sometimes even risking their own lives in support of the civil rights movement.

In the spring of 1963 President Kennedy was finally forced to express direct and open support of the cause of the civil rights movement. On June 11, addressing the nation on radio and television, he told the nation: "We are confronted primarily with a moral issue. . . . The heart of the question is whether all Americans are to be afforded equal rights and equal responsibilities."[1] A few days later he sent to Congress a bill to ban discrimination in all places of public accommodation (hotels, retail stores, recreational facilities, etc.), to end discrimination in employment, and to strengthen the attorney general's authority to speed up school desegregation proceedings. "The Administration's civil rights bill . . . is designed to alleviate some of the principal causes of the serious and unsettling racial unrest now prevailing in many of the states," Attorney General Robert F. Kennedy explained.[2]

But the bill remained bottled up in Congress and the unrest continued to grow. In the summer of 1963, by one count, no less than 1,412 civil rights demonstrations occurred, including the 300,000-strong March on Washington of late summer. By early the following year, Kennedy was dead, Medgar Evers, secretary of the Mississippi NAACP, was dead, and four black children in a church in Birmingham were dead. On July 2, 1964, Congress passed the Civil Rights Act by an overwhelming vote. And yet the violent resistance to black rights continued, and the civil rights movement, North and South, continued to grow.

In November 1964 Lyndon Johnson was reelected by one of the greatest landslides in American political history, losing only Alaska and five states of the Deep South. In the black ghettos of the North, 95 percent of the vote went to the Texas Democrat. The Democrats also chalked up enormous gains in both houses of Congress, producing the most Democratic and the most liberal Congress since the Roosevelt landslide of 1936. The power of the Old South over the Democratic party had been shattered forever. And the far right, pinning its hopes on Barry Goldwater, was, for the moment at least, in eclipse. President Johnson moved rapidly and sharply to the left.

The parallel between the history just recounted and that of the early years of FDR's administration should be noted. In each case, a president sought to respond to a social crisis and to mounting social unrest by fundamentally conservative means. The initial response proved insufficient: the crisis continued, the social movements grew, and the nation's electoral politics shifted sharply to the left.

Faced with this constellation of political influences, in 1935 FDR responded with the Second New Deal—the creation of the welfare state. Faced with a similar set of forces, in 1965 Lyndon Johnson responded with the measures that comprised the Great Society—the Voting Rights Act of 1965, the War on Poverty, and a dramatic expansion and extension of New Deal–style welfare-state measures.

Responding directly to the southern civil rights movement and the growing northern black movement, President Johnson sent federalized National Guardsmen to protect civil rights marchers in Selma, Alabama; made a nationwide speech in which he proclaimed, along with the civil rights movement, "We shall overcome"; and sent to Congress the Voting Rights bill of 1965. The bill, passed into law in August, abolished literacy tests for voters and empowered the attorney general to send federal voter registrars into those states still practicing discrimination, to register those who wanted to vote.

The importance of these actions for blacks was immediate and great. The 1964 Civil Rights Act led to the final dismantling of the system of legalized segregation in schools and public accommodations and, along with Johnson's 1968 Affirmative Action Order, began to open up new employment opportunities for minorities. The 1965 act led to the registration of almost a million southern blacks within three years. By the mid-seventies in the South, blacks and whites were registered in numbers proportionate to their numbers in the population. With growing numbers of black voters, blacks became a bloc that required wooing by candidates for federal, state, and local elections alike. Perhaps of most immediate importance, the local sheriffs and judges, historically the principal institutional mechanism for the violent suppression of black rights, became vulnerable to the black vote. The primacy of violence and terror as a means of social control of the black population was markedly diminished.

It needs emphasis, however, that the equal rights legislation of the sixties affected only formal, legally enforceable patterns of racial discrimination. It did not eliminate racism, racial discrimination, or de facto segregation; it did not abolish racial inequality in economic status or political power; and it did not directly affect the problem of black poverty.

With the 1965 Voting Rights Act, the period of intense, federal legal assault on racial discrimination came to an end. Black community unrest in the North continued to strengthen. But the problem underlying this activism was not the legal denial of rights but the deeply ingrained and institutionalized discriminatory patterns in housing, schooling, jobs, and the provision of social services. And underlying all of these was the continued poverty and powerlessness of the black population.

Civil rights legislation, like the New Deal–style economic programs of the Kennedy administration, remained an insufficient response to the rising tide of unrest. Neither approach made major dents in the problem of poverty, in particular as it affected racial and ethnic minorities.[3]

By 1964 and 1965 the intractability of long-term poverty, in both North and South, was forced to the center of the policy planners' thinking. They observed, for example, that many of the poor did not take full advantage of the job retraining programs or the new job opportunities opened up by economic growth. When they did, handicapped by their limited education or unaccustomed to the work rhythms and time discipline required by an urban industrial society, they often failed.[4] In any case, women with dependent children were barred from the job market by their child-care responsibilities; and blacks, men and women alike, regardless of legal strictures, still faced discrimination in hiring, promotions, wages, and layoffs. Crime, inadequate schools, deteriorated housing, malnutrition, and poor health and physical or mental disability created further stumbling blocks in the effort to bring the poor and minorities into the economic mainstream.

The explanation many federal policy planners gave for the continued failure of economic growth to trickle down to the poor was what anthropologist Oscar Lewis had labeled the "culture of poverty."[5] The theory had several versions. In its simplest form, it was nothing more than the observation that prolonged poverty leads to poor health, inadequate education, high rates of marital instability, aberrant subcultural value systems and behaviors, and ultimately to individual and community apathy, lack of self-esteem, and powerlessness; and that all of these characteristics handicap people in their efforts to improve their situation. A direct and sustained attack on poverty itself would be the key to solving the other problems.

Michael Harrington, in his best-selling *The Other America*, which played a major role in calling attention to the continuing problem of poverty, extended this argument, emphasizing that the poor were caught in a "cycle of poverty":[6] poor and therefore undereducated, undernourished, sickly mothers gave birth to unhealthy infants who grew into unhealthy children. Handicapped in already substandard schools by poor eyesight, chronic infections, and malnutrition, lacking academic support and help from their uneducated parents, these children did poorly and were disproportionately likely to drop out of school. As adults, unskilled and untrained, they were unable to compete in the job market, which condemned them to poverty, malnutrition, and poor health, completing the cycle. If the cycle was not broken, Harrington argued, it would go on producing generation after generation of poor people. And because the various aspects of the cycle (nutrition, health care, schooling, housing conditions, psychological effects) were all intertwined, trying to change only one aspect of the conditions in which poor people found themselves (e.g., just schools or just jobs or just health care) was useless; all the other components of the tangle of poverty would quickly draw the poor person down into its reach again, undoing the good done in one area.

Perhaps the most arguable version of the "culture of poverty" thesis represented among major policy planners in the sixties was that of then Labor Department assistant secretary Daniel Patrick Moynihan.[7] In his report "The Negro Family," Moynihan argued that the key to the tangle of poverty in which many of the black poor were enmeshed was family structure. Slave masters had prevented "normal" nuclear families from forming among their slaves, Moynihan noted. As a result, black boys grew up in female-headed families, without adequate adult male role models. This "aberrant" child-rearing pattern produced young men who lacked the values needed for economic success. Moreoever, they were themselves unable to form stable marital units, reproducing for their children the same crisis. To Moynihan, programs to strengthen the black family were the centerpiece of any antipoverty program.

Moynihan's report touched off a storm of controversy.[8] Critics pointed out that Moynihan failed to see that poor white families were almost as likely as black families to be "female-headed" (i.e., that the "crisis" of the black family was the consequence of poverty, not the residue of slavery); that it had been urbanization, prolonged male unemployment, and welfare regulations that forbade payments to families with a male present that had disrupted the black family; that the statistics Moynihan used were both inaccurate and misinterpreted; and that poor blacks had evolved alternative kinship structures that effectively served the functions of child rearing and economic emotional support. But despite the critics, Moynihan's argument was (and continues to be) widely influential.

Regardless of the specifics, the broad concept of the "culture of poverty" led the Johnson administration social policy planners to a new set of notions as to how to combat poverty.[9]

First, the multiple problems of the poor were interrelated. To attack the problem of poor education alone or poor health alone or lack of skills alone was to guarantee that the efforts would be swallowed up by the larger, multifaceted tangle of poverty. Instead, the problems of the poor had to be attacked in a multifaceted, coordinated, and sustained way.

Second, the agencies that had traditionally been relied on for social services, whether public agencies (e.g., schools, welfare departments) or private (e.g., private family agencies, voluntary hospitals), and the professionals who had traditionally provided services (government officials, social workers, physicians, educational administrators) had failed. For various reasons—the maintenance of political power, institutional inertia, professional jealousies, racism—they were unresponsive to the needs of the poor and especially to the needs of the black poor. To enable the poor to benefit from new federal programs, the traditional agencies and local governments had to be prodded or simply bypassed.

Third, broadly targeted programs (such as the overall policy of economic stimulation and even the Manpower Training and Development Act) did not address the "culture of poverty." If the poor lacked the motivation or the hope to complete training programs, if they had internalized a low sense of self-esteem and lacked the skills and even the cognitive abilities to make use of the training programs much less to hold down jobs, if they lacked the disciplined attitudes needed for jobs even if the jobs were available, then these "macro" approaches to solving the problem of poverty would not work. Thus, more specifically targeted interventions, aimed at particular "deficits" of the poor were needed.

That is, the goal of public policy had to go beyond the amelioration of poverty and its consequences. It had to attack the underlying causes of poverty. And the causes of poverty were understood to be not simply the lack of money or the lack of opportunities but the lack of *capacity* on the part of the poor to use opportunities. It was this deficit, rooted in the culture of poverty, that had to be the central focus of an effective War on Poverty. In the words of Adam Yarmolinsky, deputy director of the task force that wrote Johnson's antipoverty program, what the poor needed was "not a hand out but a hand up."[10]

Although this formulation sems to echo the old Charity Organization Society motto of a century ago, "not alms but a friend," there were crucial differences. To start with, the Johnson antipoverty program was accompanied by efforts to stimulate the economy to create jobs and by the creation of new welfare institutions, training programs, equal opportunity laws, health services, and so on. Beyond this, although the outlook of the new poverty warriors, like that of the old Charity Organization officials, remained focused upon individual change and based on a model that blamed the intransigence of poverty on the individual deficits of the poor themselves, the problems of individuals were nevertheless seen as a reflection of the problems of the community, of economic and political and welfare institutions. The Great Society planners ultimately had an environmentalist understanding of poverty, albeit one that focused on the adverse impact of the environment on individual personality rather than on the continued obstacles that social and economic institutions placed in the way of individual achievement.

Earlier generations of social planners and social workers, as we have seen, divided sharply over whether the social problems of individuals were best met through concentrated work with those individuals ("casework," "education") or through large-scale social reform (economic growth, protective legislation, "welfare" measures). These alternatives were sharply opposed to each other, if not outright contradictory. The conception underlying the new poverty program, however, sought to unite both approaches. It linked individual change to social reform. The mode of encouraging individual change was not to be primarily individual casework, doing things for individual poor people, or individual therapy, however. Rather the focus was to be on changing institutions, changing community patterns, changing the "structure of opportunity." And the approach to making these changes was to enlist the poor, as communities, in solving their own problems. The poor themselves would be asked to provide information and other input for planning the new programs, to participate on the boards that planned and administered programs, even to perform some of the jobs that traditionally had been done by professionals.

The programs resulting from these understandings were many.[11] First, programs directly providing income (in the forms of cash, goods, or services) to the poor were dramatically expanded. In 1964 the Food Stamp program was set up. In 1965 rent subsidies, Medicaid (health care for the poor), and Medicare (health care for the aged, poor or not) were added. Public assistance ("welfare") itself was rapidly expanded: AFDC rolls, which had gone up by only 17 percent from 1950 to 1960, rose 107 percent in the eight years from Kennedy's accession to office to Johnson's departure from office; two-thirds of the increase occurred after 1964.

But more innovative were a series of programs that evolved directly from the new theories of poverty. They were aimed at chronic poverty and despair and typically targeted on the minority ghettos (and especially on young men, reflecting both Moynihan's concern for reestablishing male-dominated families and the more realistic and urgent perception that young men in the urban ghettos were those most in need of "control.") The programs were comprehensive in scope, offering a wide range of services. They stressed the prevention of poverty as well as its amelioration. They sought to create new institutions to plan, coordinate, and deliver services in new ways. They sought to increase the ability of the poor to solve their own problems, largely through encouraging massive community participation in planning, administering, and delivering the new services. And they were based on a new relationship between the federal government and localities, one in which money from the federal government went directly to service programs, circumventing the city and state governments.

The major programs that shared all or most of this outlook were the Juvenile Delinquency and Control Act of 1961, which established grants for projects for the prevention and treatment of delinquency in inner city neighborhoods and provided the model for many of the later programs; the Community Mental Health Act of 1963, which established a network of Community Mental Health centers to provide both preventive mental health programs and community-based treatment; the Elementary and Secondary Education Act of 1965, which provided educational services and programs for disadvantaged children; the Partnership for Health Act and Regional Medical

Plan Act of 1966, which provided incentives and structures for the coordination of medical services and health planning, with citizen input (combined with Medicaid, these provided the health services core of the poverty program); and the Demonstration Cities and Metropolitan Development Act of 1966, often called the Model Cities program, which provided for a concentrated and coordinated attack on the economic, social, and physical problems of selected slum neighborhoods. The Economic Opportunity Act of 1965 was the centerpiece of the entire effort. Often called the War on Poverty program (although, as I am suggesting, a number of other acts shared many of the same purposes and analyses), the Economic Opportunity Act provided for, among other programs, training and career-development programs for young people (the Neighborhood Youth Corps, the Job Corps, the New Careers programs for paraprofessionals, and the college Work-Study programs); VISTA (Volunteers in Sevice to America—the domestic Peace Corps); and, under the rubric of community action programs, neighborhood health centers, Head Start, Upward Bound, Neighborhood Legal Services, Adult Basic Educational Services, family planning services, addiction services, and a variety of other activities. The act also established the Office of Economic Opportunity (OEO), within the office of the president, to coordinate the entire effort.

The Community Action Program (Title II of the Economic Opportunity Act) was the largest, the most controversial, and the most fully characteristic exemplar of the new approach. At the local level, according to the law, a Community Action Program was "a program . . . which provides services, assistance, and other activites of sufficient scope and size to give promise of progress toward elimination of poverty or a cause or causes of poverty through developing employment opportunities, improving human performance, motivation, or productivity, or bettering the conditions under which people live, learn, and work."[12] Thus, the Office of Economic Opportunity was to provide money for a group of community organizations to set up a Community Action Agency to develop, coordinate, and mobilize a whole range of programs, services, and community development projects, existing or newly created, designed to reduce poverty. Beyond simply coordinating existing programs, the Community Action Agency was expected to plan and prod and seek to develop or alter the structure of community services to make them more integrated, more comprehensive, and more responsive to the needs of the poor. To ensure this latter function, it would encourage the "maximum feasible participation of residents of the areas and members of the groups served."

No part of the Economic Opportunity Act was more controversial than those three innocent-sounding words "maximum feasible participation." To those who drafted the law, the original idea had seemed relatively innocuous. To some, it had meant only that a mechanism should be built in to ensure that black communities in the South were not excluded from the benefits of the law by white policy-making agencies. To others, it suggested that the poor should be consulted in planning the programs and that, wherever possible, the program should employ community residents as clerical workers, custodial workers, and in paraprofessional roles.

But whatever it meant to the original planners, to militant civil rights organizations in poor black communities, it represented an opening, a chance to get some real power to force changes in the community. As soon as the first program proposals arrived in Washington, protests started flooding the desk of Sargent Shriver, OEO director: the poor, the minority organizations, residents of the target communities, had been systematically excluded from the planning process, contrary to the law's provisions. The law, insisted the community groups, meant that the poor were to play the major role in both planning and directing the services they selected. Shriver and other OEO officials quickly accepted this definition of maximum feasible participation. In fact, the level of unrest in the community and the level of organized demands upon them left little choice: either community action would fully embrace the participation of the poor, or it would not happen at all. The following year Congress formally amended the law to require that at least one-third of the board of directors of the local Community Action Agency be representatives of the poor, chosen by residents of the target area.[13]

The notion of maximum feasible participation was, perhaps, the single most innovative policy of the entire decade. It represented, implicitly at least, an important modification of the "culture of poverty" analysis: in defining "poverty," lack of *power* was as important as lack of *resources*.

Taken at face value, maximum feasible participation implied nothing less than a total restructuring of local power systems. It meant not simply "helping" the poor but empowering the poor to help themselves and to challenge anyone who got in their way. Attorney General Robert F. Kennedy told a House committee:

> The institutions which affect the poor—education, welfare, recreation, business, labor—are huge, complex structures, operating far outside their control. They plan programs for the poor, not with them. Part of the sense of helplessness and futility comes from the feeling of powerlessness to affect the operation of these organizations. The community action programs must basically change these organizations by building into the program real representation for the poor.[14]

OEO director Sargent Shriver suggested to a Yale Law School audience in 1966 that the Economic Opportunity Act was "for the poor what the National Labor Relations Act was for unions. . . . It establishes a new relationship and new grievance procedure between the poor and the rest of society."[15]

Increasing the power of the poor generated enormous opposition from those whose previously undisputed power was to be challenged by the poor—mayors, agency heads, local businessmen, local union leaders, and the like. Up to a point, OEO officials continued to support maximum feasible participation, regardless of the uproar. "I said to Congress that if our activities did not stir up a community, then Congress should investigate it," OEO director Shriver told a 1965 meeting of social workers. "In community action we are asking the various establishments to share their power with those they purport to help. We must insist that this be not a token involvement but a genuine one."[16] In the end, however, the mayors, agencies, businessmen, and unions continued to hold the reins of power. As we shall see, maximum feasible participation in any real sense was unable to survive.

Maximum feasible participation was more than a formal power-sharing arrangement, however. It became an ideology, giving a degree of reality to the "participatory democracy" of the early civil rights movement, and merging into the new demands for "community control" of schools, local businesses, hospitals, and other community institutions that community activists were beginning to develop. Maximum feasible participation was not merely an abstract idea created by policy-making intellectuals and bestowed upon a passive population, nor was it simply an attempt to co-opt community leaders. If it had any meaning, it was meaning given it solely by the struggles of community activists. When community residents besieged the mayor's office demanding more summer jobs for young people, that was maximum feasible participation. When local residents joined with paraprofessional hospital workers to demand that hospital policies be determined by the needs of patients rather than by doctors and administrators, that was maximum feasible participation. When welfare recipients, organized into the National Welfare Rights Organization (in part by VISTA and other poverty program workers), demanded financial support from social service agencies and changes in welfare regulations, that was maximum feasible participation. In short, the phrase helped generate, and was sustained by, the full range of social activism that drove the reform movements of the late sixties.

Maximum feasible participation also provided a key link between institutional changes and broad social reform, on the one hand, and individual personality change, on the other—what some called "sociotherapy."[17] Harlem Youth Opportunities Unlimited, a pioneer community action program that provided one of the models for the Economic Opportunity Act itself, explained its strategy this way:

> If concrete successes of these forms of mobilized community power are obtained, then one can expect that these will stimulate, increase, and reinforce self-confidence and pride in Negro adults and youth.
>
> Given an increase in the positive self-image of Negro youth, based upon the realities of effective social action and demonstrated social change, there should emerge a solid basis for a new cycle of greater personal and community effectiveness. . . . A positive self-image cannot be obtained by exhortation or by mere verbal demands. It must be created and reinforced by reality experiences. . . .
>
> It is not the primary objective of these programs to bring under-achieving delinquents or delinquency-prone youngsters into a helping relationship with a caseworker, group worker, or remedial specialist. . . . This aspect of HARYOU's program puts stress upon a restructured *culture*, or redirected way of life, rather than on the therapeutic problem-solving relationship with a helping person, as the source of new perspectives, motives, and behavior patterns.[18]

George Brager, an executive director of another pioneering community action program, Mobilization for Youth on Manhattan's Lower East Side, similarly argued: "We believe that the personal sense of powerlessness felt by low income people is a major cause of their isolation and apathy. . . . To encourage education and social learning, therefore, it is necessary to decrease the sense of powerlessness."[19] To the Mobilization for Youth planners, encouraging militant self-assertion by poor people would enhance their self-confidence.

Numerous observers had already noted the association between involvement in social action and improved "mental health." For example, it was reported that crime among black youths in Montgomery, Alabama, had declined sharply during the year of the bus boycott.[20] Psychologists noted that students involved in the sit-in movement used that experience of "prosocial acting out" to serve constructive developmental tasks.[21] Later in the decade, some outstanding successes in the treatment of drug addiction were achieved by the Black Muslims and by militant community groups such as the Black Panther party and the (Puerto Rican) Young Lords organization, who found that participation in militant movements for social change provided the motivation and context for startling personality change. In the same vein, participation in the women's liberation movement at the very end of the decade was to prove a powerful vehicle for personal change as well as for helping achieve social reform.[22] Thus, maximum feasible participation was central to bridging the traditional gap between "macro" and "micro" approaches to dealing with social problems.

A second enormously innovative approach taken by the Community Action Program was its response to professionals and to traditional social service agencies, public and private. The early poverty program planners realized that the existing structure of services, both public and private, was simply not working, despite the enormous amounts of money flowing through it. Sargent Shriver, scolding social workers for their failure to meet the needs of the poor, cited a study of social services in Detroit:

> There are many voluntary agencies in the group service and recreation field in Detroit, but with few exceptions they serve relatively few from low-income families. . . . Of those agencies which actively do reach the poor, all of them are extremely limited in size, and in spite of some commendable effort, their total impact is still negligible with respect to the total needs of the poor. . . .
> Public tax-supported agencies were the chief resources used by the poor. Excluding hospitals, only 10 per cent, 10.1 per cent of these poor families, reported any contact with any voluntary agency. This includes the visiting nurse service, the legal aid, the family and child welfare services, the recreation and youth services, including the

YMCA and the YWCA, the Boy Scouts, the Girl Scouts, the Catholic Youth Organization, the Boys Clubs, and all the neighborhood church related programs and services.[23]

Other poverty program planners made similar charges with respect to schools, legal institutions, health institutions, and mental health services.[24]

Mitchell Sviridoff, a New Haven poverty program planner and another influential designer of the Economic Opportunity Act, described the planners' response to this problem:

> The prime problem was that the established systems were rigid and unresponsive. . . . This suggested "the social application of the art of jujitsu"—the process of bringing small amounts of resources to bear at points of leverage to capture larger resources otherwise working against (or ignoring) socially desirable ends. Community action, then, was not conceived as a new service concept. Services would be provided, of course, but mainly as a challenge to established institutions— a spur to social reform.[25]

In practice this resulted in not some orderly process of "planning" and "coordination" but an immensely vital, often uproarious process of social change.

Maximum feasible participation provided the key mechanism for developing the power to mount popular challenges to existing agencies. The community-controlled board of a Community Action Agency could make demands on participating agencies as a condition of funding them. But under the "community action" rubric, OEO also set up a variety of programs that directly challenged existing practices.

Of these, perhaps most important was the Neighborhood Legal Services Program.[26] By 1968 some 250 Legal Services offices and 1,800 lawyers were initiating more than 250,000 cases per year. Originally, Legal Services had been seen as simply a way of meeting the legal needs of poor individuals in divorce cases, criminal cases, consumer finance problems, landlord–tenant proceedings, and the like. But under the impact of maximum feasible participation and the growing radicalization of the young lawyers who staffed the offices, many Legal Services projects soon became aggressive advocates for the people of their neighborhood. They pressed legal challenges to administrative procedures in the welfare department and school systems, initiated class actions on issues ranging from consumer fraud to a patient's right to treatment in mental institutions, lobbied to reform laws that had an adverse impact on the poor, and represented neighborhood organizations and political groups formed by poor people in their dealings with the police, the city administration, and the courts.

OEO and the other similar antiproverty programs also provided money for setting up new service agencies. These were expected not only to provide more service but to provide new models for service delivery. Community Mental Health centers were expected to offer decentralized, community-based mental health services, replacing the highly centralized and bureaucratic state hospitals, to provide educational and consultative services for the community and for other community agencies, and even to initiate programs aimed at dealing with the presumed environmental sources of emotional disorder, including poor schools, exploitative landlords and employers, and racism. Neighborhood Health centers were to offer a model of comprehensive, continuous, family-centered care, as an alternative to the badly fragmented and impersonal services delivered by hospital outpatient departments. And OEO funds were expected to entice traditional social work agencies, which had long ago lost interest in serving the poor, to resume activities directed at poverty populations.

Finally, OEO underwrote experimental reorganizations of services. The most widespread and enduring form of this reorganization was the use of "paraprofessionals" (again, the maximum feasible participation concept).[27] In legal offices, health and mental health centers, welfare offices, schools, and family service agencies, local residents were trained to perform at least some of the functions previously done by professionals. The use of paraprofessionals vastly increased the manpower available for the delivery of the now-expanded services. And it provided jobs for tens of thousands of residents of poor communities. In a number of cases, "career ladders"—job advancement patterns based on mixtures of on-the-job experience, in-service training, and released-time training programs—made these positions seem to promise not a long-term dead-end job but a career.

The use of paraprofessionals posed a basic challenge to traditional models of providing services. For one thing, it rejected the assumption that only highly trained professionals could deliver human services: advocates of the use of paraprofessionals argued that the very education that created professionals also created social barriers between them and the poor populations they were to serve. Because the paraprofessional was a member of the community to be served, such social distance was minimal, and consequently, the planners hoped, the paraprofessionals would be able to provide services more effectively than professionals.

This turned the professional model on its head: traditionally, professionals had defined a knowledge base and had claimed a monopoly over the acts that sprang from that knowledge base. The use of paraprofessionals suggested replacing this model, based on formal education, with a model based on a hierarchy of competence. Beyond this, in a number of instances the paraprofessionals identified more strongly with their communities than with their employers. In institutions such as New York's Lincoln Hospital Mental Health Services, the paraprofessionals took a leading role in demanding major reorganizations and reorientations of the services themselves.[28]

Before the War of Poverty, most governmental social policies directed to the poor had been content to add new services. The poverty program, partly by design, partly through the vagueness of the law, and partly by the pressures created by community unrest, allowed the organization and delivery patterns of the services themselves to be challenged. The traditional institutions, the traditional "professional" ways in which staffs related to clients, the technology and skills on which professional monopoly and status was based, the underlying purposes of the services themselves, all came under question and often under attack. Even the schools that trained professionals came under scrutiny: professional schools were forced to reorganize their curricula to train students to respond better to the needs of poor and minority clients, open their admissions policies to recruit more minority and poor (and later female) students, and permit students a greater input into school decision making.

This picture of the poverty program is, of course, vastly oversimplified. In actuality, the process was much less orderly and systematized: it was, in Mitchell Sviridoff's words, a "long, slow, messy process"—chaotic, contradictory, disruptive, rhetorical to excess, polarizing, often extremist, occasionally violent, sometimes counterproductive. And in the end, despite the successful reorganization of many agency practices and attitudes, the poverty program failed to reform the service delivery system, much less to eliminate poverty. The central reason for this failure was the reliance of the program on "culture of poverty" theories and a corresponding inability to understand the basic politics and economics of poverty in America.

Perhaps the most important immediate reason for the failure of the poverty program was its misconception of power. The whole idea of "community action" implied there was a "community" that could be cajoled or pushed into a coordinated, cooperative effort to end poverty. The old Progressive Era idea of the ultimate harmony of interests of the rich, the middle class, and the poor was deeply embedded in the whole concept of the War on Poverty. It was assumed that no one had a vested interest in maintaining poverty and that the culture of poverty was a sufficient explanation for the persistence of poverty in the face of overall affluence.

But, in fact, the poor (black, Hispanic, Asian, and white), the middle-class professionals and local politicians, the public and private agency officials, landlords, retailers, and large employers did not constitute a "community." American society was torn asunder by war, racial polarization, growing generational tensions, tensions in the family, and class and sectional interests. Racial and ethnic minorities, women, and students were making demands on American society for power, which meant that someone else would have less power, and for resources, which meant someone else would have fewer resources. Landlords seeking exorbitant rents, merchants seeking excessive mark-ups, employers seeking low-wage labor, professionals seeking to protect their institutional power and social status, all benefited from the continued existence of poverty. There was simply no basis for the kind of social cohesion essential to the success of community action.

Nevertheless, had the economy grown at a sufficiently rapid pace, some of the needs of the poor could have been met without threatening other groups with loss of income or power. But the designers and administrators of the poverty program never came to grips with the inability of the American economy of the 1960s to provide steady employment at adequate wages for all. The War on Poverty itself represented a "service strategy": it was aimed at rationalizing and improving the delivery of services to the poor. It was not an "income strategy" designed to provide adequate incomes for all. And, in the words of John G. Wofford, an OEO

177

official, it was "not a job creation program. We have to assume that the economy, spurred on by the tax reduction, will create the jobs."[29]

As we have seen, the poverty program was accompanied by efforts to stimulate the economy. But for the most part, these were broad efforts. They were not effectively targeted at creating jobs appropriate to the location and to the skills of the poor. To do this would have implied a direct governmental role in corporate investment decisions, a step that Johnson-era America was not ready to take and that the poor never gained enough power to demand. In fact, by the sixties the American economy was not able to create jobs and income for the poor, even at high levels of overall economic activity. Ironically, it was the war in Vietnam, not the War on Poverty and not the tax cut, that both stimulated the economy and provided "jobs" (although often fatal ones) for many of the poor.

The War on Poverty also represented a "localist" strategy: it was based on the belief that an extensive local expansion of services could meet the needs of the poor. To the policy planners, the inadequacy of local services was unconnected to the national economy's inability to provide jobs at decent wages, unconnected to the systematic power of racism, unconnected to national systems of power. The "power" that the War on Poverty proposed to give to the poor was, at best, power vis-à-vis local politicians and professionals, not power with respect to national economic and political decision making.

Even at the local level, the War on Poverty planners believed that the existing institutions and agencies—the local school boards, welfare departments, hospitals, social work agencies, and the like—could be prodded into change by the lure of funds and the pressure of organized communities. The autonomy of the agencies was never seriously questioned. In reality, the agencies strenuously resisted change while seeking the new federal funds. Sometimes quickly, sometimes after protracted struggles, they beat back the demands for change. The Community Mental Health Centers program, expected to pioneer a new mode of services more appropriate to the needs of poor clients and to provide extensive preventive mental health care and educational services, became little more than an expansion of entirely conventional outpatient services into poor communities. "Neither accountable backward to the National Institutes of Mental Health . . . nor forward to the consumers and citizens in the community they allegedly serve," noted a Ralph Nader task force, "they have often become . . . windfalls for psychiatrists who have systematically ignored the programs' directives to serve the poor."[30] The Neighborhood Health Center program of OEO was captured by the hospitals, who used the funds available for institutional expansion.[31] The social work agencies, contrary to expectations, failed to promote social change and used the federal poverty funds to expand their traditional casework services.[32] School systems accepted funds for preschool programs (the widely popular Head Start program) but failed to engage in extensive and lasting educational innovation.[33] In the end, the old power of the professionals and the old institutions was greater than the new power of the poor. The institutions bent with the wind and slowly absorbed its force.

The mayors, too, undercut the goals of the program. They fought for control of the local poverty programs, with their accompanying funds and patronage possibilities (and, conversely, with their potential for making trouble for the mayors, should the mayors lose the battle). Mayor Robert Wagner of New York told a House subcommittee hearing: "I feel very strongly that the sovereign part of each locality . . . should have the power of approval over the makeup of the planning group, over the structure of the planning group, over the plan." Mayor John F. Shelley of San Francisco complained that OEO was "undermining the integrity of local government" by organizing the poor. A resolution at the 1966 U.S. Conference of Mayors accused Sargent Shriver of "fostering class warfare."[34]

The mayors' reaction proved effective in Congress: in late 1966 Congress cut back and severely restricted the scope of the community action program. And when the Model Cities program was passed in the same year, the notion of maximum feasible participation was reduced to the idea that the community should provide advice and mayors were given firm control of the monies. By late in 1967 Congress amended the Economic Opportunity Act itself to allow community action funds to be channeled directly through the mayor's office where the local government so elected. (Ironically, only about 5 percent of the mayors chose to exercise this option. As James Sundquist, one of the original program planners, noted: "In the others, either the program was under their control already, it was so innocuous that it did not matter, or it had such power that they dared not move against it."[35])

The concerted opposition from mayors, professional organizations, and local agencies crippled the poverty program. But the death blows were delivered first by the war in Vietnam and second by the election of Richard Nixon. During the formative stages of the poverty program, the planners had accepted Defense Department predictions that the other war, the one in Southeast Asia, would be of short duration. But by 1966 it was already becoming clear that the "light at the end of the tunnel" was far away indeed. President Johnson elected not to choose between guns and butter for American society as a whole, a choice that was to distort the American economy for years to come. But he was not so solicitous of the poor: funds for the Office of Economic Opportunity virtually never rose above the 1965–66 levels, and beginning in 1968–69 they began to decline. The Vietnam War took precedence over the War on Poverty.[36]

Then, in November 1968, the American electorate, bitterly divided over the war in Vietnam and deeply disturbed by the rising tide of racial unrest and student revolt, chose, by a narrow margin, the conservative Richard Nixon to be president. The forward motion of the 1960s reform wave ground to a halt, as Nixon sought to dismantle the poverty program, to cut back funds for social welfare programs, and to shift to more repressive means for controlling community and student unrest.

The Kennedy-Johnson War on Poverty, in its broadest sense, lasted eight years, from the Area Redevelopment Act of 1961 to the dismantling of OEO by President Nixon in 1969. In the narrower sense, the full range of community action programs called for by the Economic Opportunity Act were fully funded for only two years and were virtually eliminated after only four years. The argument that the poverty program "didn't work," often heard in the years that followed, is disingenuous; for all intents and purposes the poverty program was never even tried out.

Indeed, despite their limits, the various Kennedy-Johnson anti-poverty measures *did* have a significant effect in reducing poverty in the United States: in 1959 a little over 22 percent of the American population was poor; by 1969 only 12 percent remained below the official poverty standard. Nearly 20 million Americans had risen out of poverty (by the stringent official definitions, at least). The following years of cutback and economic recession brought no sustained improvement in overall poverty rates, and in the late seventies the rates began to creep upward again, reaching 15 percent in 1982.

180

Despite the continued massive influx of poor blacks into the central cities during the sixties, the poverty rate in central cities dropped from 34.3 percent in 1959 to 21.5 percent in 1969, rising again to the levels of the late fifties by the early eighties.[37] Some of the reduction in poverty was the result of economic growth, itself stimulated by government spending, but according to the Final Report of the National Advisory Council on Economic Opportunity, established by the Economic Opportunity Act, "virtually all of the reduction in poverty since the mid-1960s has come about through the expansion of social insurance and income transfer programs"—that is, welfare, Food Stamps, Social Security, rent supplements, and the like.[38]

The impact of the entire Kennedy-Johnson social reform effort went far beyond the immediate, quantifiable improvement of people's material well-being, however. Responding to the civil rights and black liberation movements and related movements of other minority groups, the rights and opportunities available to racial and ethnic minorities were dramatically expanded. Laws, regulations, and policies that had previously restricted these rights were eliminated; the system of legalized racial segregation in the South was entirely dismantled; and antidiscrimination legislation and affirmative action regulations and programs enormously expanded economic opportunities for minorities. The provisions of the Voting Rights Act, in concert with the growing political consciousness of minorities, enormously facilitated the entry of minorities into the political process. Black and Hispanic officeholders increased in number in the years that followed. By 1984 black mayors had been elected in, among other cities, Chicago, Los Angeles, Philadelphia, Detroit, and Atlanta, and the Reverend Jesse Jackson had emerged as a major presidential candidate.

The improved legal and social status of minority groups both stemmed from and led to a greater assertiveness on the part of these groups. Whatever the political or economic gains, the cultural change and the weakening of age-old patterns of self-hatred and lowered self-esteem are likely to have positive impacts on the mental health, as well as the political and economic health, of these groups for years to come. Participation by clients in decision making with respect to the services they receive, though far weaker now than in the heyday of maximum feasible participation, has also not disappeared. Old paternalistic patterns, if not dead, were dealt a severe and lasting blow.

Finally, the Kennedy-Johnson programs provided apparently permanent additions to the American welfare state. Social Security benefits to the aged, the disabled, and the blind were materially improved; welfare eligibility standards were simplified; and health benefits for the aged and the poor became an integral part of the Social Security System. Although the precise levels of benefits under these systems may be whittled away in the future, their existence as part of the welfare state seems fairly well assured.

I have suggested that the Kennedy-Johnson reform era came to an end with the inauguration of Richard M. Nixon in January 1969. But it is too simple to end the story of the social reforms of the sixties at this point. For one thing, the social conditions that gave rise to the Kennedy-Johnson social reforms had not gone away. That the last of the major ghetto "riots" took place in 1968 did not become evident for several years. In 1968–71 new militant organizations such as the Black Panther party sprang up in minority communities around the country. The demand for "maximum feasible *participation*" was succeeded by the more extreme demand for "community *control*" of community institutions. Student take-overs of universities, not infrequently triggered by black student or community demands as well as by antagonism to the war in Vietnam, turned into an epidemic; by the May 1970 invasion of Cambodia and killings of student protestors at Kent (Ohio) State and Jackson (Mississippi) State universities, virtually the entire college and university system of the country was closed down by a general student strike. Unrest seemed to have become a way of life. The women's liberation movement emerged as a mass movement, its maturation symbolized by a massive parade down New York's Fifth Avenue in 1970. And a growing movement of environmentalists demanded regulation of corporate destruction of the environment. Women's issues (i.e., abortion rights, day care, equality of opportunity, freedom from sexual harassment) and environmental issues were added to the nation's social policy agenda.

In this context, President Nixon's actions were forced to retain a certain ambiguity. He did seek to cut back the Great Society's social welfare programs, especially those, such as the community action program, that challenged existing power arrangements. And he did seek to destroy the community and student movements by reducing their causes through removal of American troops from Vietnam, ending the draft, and outright repression. Funds were poured into the Law Enforcement Assistance Administration instead of the Office of Economic Opportunity (which was, for all intents and purposes, dismantled). And the COINTELPRO program of surveillance and harassment of militant and radical community and student groups was radically expanded. At the same time, Nixon proposed a welfare reform program, the Family Assistance Program, which, had it been enacted, would have established a national guaranteed minimum income (albeit one at a very low level); dramatically expanded the food stamp, child nutrition, and rent supplement programs; continued to expand job training and employment programs; and extended President Johnson's affirmative action program to cover women as well as racial and ethnic minorities.

Nevertheless, the overwhelming impact of Nixon's election was to end the forward thrust of reform. To the ideologues of Nixonism, the "limits of social policy" in curing social woes seemed more evident than their benefits. What was needed, proclaimed Daniel Patrick Moynihan, who had participated in the planning of the Johnson antipoverty program, was a period of "benign neglect" of social problems.[39]

In 1972 Nixon was reelected, this time by a wide margin. The decline of the community, black, and student movements was evident. Exhaustion and frustration, internal divisions and antagonisms between adherents of different movements, the co-optation of some leaders and the jailing, killing, or frightening of others, the inability of the movements to create larger coalitions for change, the winding down of the American involvement in Vietnam, the impact of the economic downturns of 1969 and 1971—all played a role. But regardless of the precise causes, the social pressures that had forced the Kennedy and Johnson administrations to launch an attack on poverty and racism (or, as was the case with the first Nixon administration, had prevented its total dismantling) were dramatically weakened.

The major exception to the decline of the movements was the women's liberation movement, which remained able to win signal victories: the liberalization of abortion laws that culminated in the Supreme Court's abortion decision of 1973, the Nixon administration's extension of the federal affirmative action program to women, and congressional approval of the Equal Rights Amendment to the Constitution. But by 1974 or 1975 even this movement was weakening.

With the weakening of the movements and the strengthening of his own electoral mandate, Nixon was ready to sharpen the cutbacks. But his political ability to do so was soon undercut by the Watergate scandal. Nixon's own, ultimately unsuccessful, struggle for political survival came to take precedence over domestic social policies. In August 1974 Nixon resigned. His successor, Gerald Ford, the nation's first president who had never been elected to any national office (he had been appointed vice president after the resignation in disgrace of Spiro Agnew), inherited a weakened, delegitimized presidency and a deeply divided nation. It was a time for re-creating national unity, not for enforcing divisive social cutbacks. The cutbacks did continue, but the most abrupt and deep cutbacks were effected at the local level rather than nationally, as a growing "fiscal crisis" infected city after city.

Ford, in turn, was followed by Jimmy Carter. Carter's ability to put in motion a full program of cutbacks was also limited. Although a moderately conservative figure by the standards of the sixties, he was a Democrat: his slender electoral margin in 1976 depended on the votes of blacks and urban workers and on the organizational support of labor unions. The consequence was a continued political stalemate: welfare reform programs foundered, national health insurance proposals withered, and program cutbacks continued, although at a moderate rate.

With the election of Ronald Reagan in November 1980, along with a sharp shift to the right in the political makeup of the Congress, the decade-long stalemate was finally broken, however. The barriers that had limited cutbacks in social programs to a modest level fell, and the Reaganite program of massive cuts could be put into effect.

Recall, for a moment, the combined effects of the Progressive Era, the New Deal, and the sixties: the struggles and unrest among various groups—workers, minorities, women, students—had forced often reluctant governments to institue a whole series of measures to improve people's well-being (and in doing so, to restore social order, maintain social control, and meet various corporate needs). Some of these measures provided economic security: welfare, social security, minimum wages, unemployment compensation, food stamps.

Others provided services: medical care, legal services, educational services. Still others provided economic opportunities: job training programs, student loans, affirmative action. And yet others guaranteed certain rights: the right to join unions, the right to work in a safe environment, the right to use public facilities without discrimination, the right to get jobs, be promoted, find housing, buy insurance without discrimination.

The aggregate effect of these programs was substantial. Focusing only on gains directly translatable into dollars, the value of cash, in-kind, and service benefits, after adjusting for inflation and administrative costs, rose by 8 percent per year from 1965 to 1972 alone.[40] But the direct, economic gains and the formally instituted programs were only a part of the overall changes created by the great periods of social reform. People had collectively empowered themselves. Workers, poor people, blacks, ethnic minorities, and women had come to believe that they had rights that must be respected and that it was the responsibility of the government to protect their marketplace and political rights. The historic role of social reform in cooling out social disorder, paradoxically, had strengthened the sources of dissent and social disorder.

Frances Fox Piven and Richard A. Cloward have argued (correctly I think) that it is this new relationship between poor and working people, on the one hand, and business and government, on the other, that underlies the intensity of the Reaganite assault on the New Deal and Great Society programs.[41] The Reaganite programs represent a direct attack on the economic well-being of the poor and a redistribution of income from poor to rich (defended by the trickle-down theory: if the rich get richer, they will invest more, thus providing more jobs for everybody, and eventually everyone will be better off). But equally, Reaganism seeks to weaken the sources of opposition to unbridled corporate power: the attack on "big government" is an attack on the idea that government can or should protect people against the power of corporations, landlords, and merchants. The attack on "entitlement" programs is an assault on the idea that economic well-being is a political right. The attack on the neighborhood legal services program, on affirmative action programs, on laws regulating corporate behavior is an attack on the laws and institutions that enable people to express their rights. Thus Reaganism has a double aim: it seeks to directly benefit business and the wealthy at the expense of the poor and the working class, and it is aimed at undercutting the ability of the poor, of minorities, of workers, of women to resist. The long-term impact of Reaganism—which must wait for a later day of judgment—may lie more in the effectiveness of the latter assault than in the former. Programs that have been cut back can be easily restored; power lost is not so easily regained.

7

A House Divided: The Second
Crisis in Social Work, 1960–1980

The emergence of massive social disorder in the 1960s found social work completely unprepared. Just as in the twenties, during the
two decades of apparent social peace that followed World War II,
social work had retreated from its concern with social reform. The
social work unions, built by the leftist rank-and-file movement in
the thirties, were driven out of existence by McCarthyism. Prominent radical figures within social work, such as Bertha Reynolds,
found themselves jobless, shunned, uninvited to professional meetings and conferences.[1] Once again, dissent and reform had become
dangerous. In 1954, noting the very different perspectives of social
workers in other parts of the world, the well-known social work
educator Mary Antoinette Cannon observed: "As we look at our
own scene and note the small part played by social work in national
social action, as we note its tenuous or slack ties to labor, to education, and to other movements, we must ask ourselves whether in
our absorption in process we American social workers have not
allowed ourselves to become the most backward of all national
groups in action for the welfare of society."[2] Seven years later, a 1961
meeting of social work agency executives rejected the idea that social workers should take a more aggressive stance with respect to
the need for social change on the grounds that to do so would
threaten their funding, their jobs, and their professional status.[3]

Social work's progressive withdrawal from its historical client constituency, the poor, undoubtedly accounted for some of the profes-

sion's social apathy.[4] A 1948 study showed that no less than 60 percent of referrrals to privately supported child guidance centers came from upper income populations.[5] The new middle-class clientele, unlike the poor, was a potential source of income. Although child guidance centers and other medically controlled social service agencies had long charged fees, the practice remained virtually unknown among other traditional social work agencies. In 1943 the Jewish Family Service of New York broke with this tradition, announcing an experimental fee schedule; other agencies soon followed suit.[6]

With a potentially paying clientele appearing, private practice beckoned many social workers. Although a handful of social workers had tried individual entrepreneurship as early as the 1920s, the practice had not spread very widely: a 1951 study was able to identify only fifty-three social workers with any private practice (full-time or part-time) in the entire New York metropolitan area. By 1963 a questionnaire to the membership of the National Association of Social Workers found that about 5 percent of respondents reported some private practice. Amidst much discussion of the new phenomenon in the professional literature, a 1959 NASW commission declared private practice as a mode of practice within the proper domain of social work.[7]

In working with middle-class clients, "environmental manipulation" (much less social action) seemed relatively unimportant. "Casework" came more and more to resemble psychotherapy. Ego psychology increasingly dominated casework theory and practice, although the resulting professional problem of distinguishing social workers from other varieties of psychotherapists continued to disturb many. (One review of the latter problem listed some fifty articles on the topic in the period 1935–55.)[8]

Meanwhile, social work professionalism continued to advance. The number of social work schools and social work students continued to grow, and in 1952 the Council of Social Work Education, a common accrediting body, was formed. In 1955 the major professional associations (including the American Association of Social Workers and six smaller organizations) merged to form a unified National Association of Social Workers. By 1957, when University of California social work professor Ernest Greenwood returned to Abraham Flexner's old question, "Is social work a profession?" he responded with an unambiguous "yes": "Social work is . . . a profession; it has too many points of congruence with the [sociological] model [of a profession] to be classifiable otherwise. Social work is, however, seeking to rise within the professional hierarchy." But, he noted, social workers "might have to scuttle their social action heritage as a price of achieving the public acceptance accorded a profession." To most of those caseworkers of the late fifties who abjured social action, it hardly seemed a major sacrifice.[9]

And yet a small group of professional leaders retained, rhetorically at least, a social conscience and continued to nag their colleagues. "In recent years the profession has not made highly significant contributions to the field of social action," lamented Eveline Burns in 1947. "Put the social back in social work," casework theoretician Helen Harris Perlman urged her peers in 1952. But, noted Hyman J. Weiner a decade later, although many articles in the social work literature had urged greater social concern and a return to social action, fewer specified issues of concern, fewer still, the obstacles to action, and almost none, methods for achieving social change. Philosopher Charles Frankel, addressing the 1961 National Conference on Social Welfare, observed: "The Social Worker, unhappily, has become one of the best examples of the decline of our society's capacity to imagine its future. He is doing his job efficiently, and he is also encasing himself in his job. He is tinkering with the broken products that are brought to the repair shop, but he is not asking himself why so many of these broken products are being brought in."[10]

Marion K. Sanders, in a widely discussed 1957 article in *Harper's Magazine,* suggested that the problem lay in social workers' obsession with professionalism: "Social workers—the specialists in good deeds—seem to have lost track of what particular good needs doing by them. Preoccupied with a strange game of musical chairs called the search for professional status, they have yet to settle in a seat that suits their current hopes and capacities." If social workers would only stop worrying about their status, she argued, "they might lift their eyes from the trees of individual behavior to the woods full of social problems, moving in large numbers from the backwaters of private philanthropy to the mainstream of public welfare." Bitterly portraying social work in the late fifties, she proposed the following parable: "The day after the bomb fell, the doctor was out binding radiation burns. The minister prayed and set up a soup kitchen in the ruined chapel. The policeman herded stray children to the rubble heap where the teacher had improvised a classroom. And the social worker wrote a report; since two had survived, they held a conference on 'Interpersonal Relationships in a Time of Intensified Anxiety States.' "[11]

With the challenges of the sixties about to break over them, social work was hardly poised for advance. And indeed, social work was slow to respond to the growing social crisis of the early sixties. While a handful of social workers, working with city planners, sociologists, and foundation officials, had developed pioneering programs—New York's Mobilization for Youth, Oakland's Inter-Agency Project, and New Haven's Community Progress Incorporated— experiments that were to provide much of the experience and many of the ideas for the new approaches to community action of the mid-sixties, most social workers remained completely ignorant of these efforts.[12] The social work journals, despite occasional editorial comment on the need for social concern, remained filled with articles on casework: on the individual treatment of alcoholism, delinquency, family problems, schooling problems, and the like. By contrast, the growing civil rights movement merited only two articles in the NASW journal, *Social Work,* in the years preceding 1963; the threat of nuclear war only one.

Only after President Lyndon Johnson's spring 1964 announcement of the poverty program did social work's interest, as measured by published articles in professional journals, shift to social issues. To read the April 1964 issue of *Social Work* is to read an entirely new journal: suddenly, organized social work discovered poverty, civil rights, the welfare crisis, and political action. But the discovery was in response to the leadership of the journalists and the politicians; it was not social work, concerned with social problems, that led the way. Samuel Mencher's January 1963 review of Michael Harrington's *The Other America* in *Social Work* ruefully commented: "This is the kind of book that at least some in the profession will say a social worker should have written. Would it were so." (Mencher, noting Harrington's assertion that social workers served only a minority of those in need and had not been a major force for social change, proposed that the journalist be awarded an "honorary ACSW [Academy of Certified Social Workers].")[13]

As the poverty program got rolling, national social work leaders and professional editors were enthusiastic. But at the rank-and-file level, and especially among social work agency leaders, there was less enthusiasm. Early in 1964 *Social Work* editor Robert Morris noted that the new efforts by the federal government to combat poverty placed social welfare and social workers "at the center of thinking and planning" and were in areas of traditional social work concern and experience.

> It comes as a surprise, therefore, to learn that these new approaches are resisted by some social workers, sometimes openly and sometimes quietly. There is a belief that national incentives unfairly favor the growth of public agencies, or a concern that new agencies will be created in which social work plays a minor partnership role, or a conviction that established voluntary welfare planning bodies will be bypassed.

Morris observed that the new programs and the social casework of the fifties did "reflect basic differences in approach. . . . For example, many established services seem to be based upon the conviction that delinquency finds its roots in the individual or in the family, whereas the new programs seek to experiment with alternative explanations for delinquency, among them being the closure of opportunity to underprivileged minorities and the poor." But he chided social workers for their recalcitrance. It was, he charged, "the welfare counterpart of the reaction to efforts to alter local living patterns (read 'segregation') or to raise the standards of education (read 'segregation'), or to improve inner city housing and living conditions."[14]

A few months later, when New York City's Mobilization for Youth found itself under heavy political attack as a result of its challenges to traditional agencies and local government officials, Morris noted that many social work agencies and social workers had "consistently opposed MFY." Although acknowledging that challenging those with power can be "dangerous, not just for the few who would step out of the mainstream, but for all who share the same profession," he urged social workers to rise above this narrow professionalism and support the embattled program.[15]

Perhaps nothing seemed so threatening to social work professionalism as the growing use of paraprofessionals and the growing involvement of social workers' clients under the "maximum feasible participation" rubric. When welfare recipients proposed to organize the National Welfare Rights Organization, the social work leaders they consulted urged caution: raising welfare issues militantly would risk the retaliation of those who opposed welfare altogether, the social workers warned; welfare reform was a matter for the experts, not for clients.[16] And although some social workers had suggested the use of paraprofessionals to deal with the chronic manpower shortage in the underpaid social services, the very idea made many nervous. Even the use of "nonprofessionals" by the Peace Corps was seen by some as a threat.[17]

The most intense opposition focused less on the more-or-less untrained indigenous community workers, who did not seem to threaten the social worker's professional identity, than on the proposals to train "social workers" at a baccalaureate or associate degree level. A 1967 proposal to broaden the NASW membership to include those without a master's degree met strong opposition. "The jobs in public assistance were mostly filled by untrained people," recalled casework theorist and educator Florence Hollis a few years later.

> The best educational level you could hope for with that huge mass of public welfare workers was the B.A. . . . So we had a great mass of workers, some of whom were positive toward social work ideas and some of whom were anything but positive toward social work ideas . . . . Personally, I didn't favor lowering the MA requirement for NASW membership. To me it seemed like a lowering of standards. I had been through the fuss and the struggle in the twenties and early thirties, when we finally got the two year standard through, and the last thing I wanted to see was backsliding.[18]

The proposal was turned down (for the moment; it was successfully revived a few years later) after a survey of NASW local chapters showed that most chapters opposed "any official relationship with social workers now outside the association." "Professionalism, not membership" was the priority. Noting that this meant rebuffing social workers who might be closer to the insights of clients than the more middle-class MSW-trained social workers and that it represented inaction on one of the few social issues that social workers themselves had the power to change, Morris's successor as *Social Work* editor, Alvin L. Schorr, denounced the decision as "a time for shame. . . . Self-interest rarely struts the stage in its own clothes. . . . We understand as well as any professionals how convincing to the rationalizer is his own rationalization."[19]

It was, then, a deeply divided social work profession that gingerly stepped onto the battlefields of the War on Poverty. OEO director Sargent Shriver complained: "They [social workers] are dedicated men and women. Yet some of them seem to think that working with the poor is their exclusive problem. They reject outsiders. They are wedded to professional opinions and ideas. And frequently those in charge of these programs resist and even resent questions about their own effectiveness, about their own cost of operations."[20] Robert Morris, noting social workers' countercomplaints that OEO "has given little attention to social work experience, methods, or practices," suggested that the only way for social work to "move from this peripheral fringe to the center of national policy" was for social workers to give up their obsession with professional, organizational, and individual client-centered activities and start paying attention to national policy concerns.[21]

But social work could not remain forever isolated from the growing pressure upon it. As in the thirties, its numbers were growing, with thousands of "social workers" who had not passed through the accredited professional training process filling the newly created jobs in rapidly growing welfare departments, poverty agencies, community mental health centers, preschool programs, and the like. Many new recruits were black or Hispanic, groups that historically had existed in social work eyes mainly as clients. Clients themselves emerged for the first time as an independent force, organized in part through the poverty program's maximum feasible participation model, in part by poverty program community organizers, and in part by community-based civil rights groups. And social work students, heavily influenced by the growing radicalization of students in colleges and universities throughout the country, rejected their traditional respect for their professional elders. And so it was once again from outside the professional mainstream that growing challenges to traditional social work emerged.

The first challenge to the professional path social work had chosen was from a new wave of unionism among public sector social workers.[22] Although the NASW had taken the official position that social workers had the right to join unions, many social workers remained convinced that unionism and professionalism were inimical. For a professional, client's needs, not personal needs, came first, they argued. But in the mid-sixties, public welfare workers, including both social workers (with and without formal training in social work) and non-social work staff, formed unions in New York, Chicago, Detroit, and elsewhere. Often led by radicals, the new unions, insisting that professional and unionist demands were not contradictory, refused to accept conventional boundaries between social worker and client.

In New York in 1964 the Social Service Employees Union (SSEU) demanded not only improvements in salaries and working conditions but better training for welfare workers, physical improvements in welfare facilities to afford clients and their social workers greater privacy, and reduced caseloads to enable workers to spend more time with each client. The city offered to negotiate wages and hours but insisted that client-related issues were nonnegotiable. The impasse led to a strike, in which many of the workers' demands were met after they gained support from the citywide Central Labor Council. The following year, the 6,500-member union upped its client-related demands to include improved welfare benefits with built-in cost-of-living increases for clients. The city again refused to negotiate on client-related issues. This time the Central Labor Council refused its full support, and the union, divided internally, was defeated in the ensuing strike.

SSEU also provided support for clients outside the collective bargaining process. It joined with the burgeoning movement of welfare clients in actions against the New York City Department of Social Services and other local welfare agencies. SSEU's biweekly newsletter, *The Facts*, aimed at the community, presented simplified explanations of new welfare procedures. The union also published more detailed manuals to help social workers help their clients, including a twenty-two-page pamphlet, "How to Fight the Slum Landlord," which concluded: "Don't mourn misery in your little black book. Help your clients organize to end it."

In Chicago a similar tale unfolded. The Independent Union of Public Aid Employees won its first strike, for recognition, in 1966. But the following year, when the union demanded greater flexibility for social workers in meeting client needs, the publication of a handbook for clients detailing their rights, and better salaries and benefits for social workers, the city forced another strike. This time the union lost on the policy demands. The Welfare Employees' Union in Detroit also took stands on both welfare and community issues and in

1968 joined the picket line with their clients to demand increased clothing allowances.

Meeting with fierce opposition from their employers, especially over demands related to the substance of their services, the early radical welfare worker unions were, for the most part, soon absorbed into larger unions of state workers. Their service demands became more rhetorical, although their effectiveness on immediate social workers' needs continued to grow. The pattern set in the sixties continued into the seventies. By the mid-seventies the largest of the unions representing social workers, the American Federation of State, County and Municipal Employees, claimed some 35,000 professional social workers as members; another 20,000 social workers were members of the Service Employees International Union, and additional thousands were in the National Union of Hospital and Health Care Employees (1199) and other unions. (By way of comparison, NASW membership, although drawn from a somewhat different pool, was 70,000 in 1976.) For tens of thousands of social workers seeking to improve their material well-being, status, and ability to serve their clients, unionism had become an ongoing alternative to conventional professionalism.

The next group to emerge to challenge the social workers were clients themselves. Partially, at least, in response to studies and proposals circulated by activist-scholars Frances Fox Piven and Richard A. Cloward, the first welfare-recipients' groups were organized out of local OEO agencies in late 1965 and early 1966. By spring 1966 demonstrations of welfare recipients, together with ministers, social workers, and other sympathetic citizens, against the abuses of the welfare system took place simultaneously in some seventeen cities. Later that summer, some one hundred welfare recipients, civil rights workers, poverty program workers (many of them from VISTA), and Students for a Democratic Society organizers met to establish a National Coordinating Committee of Welfare Rights Groups and to devise plans to promote and coordinate a series of nationwide welfare demonstrations in the fall of 1966. The following summer a founding convention established the National Welfare Rights Organization (NWRO). By 1969 the organization had more than 22,000 dues-paying members in 523 local groups.[23]

The newly formed movement rejected the passive compliance traditionally expected of welfare recipients. Clients "cast off the mantle of supplicant in favor of that of petitioner, lobbyist, and demonstrator," noted Charles Grosser.[24] They militantly and aggressively demanded communitywide publicity regarding available benefits, client participation in decision making by welfare agencies, an end to undignified and degrading procedures, and liberalization of benefits.

NWRO organizers prepared handbooks on clients' rights, (often after extended struggles and even sit-ins to wrest copies of the official regulation manuals from local welfare departments). They organized welfare recipients in the waiting rooms of local welfare offices, in churches, stores, and elsewhere throughout the nation's urban ghettos. Much of their energy went into pursuing individual grievances: the problems of the client who had not received his or her check, or who had received less than he or she was entitled to, or who had been arbitrarily terminated, or who had been abused and demeaned by welfare workers.

NWRO chapters also staged demonstrations around common grievances. By spring and summer 1968 the New York City Welfare Department had to establish a "war room" in its main headquarters, staffed and equipped with banks of telephones, to keep track of the literally hundreds of demonstrations occurring at the district welfare offices on an almost daily basis. In Philadelphia, NWRO members appeared en masse to sell their blood to get more money for shoes and winter clothing; of the twenty-seven prospective donors, twenty-five were rejected because of anemia resulting from poor nutrition. In Detroit, women and children sat-in at the Housing Commission. In Cleveland, welfare recipients demanded that the United Nations investigate the denial of human rights to Ohio welfare recipients.

Throughout the country similar demonstrations occurred, often drawing in nonprofessional welfare workers, social workers, and other sympathizers as well as welfare recipients. In New York City in 1967–68 some thirty-two social workers were arrested for actions growing out of such support activities. But despite growing participation by social workers, the welfare rights movement was directly controlled by welfare clients themselves; social workers had no special status or privileges in it. The clients, not the professionals, defined goals and methods of achieving them.

Thus the "basic assumption of professionalism, that standards are set by colleagues rather than clients," was opened for reappraisal. Social workers and social work students who worked with welfare recipient organizations "were obliged to conform to the group's styles and purposes, even when these violated professional or community norms," noted community organizing theorist Charles Grosser. Partisanship and advocacy had to become part of the social workers' methods. The social worker-participant was forced to reappraise the basic tenets and methods of his or her profession.

The new movement received a confused and cautious response from the social work leadership, some of whom urged welfare recipients to "go slow" and to leave welfare reform to the experts. Des Moines, Iowa, welfare rights groups responded with a song:

> The welfare moms marched up the hill
> To fight the anti-welfare bill.
> They testified but stayed too long.
> The liberals came and sang this song:
>
> [Chorus]
>
> "You're only hurting your cause this way"—
> That's what all of us liberals say,
> "Nobody likes things the way they are.
> But you go too fast and you go too far."[25]

Welfare recipients were not the typical clients of private-sector social work agencies, of course, and some public-sector social workers' unions and local NASW chapters did aid local welfare rights groups. But ultimately it was the social work/social welfare establishment that was being attacked. Mrs. Johnnie Tillman, a Watts AFDC mother who was the NWRO chair in 1970, told the 1970 National Conference on Social Welfare meeting: "If it hadn't been for you people who administer social services, we would have no organization. We organized because we were tired of being beat around by social workers."

Discontent appeared in social work schools as early as 1967.[26] By 1968 and 1969 student strikes broke out at a number of schools. The student activists charged that the agencies in which they trained were more concerned with their own aggrandizement than with the needs of clients; that the welfare bureaucracies with which they had to work were unchangeable; that welfare programs degraded the recipients; and that social work as a whole had responded only glacially to the black revolution. "M.S.W." should stand for "Maintaining Social Wrongs," proclaimed a sign displayed at one student protest.

Much of the students' fire was directed at the social work schools themselves. Sixteen new master's degree programs had been established during the sixties, and the numbers of students had soared from 4,900 in 1959 to 11,700 in 1968. But as a casework student at the University of Michigan School of Social Work wrote in summer 1968: "At a time when the people and institutions which all of us will have to deal with meaningfully as social workers literally scream out in pain and confusion, our School continues complacently to design courses, hire professors, and plan field placements in order to turn out 200 more social workers to be fed into establishment agencies which maintain and strengthen the system which inflicts the confusion and pain."[27] The social work schools proclaim that social work is concerned with the things that go wrong in society, but the schools and the profession had not responded adequately to human need, the students charged: they had not moved to include clients in decision making. They "have given scant attention to the needs, culture, and life circumstances" of both black clients and black social work students. "Our training at the School of Social Work is simply not preparing us to deal with the tasks we confront outside," wrote one Columbia University School of Social Work student, two months after the massive student occupation that had closed down the entire university. "We are on the line and find ourselves unprepared to deliver."

In response, the schools did change. The curriculum became more flexible and varied. Community organization and social policy tracks were established in many schools, and many students took advantage of them. In 1958 only 40 students, less than 1 percent of the total, were in such tracks. By 1968, 1,017 students, 9 percent of the total, had taken up these opportunities. New settings for fieldwork were developed, ranging from alternative schools to community organizing projects to working with militant community groups. Courses provided a greater emphasis on social problems and on the systematic sources of those problems; prevention became as respectable in the curriculum as treatment. Perhaps most strikingly, courses on blacks and on ethnic minorities became a new curricular requirement, and minority enrollments soared. By 1970–71 almost 25 percent of entering students were members of minority groups.

The growing numbers of black social work students and black social workers led soon to the organization of black social workers as well.[28] The first to organize were black students at the Columbia

University School of Social Work. Black social worker groups also emerged in Chicago, Detroit, Los Angeles, Philadelphia, Pittsburgh, and elsewhere.

The critical turning point occurred at the 1968 National Conference on Social Welfare in San Francisco. The black caucus, some 500-strong, protested that the conference, the annual get-together of social workers and social policy workers from all over the country, was completely irrelevant to black needs. Social workers had to recognize, said the caucus, that white racism, not delinquency or alcoholism or family instability, was "America's number one mental health problem." Finally walking out of the conference, the caucus left this challenge: "We are committed to the reconstruction of systems to make them relevant to the needs of the black community, and are pledged to do all that we can to bring this about by any means necessary."

After the conference, many caucus participants attended a number of meetings that led to the formation of the Association of Black Social Workers early the following year. The association continued to hammer away at the insensitivity of white social workers to the problems of black Americans. They scrutinized the role of black social workers in the black community and examined social welfare policies. And they examined the structure and actions of the NASW and other professional organizations.

Discussions soon led to action. The 1969 National Conference on Social Welfare meeting in New York was "the most tumultuous Conference in NCSW history." Picketing, leafleting, and demonstrations disrupted the entire meeting, as dissidents, mostly new members of the profession, attacked the conference and its constituent organizations. The National Welfare Rights' Organization and the Association of Black Social Workers, joined by the radical, student-based Social Welfare Workers Movement, a newly formed women's liberation organization, Women of the American Revolution (WAR), and a number of other groups, took over the first general session. All exits to the room were barred, and the demonstrators demanded that the National Conference donate $35,000 to NWRO and that conference attendees add another $25,000 before the doors would be opened. After several anxious hours, a truce of sorts was declared, and negotiations began. The National Conference negotiators agreed to seek to increase minority membership on the conference's board and committees, to focus the following year's conference program on poverty and racism, to encourage political and social action by social workers, to seek to reform social work education to make it deal with urban conditions, racism, and the condition of minority groups, and to encourage maximum feasible participation of client groups.

The protest was summed up by Howard E. Pruntz, a participant:

> Social workers did not begin the demands for change. These demands were started by the consumers of social services as well as by minority groups and organizations. Unfortunately, the response of social workers and social welfare organizations has been one of defensiveness and, in some instances, of actual opposition to the kind of changes demanded. Now NCSW, as well as other social welfare organizations, has been challenged by different groups—hippies, blacks, students, and welfare rights organizations. These groups are all linked together in their protest against the discrepancies between the promise and the performance of the materialistic society, and their demands for a radical restructuring of services. Efforts to slow down this wind of change cannot be successful, except temporarily and over the short haul.[29]

In this context of widespread ferment and attacks on social work, the very pillars of social work's sense of self-identity—the value of professionalism, the beneficence of casework, the ethical commitment of the profession to social service—came under attack, from within the ranks of social work as well as from without.

Radical critics, launching an assault on the professional model of service delivery, charged that the professional mode of organizing services, contrary to its pretenses, assured society of neither high standards of service nor lofty ethical standards.[30] In fact, it often seemed antithetical to both. Professionalism, they continued, was not necessary for carrying out the ostensible functions of the professionals. Rather, it was a defense of authoritarianism, of privilege, of the monopolization of knowledge, and of the exploitation of those supposedly being served. The professions were mechanisms of social control; and social control in an exploitative society could only mean social control of the exploited, a mechanism for the maintenance of an unjust social order.

Professionalism also served to exclude racial minorities and the poor from almost all professional occupations and women from the higher status professions, charged the critics. Even in social work, men were often given leadership positions to "raise" the occupation's professional status. This exclusion was unjust per se. Moreover, it had a devastating impact on clients: the relation of dominant professional–subordinate client, common to all professions, reinforced the parallel structure of dominance and subordination in society as a whole; thus, *male* doctor, *female* patient; *white* social worker, *black* client. And, added the critics, common professional theories, such as the importance of maintaining appropriate "boundaries" between social worker and client, of avoiding "overidentification with clients," had no real theoretical legitimacy. They were mere rationalizations, designed to protect the social worker from having to acknowledge the inequality in power and resources between professional and client.

The new social work activists also critiqued casework, the central method of social work. The charges, on the surface, were a bit contradictory. First, caseworkers were accused of abandoning the poor, of systematically excluding "many of the persons most in need of attention from caseworkers."[31] Richard Cloward and Irwin Epstein's study of family service agencies, as well as a number of other studies, had documented the systematic withdrawal of caseworkers from the poor, a process that originated in the 1920s, as we have seen.

Belatedly, prodded by their critics and drawn by the lure of federal dollars, many social workers were once again trying to reach poor clients. But as they did so, the effectiveness of casework as a tool came under attack. Several studies during the sixties to determine the validity of intense individual and group work—whether they reduced delinquency rates and improved school behavior, family functioning, and social adjustment—showed little or no improvement in the "treated" groups as compared with control groups.[32]

Meanwhile, social workers in the new poverty agencies were proposing a variety of new modes of casework intervention: "radical casework" (serving as an "insurgent" within the social service bureaucracies),[33] "sociotherapy" (engaging people in collective action, ranging from self-help to participation in social action, as a therapeutic tool as well as a means of directly accomplishing the particular ends of the project),[34] and client "advocacy."[35]

The traditional caseworker's attitude, wrote Martin Rein, after an extensive study of the new community action projects, is described in the words of one caseworker: "The client's personal adjustment must include a sound, realistic social adjustment, because as an individual he lives in a definite social community. . . . The function of the caseworker is to help the client accept and adjust to these standards."[36] By contrast, the new community social workers refused to accept the given social reality as something that clients should "adjust" to. Rather, the social worker's role should be to promote social change, to ally with the client, to change the reality that creates problems for the client. Charles Grosser described the role of the caseworker who employed these techniques: "The worker is not enabler, broker, expert, consultant, guide, or social therapist. He is, in fact, a partisan in a social conflict, and his expertise is available exclusively to serve client interests. . . . This is one of the orders of today's business. . . . The community organizer must decide which side he is on. The same logic that legitimates the roles of broker and advocate leads inevitably to another role, that of activist."[37] An *ad hoc* committee of the NASW in 1969 even suggested that the social workers' code of ethics be formally amended to require social workers to take on advocacy roles to fulfill their professional responsibility and argued that the profession as a whole had a duty to defend any social worker placed in jeopardy because of his or her advocacy activities.

Conventional caseworkers were under attack for ignoring the poor and for being ineffective in any case. At the same time they were attacked for what they *did* do. Caseworkers, several studies indicated, were less committed to an ideal of service than were social workers engaged in other types of social work practice. Faced with a choice between meeting the client's needs and violating agency policies, most caseworkers said they would adhere to agency policies.[38]

Moreover, the role of social work in poor communities, some activists argued, was not social service at all. It was unmitigated social control. Henry Miller, arguing that social work in the ghetto was a form of "philanthropic colonialism" in which social workers saw themselves as bearing the "white man's burden" in a brutalized, uncivilized ghetto, quoted a 1959 social work text to make the point:

"You as a social worker are an institution of social control. You represent the community's interest to influence people to accept social control, rather than force them to submit." . . . Social work's unique contribution to the ideology of the white man's burden could be called *clinicalism. . . .* It is founded on a presumption of damage—that is, as a result of the sad and brutal history of the Negro people, the individual member of that race is likely to have been psychologically injured. . . . The philanthropic solution to this damage is directed at the very soul of black culture. The family must be molded into a different kind of structure.

Social workers had to understand, Miller argued, that "nations cannot be backward, men are not children, and ethnic diversity is necessary to the good life."[39]

Casework was under attack from all sides—for being ineffective and for being too effective, for ignoring the poor and for controlling the poor. As Scott Briar commented in early 1968: "Lately monarchies have fallen on hard times everywhere, and the caseworker is no exception."[40] Alvin Schorr, noting that the prestige of casework had been transferred to social policy and social action, wrote: "The dazzle that once hovered over casework—especially psychiatric social work—now lights up social policy. Those who were interested in social policy ten years ago could have held their conventions in a telephone booth (if they had a dime); today they deliver the major addresses at our national conferences."[41] Social work's casework–social policy pendulum had swung once again.

Social work was in a state of growing disarray. By 1968 articles began appearing in social work journals on the "crisis" in social work. But, in fact, some of the worst blows were yet to come.

In the late sixties, the women's liberation movement had begun to emerge. Social work, of course, had always viewed itself as a woman's profession par excellence. Along with teaching and nursing, it was one of the few occupations in which women were able to participate on an equal (if not superior) footing with men. The profession's Pantheon—from Jane Addams and Mary Richmond through Mary Jarrett, Bertha Reynolds, Virginia Robinson, Jessie Taft, Gordon Hamilton, and Florence Hollis to such theorists of the sixties as Virginia Satir and Helen Harris Perlman—was filled with women. Women were deans and administrators, writers, researchers, and practitioners.

But when the new feminists turned their eyes to social work, they found a very different story.[42] Repeatedly, the social work profession had seen its largely female composition as a cause for concern rather than pride. Only by recruiting men into key positions in the field would social work gain in power and prestige, argued Mary Rich-mond and other social work leaders at the turn of the century; late fifties and early sixties writers had echoed their agreement.

Studies of officers of the major social work professional associa-tions, deans and directors of social work schools, contributors of journal articles, and agency administrators found an enormously disproportionate number of men in these roles. For example, from 1874 to 1974 of the 100 presidents of the National Conference on Social Welfare, only 19 had been women. In 1970, 10 out of every 11 social work school deans and 60 percent of agency executives were male, although less than a third of the direct service workers in agencies were men. And the disparities continued to grow: in the sixties and early seventies men were replacing women in adminis-trative positions at the rate of 2 percent per year. Feminist research-ers concluded that, except for a brief period in the late thirties and early forties and except for the fields of medical social work and psychiatric social work, men had dominated social work leadership positions since the profession's beginnings.

The feminist studies showed that in social work, as in non–"female dominated" professions, women received lower salaries than men and were less likely to be promoted. Women and men also chose different paths within social work: in social work schools in the late sixties, men were far more likely to pursue community organization and social policy (which offered higher salaries, among other things), whereas women dominated the casework tracks. (Whether the shift of social work toward social action in the sixties represented a male "take-over" is arguable, although, according to George Brager and John A. Michael, social work school activists were disproportionately male and the major theoretical contributors to the community organizing literature, unlike those to the casework literature, were male; even within casework, the best-known proponents of "advocacy" as a method were men.)

Finally, feminists uncovered systematic biases against women deeply embedded in social work theory. The psychiatric orientation that social work had adopted was rampant with sexism. For exam-ple, one study showed that mental health professionals, male and female alike, used different sex-stereotyped characteristics to define mental health in men and women and that a "mentally healthy" adult (no sex specified) was seen by the professionals to have the traits of a "mentally healthy" male. That is, "normal" women were seen as intrinsically less healthy than "normal" men. This, along with many other studies, suggested that in buying a psychiatric knowledge base the "woman-dominated" profession had bought a sexist self-image of women themselves.[43]

Ironically, it was not primarily women social workers but women psychologists—from the early writings of Naomi Weisstein and Phyllis Chesler to the later work of Nancy Chodorow, Miriam Dinerstein, and Carol Gilligan—who took the lead in discovering the sexism underlying much of social work's knowledge base. An early social work writer on sex discrimination in social work, C. Bernard Scotch, asked in 1971 whether, "as in the War on Poverty and the civil rights movement, the social work profession will be found lagging as the current struggle for women's liberation gathers momentum?" The early answer, at least, seems to have been "yes."

Social work's response to the social movements and social reforms of the sixties was deeply contradictory. For the first time, the social work profession itself was the target, rather than the ally, of a movement for social justice. But the criticism was from within as well as from without: social workers lined up on both sides of the battle. Some played a major role in developing and carrying out the new approaches to social problems that characterized the War on Poverty, whereas others had to be dragged, kicking and screaming, into a renewed social concern. Under the pressure of the community movements and the new institutional arrangements, long-accepted social work methods came under scrutiny—often by social workers themselves. The curriculum of social work schools was equally targeted for criticism—by young social workers in training. And the major social work institutions—that National Association of Social Workers, the National Conference on Social Welfare, the social work schools—after an initial defensiveness and hesitation, did respond to the pressures in a substantial way.

It is tempting to see the whole experience in a very positive light, as evidence of a capacity within the social work profession for a periodic renewal, a creative (if disorderly) rethinking of professional goals and methods. And the widespread involvement of social workers themselves provides some support for this view. But the opposition to change within the profession was very powerful. More important, it took a social movement powerful enough to shake American politics and institutions to set off the renewal process in social work. Not coincidentally, that social movement represented an effort by the poor—social work's traditional clientele—to solve their own problems in their own way rather than through the ministrations of social workers with their time-honored "expertise." That is, the very existence of the civil rights and community movements and the War on Poverty bears testimony to the failure of social work to deal with its ostensible concerns and to revitalize itself without prodding.

Finally, the social work response to the sixties movements never became self-sustaining. As soon as the movements themselves died down, the impetus for change within social work also faded. (Other factors, such as the increased risk of openly opposing agency administrators as the job market softened in the seventies and the real, if limited, successes in changing social work school curricula and in recruiting minorities into social work, no doubt also played a role in the decline in ferment within the profession.)

By 1970, with the "dazzle" lighting up social policy scarcely five years old, the excitement over the new approaches to social intervention was already beginning to fade. A new pessimism, born of the Nixon counterrevolution as well as of the increasingly evident failures of the social movements to maintain their momentum, was growing. After the drama of the 1969 National Conference on Social Welfare, the 1970 meeting in Chicago found a much lower level of activism. Despite occasional disruptions and the massive participation in sessions by representatives of the National Welfare Rights Organization, the Social Welfare Workers Movement, La Raza Unida, the Young Lords, and various American Indian organizations, a growing mood of indifference, passivity, and resignation characterized the meeting.

By the following year's conference in Dallas, it was almost as if the disruptions of the late sixties had not even occurred.[44] The social policy and social action drive within social work had collapsed, although social casework had not yet regained a dominant role. Confusion reigned: papers appeared in social work journals on ethnicity and race, on "Marxist approaches to social work," and on the continuing "crisis." Casework was again defended, in a *Social Work* editorial, as "The Real Thing," while another author still found it necessary to write an article "The Case for Activism in Social Work." One widely discussed article proclaimed that "the social work profession is undergoing fundamental change and may even be approaching its denouement," a result of the spread of what the author called the "ideological currents" of "activism, anti-individualism, communalism, and environmental determinism." Another highly influential essay, Frances Fox Piven and Richard A. Cloward's book-length *Regulating the Poor: The Functions of Public Welfare,* by contrast, argued that historically it was only activism and the rise of civil disorder that had produced expansions of the welfare state: "The moral seems clear," Piven and Cloward concluded. "A placid poor get nothing, but a turbulent poor sometimes get something."[45]

In the years that followed, social work tried to put itself together again, but to no avail. The assumptions upon which the profession had been built had been shattered. Throughout the seventies and early eighties issues that had been raised by the movements and internal social work dissidents in the sixties—ethnicity, race, clients' rights, sexuality, poverty, social policy initiatives, and methods of casework with the poor—continued to receive widespread discussion. And the more self-critical stance toward the profession and toward agencies continued, at least with respect to the problems of sex and race discrimination within the profession.

At the same time, the sixties-born rediscovery of social action was quickly forgotten. Enrollments in community organization courses in social work schools dropped as dramatically as they had risen, and the critiques of professionalism and of social work's social role disappeared. Some social workers once again openly embraced the idea that their roles were centered around "adjusting" people to their situations and maintaining social order. "In today's cynical society, altruistic rationales are not marketable," wrote Charles D. Cowger and Charles R. Atherton in 1974. But:

> the concept that social control is the primary function of welfare and that social control involves providing constructive services—that is a marketable idea. . . . The task of the social services should involve the provision of evidence that the best way to control disorder and deviance in the society is by responsive, universal, and flexible social services focused on (1) alleviation of individual problematic behavior, and (2) intervention in the ongoing process of the society.[46]

Many "clinical" social workers (as caseworkers with a strong psychotherapeutic orientation were coming to call themselves) felt betrayed by the NASW's belated embrace of social activism and, in 1971, formed their own professional organization, the National Federation of Societies for Clinical Social Work.[47] Others, seeking freedom from agency constraints, or higher incomes, or clients with fewer "objective" problems, fled the profession's traditional institutions for private practice, which grew dramatically. As social workers more and more became psychotherapists and more and more concerned with the life-cycle problems of the middle class, their theoretical base widened: behavior modification and learning theory, existentialist and humanist therapy, transactional analysis and gestalt therapy, systems theory and "social ecology," and a dozen varieties of family therapy and group work joined the more-or-less Freudian psychodynamic theories as part of many social workers' armamentarium of approaches and techniques. What was "social" about these techniques, few even asked.

By the end of the decade, the disarray was serious indeed. A series of conferences on the knowledge base of clinical social work showed little agreement even among clinicians; and between clinicians and social workers in medical settings, child protective agencies, welfare departments, and the like the gulf grew even larger. In a deteriorating job market, created by cutbacks in federal programs, social workers fought over the respective roles and training of B.S.W. social workers and M.S.W. social workers and over the relative efficacy of unions and professional organizations in responding to downward pressure on wages and upward pressure on caseloads.[48] Flexner's old question, "Is social work a profession?" or, equally disturbing, "Is it one or several professions?" loomed larger than at any time since the early twenties.

8

The Next Phase

Social work and social policy have evolved through a series of crises. The social ferment of the Progressive Era, with its conflict between the individual approach of the old Charity Organization Society and the social-reform–oriented approach of the settlement houses, was "resolved" by the collapse of liberal social policy and the rise of professional casework in the twenties. The revival of social action in the thirties set off a new period of ferment: the limited social reforms of the early New Deal gave way to the creation of the modern welfare state. Within social work, the rank-and-file movement challenged the professional model of social work practice altogether, and the "functional school" of casework raised major challenges to traditional casework practice. But once again, with the return of social peace in the forties and fifties, the crises were "resolved": the welfare state was cut short in its further development, and social work returned to its pre-Depression trajectory of professionalization around a psychotherapeutic model.

From the sixties through the eighties, however, the pattern had a different outcome. Once again, the revival of social action—above all, the black movement, in both the north and the south—prompted a new wave of social reform. Beginning with little more than an expansion of the New Deal pattern, presidents Kennedy and Johnson soon evolved a unique approach that combined legal prohibitions on racial and gender discrimination, macroeconomic stimulation, expansion of more or less traditional welfare state measures, a major expansion of social services, and an effort (however halfhearted) at empowering the poor. Social work responded slowly, even reluctantly, but by the late sixties, social workers were once again reexamining their traditional practice modes, inventing new approaches or reinventing old approaches, and rethinking the entire professional model.

But unlike the earlier crises, the ferment in social policy and social work of the sixties and early seventies has not subsided as rapidly as the social movements that engendered it. In the early eighties, with most of the major social movements of the sixties dead a decade or more, both social policy and social work remain in more disarray than at any time since the years immediately preceding the Depression. The battles and issues of the sixties remain as alive as ever, if in a changed social and political context.

Social work appears rudderless, insecure, suffering from a loss of unity and a clear sense of self-identity. Not since the twenties has the profession seemed like such a collection of disparate occupations, with no clear basis for unity as a single profession. Is social work concerned with psychotherapy? Organizing communities? Administering social services? Developing social policy? What do workers in child protective services, hospital social service departments, welfare department bureaucracies, and the private practice of psychotherapy have in common? In 1928 the Milford Conference concluded that social workers in a variety of casework situations (hospitals, schools, family services) shared a common set of "generic" skills as caseworkers. But today casework is crowded from one side by community organizing, administration, and policy planning and evaluation and from the other side by a psychotherapy relatively innocent of efforts at environmental awareness or manipulation. Do social workers still share a common knowledge base, a common set of attitudes or skills? Do BSW-trained case aides and MSW-trained administrators and therapists share in a common profession?

If what makes social work unique is its "recognition of social forces as determinants of life experience,"[1] then what are we to make of the rush of social workers to private practice with middle-class clients, clients who presumably are less the helpless pawns of social forces than are poorer, less powerful people? And how shall we interpret the appearance of a new group of social policy professions—city planners, public administrators, policy analysts—who share the "social forces" perspective yet are not social workers?

The Next Phase

The question asked so long ago by Abraham Flexner, as the basis for his rejection of social work's claim to professional status, has once again emerged: does social work have a unique role of its own, and if so, what is it? Or contrariwise, is social work's role simply to be the "humanizer" of other less humane services, the "individualizer" in the face of the "isolating, technological, specialized, and hopelessly complex world in which we live"?[2]

Social policy appears equally adrift. The certainties and optimism of the sixties gave way to doubts and pessimism in the seventies and to open assaults on the very possibility of governmental intervention to solve social problems in the eighties. A quarter century ago, Harold Wilensky and Charles Lebeaux distinguished between the "residual" and the "institutional" approach to social welfare.[3] The "residual" approach, they suggested, saw the family and the market economy as able to meet individual needs under most circumstances. The role of social policy was literally "residual": to deal with the relatively few who, for whatever reasons, could not make it on their own. By contrast, the "institutional" perspective, embodied in the welfare state, perceived that in modern industrial society the family and the market economy could no longer meet all human needs. The inability of individuals to provide for all their own needs had become normal and expected, not exceptional. It was up to the state to provide for such unmet needs on an ongoing, institutionalized basis.

From the thirties on, the institutional approach has been the dominant mode of American social policy. But under President Reagan, a return to a residual concept—with only very low-hung "safety nets" providing for those who could not cope—was for the first time in decades again proposed as a viable option for American society.

Startlingly, both liberals and the left were paralyzed by the Reagan assault. The paralysis stemmed from a series of dilemmas: first although public support for many of the major welfare state services and guarantees (e.g., unemployment insurance, Social Security pensions, food and medical care for those in need) remained high, public support for large-scale public spending for such services had reached a breaking point. It was especially low for direct income maintenance, which was perceived as a handout to racial minorities. Second, although many liberals wanted nevertheless to restore the cutbacks in funding for desperately needed programs, others remembered that only a few years earlier these same programs had been attacked as inadequate and humiliating. Should funds be restored to programs that were admittedly inadequate? Third, the sixties programs, at least, were conceived in an age of prosperity, of economic expansion apparently without limits. But the "age of limits" had dawned; the economic environment of the seventies was one of economic stagnation: sharing even a growing pie had engendered massive intrasocial conflict. With a declining pie, the threat of ethnic, regional, and class conflicts inhibited the most optimistic policy planner and altogether discouraged most. Finally, the New Deal coalition, that alliance of labor unionists and ethnic and racial minorities, was coming apart at the seams. A new coalition of those in need of services, social service professionals (now grown to number in the millions), and even businessmen, who desired to socialize labor costs that otherwise would have to be paid in the form of individual wages, seemed a possibility, but these disparate groups lacked an overriding, common class interest. At best, it seemed a problematic, troubled alliance.

Thus two decades after Lyndon Johnson proclaimed the imminence of the Great Society, even those social policy planners who still believed in that dream remained deeply divided, uncertain of how to proceed, and powerless.

How can these impasses be surmounted? There are no simple, formulaic answers. It is not just that the problems are recent, complex, and full of dilemmas, nor is it just that to set out a program in the absence of its possible realization would be a sterile exercise in wishful thinking (although both of those concerns are real). Rather, the basic problem is that any program, if stated in any but the most vague terms, must make assumptions as to the nature of the real world in which it will operate—its political, social, and economic parameters. But if there are any lessons to be drawn from the history recorded in this book, they are (1) that no real social reforms, no major advances in social policy have occurred in twentieth-century America in the absence of pressure from massive social movements of the poor and dispossessed; (2) that such massive social movements redefine, often in surprising and unpredictable ways, the social needs to which social policy must respond; and (3) that social movements radically alter the objective possibilities and subjective perceptions that underlie social policy formation.

It is quixotic, therefore, to devise new programs in the abstract. What is not so senseless, however, is to draw from the history presented here an analysis of the present situation in relation to the lessons of the past. For organizers, policy makers, politicians, and social workers (whether working with individuals, groups, or communities), this would seem to be an appropriate starting point. In the remainder of this chapter I will seek to examine the new environment within which social policy and social work practice take place and to reconsider some of the "lessons" of the past.

The starting point in responding to the crisis that has so infected both social work and social policy is to identify the changes in the economic, political, and social situation. The world economic crisis and the evolution of the American economy, shifting political and social patterns, and the inroads of Reaganism on the welfare state have made the mid-eighties a very different world from that of even two decades ago. To *begin* to address the crisis, the new environment must be analyzed and understood—not as a fixed "given," within which we must function, but as a present environment and a starting point for future change.

Social needs and the economic, social, and political constraints on responding to them have changed. Poverty, the target of so much social policy and social work practice in the past, is still the single, overwhelming domestic problem and remains disproportionately concentrated in the black and Hispanic population. But at the same time, the poverty of the eighties is not identical to that of the sixties.

Improvements in Social Security benefits have reduced (although by no means eliminated) poverty among the aged. The lot of elderly men, especially, has improved; elderly women who had no history of independent employment or who worked in less well paid jobs have benefitted less. At the same time, Medicare and Medicaid, while ostensibly funding medical services for the old and the poor, respectively, fueled an enormous inflation in medical care costs. But Medicare does not cover all services and includes a system of co-payments by the patient; thus, by the eighties the elderly were paying more out-of-pocket for medical care than they had before Medicare. And with the low levels of Medicaid eligibility, the increase in medical care costs left millions of Americans too "rich" for Medicaid but too poor to buy private medical insurance, that is, frozen out of the medical care market altogether.

During the seventies the country also experienced what sociologist Diana Pearce has termed the "feminization of poverty."[4] By the early eighties, of every three adults with incomes below the poverty level, two were women.

So rapid was the shift in the gender distribution of poverty during the seventies that the National Advisory Council on Economic Opportunity (set up by the 1965 Economic Opportunity Act) predicted in late 1981: "All other things being equal, if the proportion of the poor in female-householder families were to continue to increase at the same rate as it did from 1967 to 1978, the poverty population would be composed solely of women and their children before the year 2000."[5]

The feminization of poverty has three roots. First, discriminated against in the job market, women remain less likely than men to be hired and promoted to relatively well-paying jobs; and women are still paid lower wages for equivalent work. That the jobs available in large numbers to women are low paying is equally serious, however. Of employed women, 80 percent work in only 20 of the 420 occupations identified by the Bureau of Labor Statistics—in low-wage sectors such as clerical, light manufacturing, and service work. Thus, men and women fare differentially in the job market: a job frequently lifts a man and his family out of the poverty category; for women, confined to the low-wage sector of the work force, a job may not be a solution to poverty. According to the National Advisory Council on Economic Opportunity, of those mothers with children under age eighteen who worked outside their home, more than a quarter had incomes below the poverty line.

Another factor contributing to the poverty level of women is the rising rate of divorce in the years since 1965. Of all American women, 85 percent can expect to support themselves, as a result of divorce, separation, or death, at some point in their lives. Less than two-thirds of divorced fathers pay anything at all toward child support, and the average payment is less than $2,000 a year. Only 7 percent of divorced women collect alimony.

Finally, the recent cutbacks in social programs have had a disproportionate impact on women: 85 percent of food stamp recipients are women and children, 61 percent of Medicaid recipients are women, 93 percent of Aid for Families with Dependent Children recipients are women, and 67 percent of Legal Services Corporation clients are women.[6]

The possibility of meeting social needs has been affected adversely also by the American and worldwide economic situations.[7]

The worldwide economic collapse of the 1930s was ended by World War II. From the forties through the sixties, industrialized countries experienced an economic boom. But in the seventies and eighties, what appears to be a long period of economic stagnation set in. The economy of the eighties no longer appears to respond effectively to the Keynesian remedies of the earlier period: the structure of the economy has changed so that the rates of investment necessary to provide even close to full employment (i.e., 5 or 6 percent unemployment) lead to unacceptably high levels of inflation.

At the same time, the American economy is "de-industrializing." Manufacturing jobs, which provided low-and medium-skill jobs for previous generations of the poor, are disappearing. Many jobs are simply exported overseas, to the third world; other manufacturers flee to the American South and Southwest in search of a non-unionized, low-wage, low-benefit work force. Still other jobs are lost to automation; and as corporations shift excess funds to mergers and speculation rather than reinvestment, still other jobs are lost. As a result, even substantial levels of aggregate economic growth no longer produce masses of semiskilled and skilled jobs. The "middle" of the job structure is disappearing, leaving dead-end, low-skill, low-wage jobs at the bottom and technical and managerial jobs at the top. The job a new entrant into the unskilled labor market may get may not lift him or her out of poverty or lead to a job that does.

The outlook for social policy has been affected as well by the transformation in the American political environment in the eighties. Benefiting from the civil rights activity of the sixties that removed legal barriers to black voting, massive voter registration drives and efforts to increase the black vote began to pay off in the early eighties. In cities such as Chicago and Philadelphia in 1983, black mayors were elected for the first time. With the black vote far more supportive of social programs than the white vote, a massive voice for renewed social reform can be anticipated.

In the same vein, in the early eighties "gender gap" entered the vocabulary of American politics. American women, perhaps influenced in part by the feminist movement, began to diverge sharply from men in voting patterns, taking more liberal stands on both foreign policy and domestic issues.

Finally, one of the creations of the New Deal and the Great Society was a massive stratum of public employees, employed above all in human services. Although the needs and concerns of the millions of

215

health and hospital workers, schoolteachers, and social workers and other welfare workers are by no means identical with those of their clients, they do share with clients an interest in full public funding of their agencies and expansion of their programs.

It remains to be seen whether or not these changes will give rise to a new coalition in American politics, one rivaling in significance the emergence of the New Deal coalition of the thirties and forties. But the potential for major realignments in American politics is more real today than at any time in the last four decades.

Thus far we have been concerned with changes in the structure of social need and in the overall political, social, and economic achievement. Other changes affecting the world of social work and social policy more directly have also taken place in the last two decades.

Social work and social policy, now thoroughly integrated into the American economy, play an increasingly important economic role. Directly, the social institutions and programs created by social policy—schools, health institutions, social welfare systems—provide jobs for some 15 million people, or 14 percent of the American labor force. The institutions are also enormous consumers: hospitals alone spend some $30 billion a year for supplies ranging from drugs and medical equipment to food, mattresses, and linens. Schools, nursing homes, and other social service institutions spend billions more for goods and services. The public welfare systems supervise the transfer of $78 billion a year in benefits of all varieties to low-income families and individuals.[8]

Beyond their direct economic impact, the institutions of social policy play a major role as regulators of the labor market: they keep millions of people, who would otherwise be unemployed, out of the labor force entirely. The Bureau of Labor Statistics (BLS) distinguished three, not two, major groups with respect to employment. There are *employed* (full time, part time, well paid, or underpaid). There are the *unemployed*, defined as people who are not working at present, who have made specific efforts to find a job in the four weeks immediately preceding the BLS survey, and who are ready to go to work immediately if work is available. And finally, all others are classified as "not in the labor force"—what might better be called the *nonemployed*, to keep the syntax and the social content parallel. The latter group includes not only the "retired" (a group whose enormous numbers are made possible by the Social Security System) and "housewives" (i.e., unpaid domestic laborers) but what might be called the institutionally nonemployed—the millions of people engaged in institutionally based daily activities that are not classified as "gainful employment." These include students, prisoners, inmates of psychiatric hospitals and nursing homes, and, until 1983 (when the BLS reclassified them), those on active duty in the armed forces.

In fact, the number of unemployed and institutionally nonemployed people over the age of 14 (recalling that until the 1930s, 14—eighth grade—was the typical age for leaving school and going to work) rose slightly from 20 million people (23.3 percent of the potentially economically active population) in 1933, the worst year of the Depression, to more than 35 million people (23.9 percent) in 1978–79, the most prosperous period preceding the serious economic slump of the following half decade.[9]

The American economy, since the thirties, has been unable to provide full employment, even with the benefit of enormous government spending for military and nonmilitary purposes. If all the potentially employable were to seek jobs, the unemployment rates would be at Depression levels. Maintaining low levels of *un*employment has required maintaining high levels of *nonemployment*. The great sponges are the institutions and programs with which social policy has traditionally concerned itself—schools, hospitals, correctional facilities, residential treatment centers, Social Security System—and the military. Absorbing adults who would otherwise be looking for nonexistent jobs, the institutional programs transform the socially undesirable and politically dangerous category "unemployed" into the benign category "not in the labor force."

The implications of this analysis are several. Most obviously, the employment-related impacts of changes in government social spending are not limited to the direct effect on the employees involved in running the programs nor to the direct effect of changes in levels of benefits. They have an equally large impact on the employment status of the recipients of services. The level of government aid to education; the age of retirement, which makes one eligible for Social Security benefits; the standards for admission to mental hospitals—all have employment impacts as well as direct economic or service impacts.

The role of social services in the economy also has a major impact on the nature of the services themselves. The vast economic and political power of the "medical industrial complex" maintains a structure for the government financing of health services that encourages capital-intensive, centralized, and often "dehumanized" modes of health care.[10] The need to extend the years of schooling to sop up the potentially employable, at a rate considerably more rapid than the need for additional educational preparation of the work force requires, has the effect of extending the number of years of schooling disproportionately to the amount of educational content. (Conversely, the educational content per school year is degraded—one of the underlying sources of the decline in reading achievement of recent years.) And, as Frances Fox Piven and Richard A. Cloward have argued, the expansion and contraction of the welfare rolls plays a major role in regulating wage levels and pushing people into low-wage employment, thus creating a welfare system that is intrinsically "interfering," one that merits the enmity of the very people it supposedly assists.[11]

Social work and social policy, back in the days when they served a "residual" function, were peripheral to the American political process. But with the institutionalization of social welfare policy, they have become central to the political process and government operations.

Most social work and most social policy functions and institutions, both public and private, are financed, in whole or in large part, by government (at all levels—federal, state, and local). By 1973, according to one study, 51 percent of the income ($561 million) of Jewish-sponsored agencies came from public sources, up from 11 percent ($27 million) in 1962.[12] Overall, 42 percent of health care expenditures, 86 percent of educational costs, 87 percent of welfare services of all kinds are paid for by governmental sources. Half the federal budget goes for health, educational, welfare, and income maintenance purposes; almost half the expenditures of state and local governments are allocated similarly.

As a consequence, social policy has become fully politicized. The budgets and the very existence of agencies providing social services are extraordinarily dependent on the vagaries of local, state, and national politics. Few agencies serving public welfare purposes are, in any real sense, fully private institutions any longer; all are, to a greater or lesser degree, directly or indirectly controlled by government. The levels of operation, clientele served, regulations and procedures, and the organization of services in schools, hospitals, mental health centers, and family welfare agencies are increasingly determined not by the institutions, not by the relevant "professions," but by political decisions often taken at national levels.

Although social policy and social work are increasingly *financed* by government, they are less and less likely to be based in governmental institutions in the traditional sense, however. A growing number of social policy functions have been turned over to private institutions, both voluntary (nonprofit) and proprietary (profit making).[13] Historically, local governments operated public schools and county and city hospitals; state governments operated psychiatric hospitals; localities ran (and federal and state governments helped pay for) welfare. But lured by the huge amounts of government money going into these activities by the sixties, and assisted by legal provisions such as the "reasonable cost reimbursement" provisions of Medicare and Medicaid and the provisions of the 1967 and 1974 Social Security amendments, which encouraged the contracting out of services, a massive private social policy sector has arisen.

Many cities have closed their public hospitals, contracting with local privately controlled hospitals to care for the poor or allowing Medicaid to cover the costs of health care for the poor on a case-by-case basis. Increasingly, profit-making hospitals have emerged, skimming off paying patients with low mortality diseases and leaving a poorer, sicker patient group for voluntary and public hospitals to care for. By 1983, five large national chains of proprietary hospitals owned among them no fewer than 909 hospitals and collected more than $8 billion a year in revenues.[14]

Fed by Medicaid and Medicare revenues, private nursing homes also boomed. In significant measure, their patient load came from among people previously cared for in state psychiatric hospitals: between 1963 (pre-Medicaid) and 1969 (four years post-Medicaid), the number of nursing-home boarders "afflicted with mental disorders" doubled, from 222,000 to 427,000. By 1978 more chronically ill mental patients were housed in Medicaid-approved nursing homes that in psychiatric hospitals.[15]

Even traditional social work services increasingly were handled by private agencies. Day care, home care, elderly services, job training, outpatient mental health services, individual and family counseling, drug abuse and alcoholism services, and family planning services were among the services "contracted out" by state and local mental health and welfare departments. In Massachusetts, the Department of Mental Health laid plans, in the words of a memo from its deputy commissioner, to "minimize its role as a direct service provider. . . . The long range effect of this proposal would be the complete conversion of all delivery of service in the community to contracted human service providers."[16] Schemes to establish "voucher systems" to enable people to pay for schooling, health care, and other services threaten to expand this trend to yet other sectors.

The dismantling of the public-sector social service delivery system has been defended as a way to obtain cheaper, more effective, more flexible and efficient, and more innovative services. In practice, according to the limited number of studies of the impact of contracting out, few of these benefits have been realized. A study of some sixty-two municipal service agencies engaged in the practice reported that the more services are contracted out, the less citizen participation is found, the less oriented services were to overall service goals, and the more oriented the agencies were toward institutional mainte-nance goals. Contracted-out services were no cheaper than those performed by the public agency itself and were more difficult for the public agency to monitor. In other words, the anticipated gains did not materialize and the services became less accountable.[17]

Thus, ironically, the growing dominance of the public sector in financing social services has been accompanied by the deterioration of mechanisms for public control of the services.

The social work and social policy environment of the eighties will be very different from that of past periods. The economic and political environment has become more restrictive; the composition of target populations has changed; and the relationship between the institu-tions of social policy, the state, and the economy has changed. Nevertheless, not everything has changed. Many lessons of past generations in dealing with social policy concerns remain to be ab-sorbed into American political wisdom. Easily forgotten amidst the rhetoric and cuts of recent years, they are essential to rebuilding a humane social policy. In the final part of this chapter, I will outline some of the principal lessons of the past.

First, "big spending" and "big government" *did* solve social prob-lems (and, conversely, cuts in the big spending programs in the seventies and early eighties made social problems a lot worse). The social programs of the New Deal significantly alleviated the financial plight of the elderly; provided buffers against the impact of unemployment and disability; helped maintain relatively high levels of employment; and empowered millions of workers, via its encouragement of labor unions, to gain higher wages and better working conditions for themselves. The Great Society programs ended legal discrimination against blacks, and, to a large measure, women; opened substantial educational and employment opportunities to women and minorities; lifted millions of people out of dire poverty; dramatically improved the access of many poor people and old people to health and mental health services; improved the nutritional status of the poor; and contributed greatly to the entry of blacks into the American political mainstream. Many of these programs were limited, of course, and it is certainly true that some groups (e.g., the elderly and men) were helped more than others (e.g., children and women). But the experience of the reform decades of the thirties and the sixties do not support the conservative conclusion that government can do nothing directly to alleviate poverty and other social problems. (The argument that we can't afford such programs is equally specious. Merely returning to the tax rate structure of 1980 would generate enough revenue to allow lifting every family in the United States above the official poverty level, without the need to make cuts in any other programs. The problem is one of priorities among tax cuts, military expenditures, and social programs, not one of the absolute fiscal impossibility of reducing poverty without adverse effects on the federal budget, inflation rates, and so on.)

A program of income redistribution (via tax reform and direct income transfers), job creation, job supports (day care, retraining programs), personal supports (counseling, health and mental health services, schooling) and support for efforts by the poor to empower themselves and thus gain a sense of hope is possible and does make a difference. The failure of the sixties was not in its attempt but in its failure to follow through on that attempt, a result of the combined pressures of the Vietnam War, political opposition from those with a stake in poverty, and the failure to develop all components of the antipoverty program consistently and coherently.

If elements of the sixties poverty programs were misadministered and wasteful, they were no more wasteful than the defense budget and certainly much less wasteful than the maintenance of poverty with its resultant social costs. There simply is no enormous mystery as to how to fight poverty. What's needed is merely the political will to do so.

221

But if governmental action can reduce poverty and help solve other social problems, the fact remains that unemployment, poverty, and inequality, the problems that the New Deal and the Great Society set out to solve, remain the central American domestic problems. Despite the efforts of Reagan administration officials to deny or conceal, millions of Americans remain in dire poverty. Children still suffer from hunger, adults are maimed in body and spirit by inadequate food, unsanitary and unsafe living and working conditions, unavailable medical and mental health care, and inadequate education.[18]

There are a variety of definitional issues, to be sure, but these beg the question. Based on their cash income, some 34.4 million people were officially classified as poor by the U.S. Census Bureau in 1982.[19] The official numbers would have been reduced by perhaps as much as 30 to 40 percent if noncash benefits such as Medicaid, food stamps, and housing subsidies were included. At the same time, however, the official poverty level, a $9,862 income for a family of four, is so extraordinarily low that a case can easily be made for raising the number officially counted as poor by 30 or 40 percent. In any case, the question of whether 20 million or 34 million or 50 million Americans are "poor" is surely an indecent one; the lowest of these figures is a national scandal. And worse yet, no matter how poverty is measured, the decline in poverty that began in the sixties slowed and then stopped in the seventies; since 1978, the numbers below the poverty level have steadily risen.

Racism, too, continues to scar the lives of millions, poor and nonpoor. Black median income remains about 55 percent of the white median, exactly where it stood in 1960 (and down from the 64 percent it reached in 1970). Of all black families, 54 percent earn less than $15,000 a year, compared with 28 percent of white families. Although the racial gap in years of educational attainment has closed dramatically, college-educated blacks and whites with high school educations earn roughly the same incomes. Blacks are three times as likely as whites to have incomes below the poverty line and more than twice as likely to be unemployed.[20] And regardless of income, racism—the systematic belief by many whites that blacks are inferior to whites—remains a reality in the lives of all blacks.

Sex inequality, rediscovered in the sixties, also remains a central feature of American life. Women make up a predominant and growing fraction of the poor. Year-round, full-time female workers, both white and black, earn less than year-round, full-time black male workers. In 1980 less than 2 percent of employed women earned more than $25,000 a year, compared with almost 18 percent of male workers.[21] But as was the case with race, income and employment figures tell only a small part of the story: violence against women, sexual harassment on the job, sexual exploitation, and pervasive sexism scar women's lives.

In the fifties many Americans believed that America was a classless society. In the 1960s race, gender, and class, the three great structural social inequalities, were rediscovered, not by dispassionate academicians, not by social workers, teachers, and others who worked with the poor, the black, and the female, but by the poor, the black, the female themselves. It was the great social movements of poor people, racial minorities, and women that reminded Americans of the existence of social injustice and that insisted its continuation was intolerable. Race, class, and gender, insisted the movements of the sixties, were not incidental aspects of an otherwise unblemished American society and culture. They were deeply embedded in American society—in its institutions, its occupational structure, its culture, even its very language. Systematically, blacks, women, and poor people were denied not only wealth and access to wealth but power and access to power. And despite the undeniable gains for some members of these groups in the last twenty years, the basic analysis they thrust upon the American people fifteen to twenty-five years ago remains as valid today as when it was first uttered.

The continued strength of race, class, and gender in determining people's life chances has immediate implications. In the late sixties, black mental health activists insisted that the "number one mental health problem in America is white racism." Adding sexism and poverty to the list, the analysis still holds. Not merely does oppression leave its mark on the oppressed themselves, but, as black and feminist scholars have repeatedly shown, our very ideas of "normal" family structure, "normal" moral values, "normal" language are themselves deeply tinged with racism, sexism, and class attitudes.

It remains essential to analyze virtually every social phenomenon in terms of how its meanings and impacts are structured by race, gender, and class. The school that educates the middle-class child acts as a barrier to upward mobility for the poor child; the benefits of conventional job-creation programs accrue mainly to men, leaving women all but untouched, while cuts in welfare or food stamps harm mainly women. What holds for policies also holds for overtly benevolent individual interactions, as well. For example, the relationship between a white or male professional and a black or female client involves not only power issues intrinsic to the professional–client relationship under any circumstances but power issues that stem from the inequality in power and status in the larger world of everyday life.[22]

It was social movements that forced issues of race, sex, and class into our consciousness. Perhaps the central lesson of the entire history of American social reform is that without social movements there is no social reform. The reforms of the Progressive Era were a response to the growing threat and reality of unrest among poor farmers, workers, and immigrants. The New Deal (and especially the Second New Deal's creation of the welfare state) was a response to the movements of the unemployed and the unionists and to the electoral threat to FDR's left. And the reforms of the sixties and early seventies were the direct result of the civil rights movement, black and other minority unrest in the North, the student movements, and the feminist movement. Again and again, when masses of people erupt into protest and action, new institutions and new programs, designed at least in part to meet their demands, are created. "Thanks to the Negro, we have developed a fourth branch of American government . . . The March," wrote Paul Ylvisaker, one of the principal planners of the War on Poverty, in 1967. "A riot is the language of the unheard," added Martin Luther King, Jr.[23] Conversely, when the social movements subsided, calls for reform went unheard, social injustice remained unseen, and, if anything, social reforms of an earlier period were weakened or withdrawn.

Social movements, of course, are concerned above all with power: power over resources, over opportunities, over economic and political and social institutions, over the fabric of everyday life. In the late nineteenth century, workers, poor farmers, and immigrants sought to escape the enormous and arbitrary power wielded by giant corporations. The middle-class Progressives, however, were able to restore social peace by regulating corporations, to a small degree, without any major redistribution of power. In the 1930s, again, industrial workers recognized that their problems were not only unemployment, low wages, and poor working conditions but a loss of any sense of personal dignity at work and a lack of power over the economy as a whole. The great industrial unions that emerged in the late thirties were, in part at least, the result of efforts to create an "industrial democracy" to parallel political democracy. But success was elusive: the unions did succeed in limiting the arbitrariness of their members' corporate employers—for the minority of workers (largely white and male) who were unionized. With the ensuing bureaucratization of the unions and the decline of militant, socially oriented unionism in the forties and fifties, however, the larger dream of class justice and individual dignity was all but forgiven.

In the sixties issues of power, or rather the lack of power, reemerged. First, in the political sphere, both legal and traditional constraints limited the political participation of blacks, the poor, and women. Only now, in the mid-eighties, are the fruits of the struggles to throw off those constraints beginning to have a major impact on American politics at the national level.

Second, the poor of the sixties and, briefly, some policy planners insisted that poverty was as much a problem of a lack of power as of a lack of financial resources. The struggles over "maximum feasible participation" and "community control," the experiments with "sociotherapy," and the battles to keep community action programs responsive to poor communities rather than to the traditional political apparatus and the social service agencies directly reflected that perception. The thesis that poverty cannot be fought by money alone, that the elimination of poverty entails a major redistribution of power in America represents the germ of truth in the notion that "you can't solve social problems by throwing money at them." It is also one of the great forgotten lessons of the sixties. Its corollary, that individual, personal "powerlessness" is profoundly linked to objective, social powerlessness, and, conversely, that personal "empowerment" is limited, if not impossible, in the absence of objective empowerment, is perhaps one of the greatest potential legacies of the sixties to social work practice.

Third, to the social movements of the sixties, "power" was not a category that applied only to economic and political institutions. Power—and lack of power—shape every facet of one's daily life, from infancy on. Power—and lack of power—influence culture, modes of speech, personality, self-image, sexuality. Social power—the power of upper classes over lower classes, of men over women, of whites over blacks—intrudes into even the most apparently egali-

225

tarian individual relationships between people of different classes, genders, races (including, not trivially, the relationship between social worker and client, social planner and "constituency"). As the radical feminist movement of the late sixties put it, "the personal is political."

To a first approximation, struggles over power are zero-sum games—for the powerless to gain power, some power must be lost by those already in power. If history teaches anything, it teaches that those with power do not give up their power voluntarily, happily, or readily. As a consequence, social movements, however self-evidently just their demands and no matter what their tactics, create conflict and disorder. It should come as no surprise that the mayors, businessmen, craft unions, landlords, and social agency administrators felt threatened by the community movements of the sixties: it was their power that was directly under attack.

But many people—even those who supported demands of the sixties social movements—felt threatened by disorder, chaos, change. Thus the reservations of many rank-and-file service professionals about the goals and tactics of the social movements of the sixties were more complex in motivation. For these groups, the zero-sum-game analysis breaks down: their self-interest is by no means identical to that of their clients; some of their autonomy and power may indeed be threatened. Yet there is a broad area of overlap of interest as well. Social workers, teachers, nurses, and other social service professionals are powerfully motivated by a service ethic. For most, that is why they chose their occupation. And to the extent that social movements demand more services and better services and better funded services, the interests of the professional coincide with those of the movements. The social worker seeking resources for a client—a day care center, a homemaker service for the elderly, a vocational rehabilitation program, a bed in a mental hospital, housing, legal services, the next day's food—has a vital interest in the social movements of the clients. For without them, the resources and services the social worker needs to do his or her job disappear.

As we have seen, social workers have sought to root their professional identity and their daily practice (including their response to social movements) in the development of a body of theory, or "knowledge base." The knowledge base of a profession reflects both the class and occupational needs of the professionals and a variety of social forces outside the occupation, however. The knowledge base is not simply a collection of "objective" assertions, or theories, about human behavior, social organization, and so on. There is no such thing as value-free theory. All theories, no matter how technical in appearance and no matter how pragmatically useful, are laden with social and political values and assumptions. Even medical science, which appears to be an objective biological science, contains assumptions about the relationships between mind and body, between social environment and physical health, between doctor and patient. How much more so the social sciences and the psychological sciences, sciences that deal with human behavior and the nature of human beings themselves. For example, the theories on which the War on Poverty was based located the source of poverty in the dysfunctional impoverished community rather than in the dysfunctional economic and political structure of the larger society. The psychological theories that have so influenced social work are based on norms of mental health that reflect the experience and needs of middle-class white males and on values that see adjustment and equilibrium as positive, conflict and change as negative. There is nothing "objective" about these theories; they serve easily specifiable political and occupational interests.[24]

There is no way of escaping value assumptions in constructing theories to explain social problems or individual problems. The challenge is to identify the assumptions clearly and to be sure that they are consistent with the larger values that the theories are intended to advance.

Social work and social policy have been characterized at different times by one of two broadly opposing sets of theories. On the one hand, there are those theories that emphasize the problems of the individual (his or her morality, character, personality, attitudes, ego structure) and see casework (friendly visiting, psychotherapy) as the solution. On the other hand, there are the theories that emphasize the problems of society (communities, ethnic groups, the poor) and see social reform (social policy) as the solution. These theories are more readily understood as the ideologies and battle cries of particular groups within and outside the profession, struggling for power in the profession, than as exclusively true, well-validated (or even capable of being validated) theories of human behavior.

In fact, the individual-societal change (casework-reform) dichotomy seems to me a false trail for social work to pursue. Even synthetic formulas that seek to bridge the gap between the two

227

poles (such as trying to look at the "person in situation" or focusing on the "relationship between the person and his or her social environment," or examining the social "ecosystem" in which the individual is enmeshed) are insufficient.[25] Social forces and social structure, the traditional arenas for social policy, are not external to, and separate from, individual personality and behavior or family structure and dynamics, the traditional arenas for casework intervention. They cannot be conceived of independently and then brought into relationship with one another. Rather they are deeply interpenetrated.

We cannot, for instance, talk about racism as distinct from self-identity: racial identity, black or white, in our racially polarized society is a central component of total identity. Similarly for gender and class: social and environmental forces—in the deepest sense of the racial, gender, and class structure and dynamics of our society as well as in the more immediate sense of the particular local social environment—are incorporated into the deepest parts of the self. Self-esteem, aspirations, cognitive styles, interpersonal patterns, coping styles and defenses, moral values, sexuality and sexual behavior, and dependency needs embody essentially accurate perceptions of one's place in the social order, as well as reflecting purely individual histories of personal development.[26]

Yet it has been the individual, not the environment, that social workers have sought to establish as the "knowledge base" of their profession. With rare exceptions, the child's school problems, the adult's work problems, and the housewife's marital problems are seen as the consequence of their individual psychological or family problems. For example, the worker has work problems because he or she drinks; not the worker drinks because most jobs in our society are demeaning, pointless, and oppressive. Even to the extent that the environment is taken seriously, it is at best in the most immediate sense of "environment": it is the child's particular school or the adult's particular boss or job that are the problems. An analysis of the overall social function, the content, the power relations expressed by schools or work or the family, disappears entirely.

This latter model would suggest that if the sources of an individual's troubles are, in some measure, social, the sources of individual change to deal with those troubles may also have to be social. Again and again in the movements of the sixties, through involvement in social action, people changed *themselves* as well as their objective social situation. That is, social change created new possibilities for individual change. Illnesses that have a social etiology, we might hypothesize, would require social approaches to "cure." Socially engendered problems may defy individual solution precisely because one source of the individual's troubles may be the very fact that he or she perceives his or her problems as individual.

The environmental-change–individual-change dichotomy may be real *in the absence of social movements.* But social movements may provide the basis for overcoming this dichotomy. For a social work concerned with helping individuals to change, this suggests that community organizing and social activism, long seen as outside the purview of casework, may be as relevant to casework as individual psychotherapy that seeks to alter family dynamics or manipulate the immediate environment.

It is also true, of course, that social policy and social change take place, in the end, as a form of individual activity. Social problems are, ultimately, matters of individual behavior (albeit socially structured and constrained individual behavior), and personality structure represents both the source of social movements and the obstacle to them. If I have emphasized the reverse side of this argument it is because social workers and social policy planners, despite rhetoric about social forces impacting individual behavior and personality, have all too often emphasized the individual and particular sources of individual troubles.

Along with the notion of a "knowledge base" for social work practice, the entire notion of social work "professionalism" is in dire need of a fundamental reconceptualization. Almost three-quarters of a century ago, Abraham Flexner asked: "Is social work a profession?" The question has been debated endlessly, more or less on Flexner's terms, and in the last twenty-five years or so social workers have answered "yes" (although often a rather defensive "yes"). But the history and analysis presented in this book suggest that they have been trying to answer the wrong question. If "professionalism" means a frantic search for status, abjuring social action, kowtowing to upper-class financial saviors, evaluating theory for its occupational benefits, defending turf against other professionals, maintaining agency or "professional" concerns as prior to those of clients, then "professionalism" hardly seems a desirable or respectable goal for social work. And yet again and again, it is precisely these goals (though often not stated quite so baldly) that social workers have pursued.

In any event, the supposed attainment of professional status has received scant reward. Social work remains a low-status profession. Salary levels hover barely above the poverty level. (In 1982 starting salaries for M.S.W. social workers in the northeastern United States were as low as $12,000 to $14,000, or only $2,000 to $4,000 above the U.S. government's 1982 poverty level for a family of four.)

The dividing line between social work, psychology, psychiatric nursing, counseling, and other helping professions remains as fuzzy as ever. Meanwhile the drive to professionalize has served to divide less trained (B.A., B.S.W. social workers from more highly trained (M.S.W.) workers. It has sent social work on a fruitless search for a "scientific" theory and thus diverted its pursuit of social goals. It has served as a shield to ward off client participation in agency decision making and thus maintained the social distance between client and practitioner. It has been a barrier to unionization, which could raise social work salaries and work standards far more effectively than "a gain in professional status" does.

Perhaps the question social workers *should* have been asking all those years is: "Do we really want to be a profession?" Professionalism must accept the judgment of its own high standards. To the extent that professionalism represents a real effort to maintain competence and high ethical standards—a commitment to client needs even when they conflict with agency rules, a commitment to openness and collegiality, a commitment to the goal and the actuality of social justice, which is at the core of social work's reason for existence—it needs no defense. But if professionialism does not measure up to, or conflicts with, these standards, it should be discarded without regret.

A FINAL WORD

As this book as been a social and political analysis of a profession that is intensely concerned with the personal, it is appropriate to end with a few personal reflections.

"Social work"—the very words are a contradiction. First there is "social," a word pregnant with connotations of collectivity, com-

munality, connectedness, of expressivity and of ties between people. Then there is "work," a word that, in our society at least, bears a
burden of negative meanings, a drudgery, instrumentality, self-
denial, individual isolation. As I explored the history and manifold
meanings of social work, the tension, duality, and contradiction
between the two words emerged again and again. There was social
work, the helping profession, ameliorating human woes, driven by
ethical, humanistic, social concerns; and there was social work, the
occupation used by those with wealth and power to maintain social
order, to moderate the social discontent that resulted from inequities
in wealth and power. There were countless social workers,
motivated by altruism, by respect and compassion for their clients;
and there were countless social workers (often the very same ones),
motivated by the desire for social status and professional turf, exert-
ing power over their clients. There were social workers struggling
for social solutions to social problems and others entering into intense, one-on-one relations with troubled clients, in each case sometimes with affection and compassion, sometimes with arrogance
and paternalism.

I have often thought that the very idea of social work in a society
such as ours, a society characterized by pervasive class and race and
gender distinctions, driven by greed and a pernicious individualism, is impossible. And yet compassion for individuals and human
solidarity and the drive for justice are just as powerful as
selfishness, greed, and self-seeking. And so social work, for all of its
flaws—its history of self-abasement before the mighty, its swift re-
treats from the struggle for social justice into one-to-one helping
relationships, its lack of self-awareness about its social role and
about the implications of its quest for professional status—has been
unable to escape its own better side, its commitment to social justice, its alliance with the dispossessed, its attachment to the values
that ennoble and empower men and women. Whatever its vices,
social work also contains within itself our hopes for a decent,
humane society.

But what, then, about all those dualities and contradictions? A
few years ago, in a course designed to examine the usefulness of
sociological concepts in clinical social work practice, a student of
mine tried to analyze a case of a junior high school boy, a client in a
field placement. He suggested that the boy's behavioral difficulties
in school might have reflected a real, and in a sense legitimate,

231

resistance to an oppressive school situation. "But," I objected, conceding to intrapsychic explanations of such behavior, "remember, he was just hitting adolescence." "Oh, no," responded my student. "He wasn't just hitting adolescents. He was hitting grown-ups!" Subjective reality and objective reality, troubled individuals in a troubled society, related, intertwined, yet distinct.

Is there any way around these dualities? I have suggested that from the perspective of a social worker working with individuals, one direction for resolution may lie in an understanding of how social structure and social forces are internalized as personality structure. That is, social realities, past as well as present, are as central as individual family history in determining an individual's personality. Conversely, social structure—indeed, all of culture—is in some sense a projection of the personalities of the people of all classes who make up the society (personalities that are, in turn, an internalization of the social structure and culture).[27] The powerful intrapsychic and interpersonal dynamics that shape individual and collective beliefs and behavior are as relevant a consideration for policy planners and community organizers as are broad economic and sociological factors. But I should emphasize here, these theses do not imply that the resolution of intrapsychic and interpersonal conflicts, whatever their origin, on a one-by-one basis is the route to achieving a just society. The evidence that people's personalities, even in adult life, are remarkably plastic and remarkably responsive to the social environment (including the structure of rewards and punishments offered by social institutions and, above all, the impact upon individuals of the social movements in which they participate) is too persuasive to allow such a pessimistic conclusion. Steadfast support for social reforms and the social movements that demand such reforms must be at the heart of social work's mission, whatever the particular roles played in such efforts by individual social workers.

Beyond this, there are no abstract, eternally valid, theoretical resolutions to social work's dualities. Only in the practice of a social work as concerned with social justice as it is with the alleviation of the problems of individuals can solutions be found.

"I think that, as life is action and passion, it is required of a man that he should share the passion and action of his time at peril of being judged not to have lived," observed Justice Oliver Wendell Holmes in his 1884 "Memorial Day Address." Perhaps the same can be said of the profession of social work, situated centrally amid the "action and passion" of our times. It must throw itself into that action, in firm alliance with its clients, on the side of human decency and social justice. Otherwise, no matter how "adequate" its knowledge base, no matter how "successful" its drive for professional status, it might as well "not have lived."

Perhaps another way of saying this is that social movements and the history of social work are concerned not only with poverty, war, and racial injustice. They are equally concerned with personal relationships, the quality of daily life, existential issues, human dignity, ethnic pride, morality, and transcendent experience. Two centuries ago, in describing the French Revolution, the social movement that virtually defined the modern era, Wordsworth wrote: "Bliss was it in that dawn to be alive, / But to be young was very heaven" (*The Prelude*, Book XI). Wordsworth was linking collective hopes and communal experience to individual bliss—precisely the goal that, however quixotically, the social work in my imagination must seek.

Living in the slums of pre–World War I Chicago, Jane Addams, who inspired so much of modern social work, took time to organize a library, an art gallery, and a theater. The sixties movements were about anger at war and injustice and solidarity with the oppressed, but they were also about play and leisure, sexuality, music and color and form, a sense of adventure and a joy in collective struggle.[28] These latter, too, are part of the historic vision and theory of social work and social policy, for without them, no matter how equitable the distribution of wealth and power, a good society will not emerge. The challenge to social work in the eighties is how to incorporate these, as well as "ego structure," "family systems," "advocacy," and "welfare reform," into its professional canon.

233

Notes

Preface

1. See Daniel M. Fox, *The Discovery of Abundance* (Ithaca, N.Y.: Cornell University Press, 1967), pp. 102–4.
2. Miriam Van Waters, "Philosophical Trends in Social Work," *Proceedings of the National Conference of Social Work, 1930* (Chicago, 1931), pp. 3–19.
3. George Gilder, *Wealth and Poverty* (New York: Basic Books, 1981), p. 68.
4. A[nne] M[inahan], "What Is Clinical Social Work?" *Social Work* 25, no. 3 (1980): 171.
5. Eda G. Goldstein, "Knowledge Base of Clinical Social Work," *Social Work* 25, no. 3 (1980): 173–78.
6. Bertha Reynolds, "Social Work and the Life of Its Time," unpublished paper, 1905, cited in Carel B. Germain, "Social Context of Clinical Social Work," *Social Work* 25, no. 6 (1980): 483–88.
7. Bertha Reynolds, *Social Work and Social Living* (Washington, D.C.: National Association of Social Work, 1975; originally published 1951), p. 174.

CHAPTER 1. *The Origins of American Social Policy*

1. Works on Progressivism that I have found useful include Robert H. Wiebe, *The Search for Order, 1877–1920* (New York: Hill & Wang, 1967); Richard Hofstadter, *The Age of Reform* (New York: Knopf, 1955); Christopher Lasch, *The New Radicalism in America, 1889–1963* (New York: Knopf, 1965); James Weinstein, *The Corporate Ideal in the Liberal State, 1900–1918* (Boston: Beacon Press, 1968); and Gabriel Kolko, *The Triumph of Conservatism* (New York: Free Press, 1963).
2. Statistics in this chapter, unless otherwise noted, are from Gilbert C.

Fite and Jim E. Reese, *An Economic History of the United States,* 2d ed. (Boston: Houghton Mifflin, 1905); Martin L. Primack and James F. Willis, *An Economic History of the United States* (Menlo Park, Calif.: Cummings, 1980); U.S. Department of Commerce, *Historical Statistics of the United States, Colonial Times to 1970* (Washington, D.C.: U.S. Government Printing Office, 1975).

3. On turn-of-the-century living conditions, see Otto L. Bettmann, *The Good Old Days—They Were Terrible* (New York: Random House, 1974), and Philip S. Foner, *History of the Labor Movement in the United States,* vol. II (New York: International, 1955), pp. 11–31, and vol. III (New York: International, 1964), pp. 11–31.

4. On immigration, see John Higham, *Strangers in the Land* (New York: Atheneum, 1971); Herbert Gutman, *Work, Culture, and Society in Industrializing America* (New York: Knopf, 1976); Foner, III: 256–81; and Herbert Gutman and Gregory S. Kealey, eds., *Many Pasts,* vol. II (Englewood Cliffs, N.J.: Prentice-Hall, 1973), pp. 183–250.

5. On industrial development 1877–1914, see Primack and Willis, pp. 244–311, and Fite and Reese, pp. 296–527.

6. On working conditions and wages, see Foner, II: 11–31, and Bettmann, pp. 67–86.

7. Cited in Foner, III: 17.

8. Cited in Philip Taft, *Organized Labor in American History* (New York: Harper & Row, 1964), pp. 178–79.

9. On worker and farmer responses to the crisis of industrialism, see Norman Pollack, *The Populist Response to Industrial America* (New York: Norton, 1962); Laurence Goodwyn, *Democratic Promise: The Populist Movement in America* (New York: Oxford University Press, 1976); Foner, vol. III; Samuel Yellen, *American Labor Struggles, 1877–1934* (New York: Monad Press, 1974); Taft, op. cit.; Norman J. Ware, *The Labor Movement in the United States, 1860–1895* (New York: Vintage, 1964); David Montgomery, *Workers' Control in America* (Cambridge: Cambridge University Press, 1979); Sterling D. Spero and Abram L. Harris, *The Black Worker* (New York: Atheneum, 1960); Gutman, op. cit.; Ray Ginger, *The Bending Cross* (New Brunswick, N.J.: Rutgers University Press, 1949); Melvin Dubofsky, *We Shall Be All: A History of the Industrial Workers of the World* (Chicago: Quadrangle, 1969); Ira Kipnis, *The American Socialist Movement* (New York: Monthly Review Press, 1972).

10. Cited in William Appleman Williams, *The Tragedy of American Diplomacy,* 2d ed. (New York: Dell, 1972), p. 34.

11. Cited in Hofstadter, p. 239.

12. Hofstadter, pp. 215–16.

13. Barbara Ehrenreich and John Ehrenreich, "The Professional-Managerial Class," *Radical America,* March-April 1977, reprinted in Pat Walker, ed., *Between Labor and Capital* (Boston: South End Press, 1979).

14. Harry Braverman, *Labor and Monopoly Capital* (New York: Monthly Review Press, 1975), pp. 85–123, 155–68.

15. Barbara Ehrenreich and John Ehrenreich, "Work and Consciousness," *Monthly Review,* 28 (July-August 1976): 10–18.

16. Samuel Bowles and Herbert Gintis, *Schooling in Capitalist America* (New York: Basic Books, 1975); Barbara Ehrenreich and Deirdre English, *For Her Own Good* (Garden City, N.Y.: Doubleday/Anchor, 1978).

17. Higham, pp. 247–48.

18. Ehrenreich and English, op. cit.; Frances E. Kobrin, "The American Midwife Controversy: A Crisis of Professionalization," *Bulletin of the History of Medicine,* July-August 1966, p. 350.

19. Stuart Ewen, *Captains of Consciousness* (New York: McGraw-Hill, 1976); Paul Baran and Paul M. Sweezy, *Monopoly Capital* (New York: Monthly Review Press, 1966), chap. 5.

20. For more thorough discussions of this phase in the history of the American working class, see Stanley Aronowitz, *False Promises* (New York: McGraw-Hill, 1973); Ewen, op. cit.; Braverman, op. cit.; Ehrenreich and English, op. cit. A contemporary example can be found in Hope Leichter, *Kinship and Casework* (New York: Russell Sage Foundation, 1967).

21. Edward A. Ross, *Sin and Society* (1907), excerpted in Otis C. Graham, Jr., *The Great Campaigns* (Englewood Cliffs, N.J.: Prentice-Hall, 1971), p. 237; Anthony Platt, *The Child Savers* (Chicago: University of Chicago Press, 1969), pp. 87–88; Weinstein, p. xi.

22. Barbara Ehrenreich and Deirdre English, *Complaints and Disorders* (Old Westbury, N.Y.: Feminist Press, 1973). On the impact of the industrial revolution on women, also see Rosalind Baxandall, Linda Gordon, and Susan Reverby, *America's Working Women* (New York: Vintage, 1976); Mary P. Ryan, *Womanhood in America from Colonial Times to the Present* (New York: Harper & Row, 1975), pp. 193–251; Linda K. Kerber and Janet DeHart Mathews, eds., *Women's America* (New York: Oxford University Press, 1982).

23. Cited in William L. O'Neill, *Everyone Was Brave* (Chicago: Quadrangle, 1969), pp. 3–4.

24. Jane Addams, "The Subjective Necessity of Settlements," in Jane Addams, *Twenty Years at Hull House* (New York: Signet, 1960; originally published, 1910), pp. 91, 94.

25. O'Neill, op. cit., cf. Ryan, op. cit.; Ellen Carol DuBois, *Feminism and Suffrage* (Ithaca, N.Y.: Cornell University Press, 1978); Eleanor Flexner, *Centuries of Struggle* (New York: Atheneum, 1972); Barbara J. Harris, *Beyond Her Sphere: Women and the Professions in American History* (Westport, Conn.: Greenwood Press, 1978); Blanche Wiesen Cook, "Female Support Networks and Political Activism," in Nancy F. Cott and Elizabeth H. Pleck, eds., *A Heritage of Her Own* (New York: Simon & Schuster, 1979); Aileen Kraditor, *Ideas of the Woman Suffrage Movement, 1890–1920* (New York: Atheneum, 1965).

26. Cited in O'Neill, p. 134.

27. Jessie Taft, "Qualifications of the Psychiatric Social Worker," *Proceed-*

ings of the National Conference of Social Work, 1919, (Chicago, 1919), pp. 593–99.

28. Kipnis, p. 216.

29. Kolko, pp. 98–110. More generally, in addition to Kolko's book, cf. Weinstein, op. cit.

30. Mabel Kittredge, "Homemaking in a Model Flat," *Charities and the Commons* 15 (Nov. 4, 1905):176–81; Mabel Kittredge, "Housekeeping Centers in Settlements and Public Schools," *Survey* 30 (May 3, 1915): 188–92.

31. Anzia Yezierska, "My Own People," in Anzia Yezierska, *Hungry Hearts* (New York: Arno Press, 1951), pp. 224–49.

32. Cited in Allen F. Davis, *Spearheads of Reform: The Social Settlements and the Progressive Movement, 1890–1914* (New York: Oxford University Press, 1968), p. 19.

33. Kipnis, pp. 227–28.

34. On early social workers' attitudes toward immigrants, see Davis, op. cit. On attitudes toward blacks, see Davis, op. cit.; Alvin B. Kogut, "The Negro and the Charity Organization Society in the Progressive Era," *Social Service Review* 44, no. 1 (1970): 11–21; Steven J. Diner, "Chicago Social Workers and Blacks in the Progressive Era," *Social Service Review* 44, no. 4 (1970): 393–410; Herbert Apthekar, "DuBois on Florence Kelley," *Social Work* 11, no. 3 (1966): 98–100. Social welfare activities undertaken by blacks are recounted and documented in Edyth L. Ross, ed., *Black Heritage and Social Welfare, 1860–1930* (Metuchen, N.J.: Scarecrow Press, 1978); and William L. Pollard, *A Study of Black Self Help* (San Francisco: R and E Research Associates, 1978).

CHAPTER 2. *Casework and the Emergence of Social Work as a Profession*

1. On feminism, see references in Chapter 1, notes 22 and 25. On postwar labor unrest and labor in the 1920s, see Irving Bernstein, *The Lean Years* (Baltimore: Penguin, 1966); Samuel Yellen, *American Labor Struggles, 1877–1934* (New York: Monad Press, 1974); Philip Taft, *Organized Labor in American History* (New York: Harper & Row, 1964); Harvey O'Connor, *Revolution in Seattle: A Memoir* (New York: Monthly Review Press, 1966).

2. On immigration (from abroad and internal) and nativism, see John Higham, *Strangers in the Land* (New York: Atheneum, 1971). On black migration and racial unrest, see Arthur I. Waskow, *From Race Riot to Sit-In* (Gloucester, Mass.: Peter Smith Publishers, 1975); William M. Tuttle, *Race Riot: Chicago in the Red Summer of 1919* (New York: Atheneum, 1970); Gilbert Osofsky, *Harlem: The Making of a Ghetto* (New York: Harper & Row, 1966); St. Clair Drake and H. R. Clayton, *Black Metropolis* (New York: Harper & Row, 1962).

3. See Robert K. Murray, *Red Scare: A Study in National Hysteria, 1919–20* (New York: McGraw-Hill, 1955).

4. See George Henry Soule, *Prosperity Decade* (New York: Holt, Rinehart and Winston, 1947); Frederick Lewis Allen, *Only Yesterday* (New York: Harper, 1957); Robert S. Lynd and Helen Merril Lynd, *Middletown: A Study in Contemporary American Culture* (New York: Harcourt, Brace, 1929); Stuart Ewen, *Captains of Consciousness* (New York: McGraw-Hill, 1976); James J. Flink, *The Car Culture* (Cambridge: M.I.T. Press, 1975).

5. Bernstein, pp. 63–66.

6. Paul Baran and Paul M. Sweezy, *Monopoly Capital* (New York: Monthly Review Press, 1966).

7. Ewen, p. 53.

8. Barbara Ehrenreich and Deirdre English, *For Her Own Good* (Garden City, N.Y.: Doubleday/Anchor, 1978), chap. 5.

9. Edward A. Filene, *Successful Living in This Machine Age* (New York: Simon & Schuster, 1931), p. 44.

10. Flink, pp. 147–48.

11. Ewen, p. 86.

12. Allen, p. 100.

13. Flink, p. 84.

14. Allen, pp. 98–103.

15. Bernstein, pp. 47–82.

16. Ehrenreich and English, chaps. 3 and 4; E. Richard Brown, *Rockefeller Medicine Men: Medicine and Capitalism in America* (Berkeley: University of California Press, 1979). A differing view can be found in Paul Starr, *The Social Transformation of American Medicine* (New York: Basic Books, 1982), pp. 420–49.

17. The functionalist view of professionalism is most clearly articulated by Talcott Parsons, "The Professions and Social Structure," *Social Forces* 17 (1939): 457–67, and reviewed in Everett C. Hughes, "The Professions in Society," *Canadian Journal of Economics and Political Science* 26 (Feb. 1960): 54–61. Many of the key functionalist articles on professionalism are reprinted in Howard M. Vollmer and Donald C. Mills, eds., *Professionalization* (Englewood Cliffs, N.J.: Prentice-Hall, 1966). Major alternative perspectives are those of Terence J. Johnson, *Professions and Power* (London: Macmillan, 1970); Eliot Freidson, *The Profession of Medicine* (New York: Dodd, Mead, 1970); and Magali Sarfatti Lawson, *The Rise of Professionalism* (Berkeley: University of California Press, 1977). For more detailed discussion, see John Ehrenreich, "Class and Professionalism: Some Comments on the Sociology of the Professions" (in preparation).

18. Jeanne M. Giovanni and Margaret K. Purvine, "The Myth of the Social Work Matriarchy," *Social Welfare Forum, 1973* (New York: National Conference on Social Welfare, 1974): 166–95. This male domination of a "female profession" has persisted to the present day, worsening since World War II (see references in Chapter 7, note 42).

19. Abraham Flexner, "Is Social Work a Profession?" *Proceedings of the*

National Conference of Charities and Correction, 1915 (Chicago, 1915), pp. 576–90.

20. Ibid., pp. 588–89.

21. See, for instance, letters in *Survey* 41 (1919): 740–46.

22. Porter R. Lee, "Social Work: Cause and Function," *Proceedings of the National Conference of Social Work, 1929* (Chicago, 1930), pp. 3–20.

23. Ibid., pp. 7–8. Also cf. Porter R. Lee, "What Is the Basis of Public Confidence in Social Work?" *Bulletin of the New York School for Social Work,* Oct. 1933, pp. 19–30, and Porter R. Lee, "A Critical Period in Education for Social Work," idem., Oct. 1934, pp. 201–14.

24. Harry Greenwood, "Attributes of a Profession," *Social Work* 2 (July 1957): 45–55.

25. Harry Specht, "The Deprofessionalization of Social Work," *Social Work* 17 (Mar. 1972): 3–15.

26. Psychiatric social work also drew on nonpsychoanalytic theories such as behaviorism; see Virginia Robinson, *A Changing Psychology in Social Case Work* (Chapel Hill: University of North Carolina Press, 1930), pp. 83–93; Frank Bruno, *The Theory of Social Work* (New York: Heath, 1936), p. 231; S. C. Kohs, "We've Gone Psychiatric," *Survey* 64 (1930): 188–90; Scott Briar and Henry Miller, *Problems and Issues in Social Casework* (New York: Columbia University Press, 1971), p. 11. By 1930, however, variations on psychoanalytic theory had become the dominant psychiatric approach.

27. Secondary sources on the history of social work to 1933 include Allen F. Davis, *Spearheads of Reform: The Social Settlements and the Progressive Movement, 1890–1914* (New York: Oxford University Press, 1968); Robert H. Bremner, *From the Depths: The Discovery of Poverty in the United States* (New York: New York University Press, 1956); Roy Lubove, *The Professional Altruist: The Emergence of Social Work as a Career, 1880–1930* (Cambridge: Harvard University Press, 1965); and Clarke A. Chambers, *Seedtime of Reform: American Social Service and Social Action, 1918–1933* (Ann Arbor: University of Michigan Press, 1967).

28. Cited in Bremner, p. 46.

29. Cited in Daniel M. Fox, *The Discovery of Abundance: Simon N. Patten and the Transformation of Social Theory* (Ithaca, N.Y.: Cornell University Press, 1967), p. 102.

30. Davis, chap. 1.

31. Cited in Bremner, p.62.

32. Mary Kingsbury Simkhovitch, *Neighborhood: The Story of Greenwich House* (New York: Norton, 1938), p. 73.

33. Cited in Bremner, pp. 129, 130. Cf. Simon Patten, "A Programme for Social Work," in *The New Basis of Civilization* (Cambridge: Belknap Press, 1968; originally published 1907).

34. On Richmond's early career, see Muriel Warren Pumphrey, "Mary Richmond and the Rise of Professional Social Work in Baltimore," Ph.D.

diss., School of Social Work, Columbia University, 1956. Richmond's shorter writings are collected in Joanne C. Colcord, ed., *The Long View* (New York: Russell Sage Foundation, 1930).

35. Mary Richmond, *Social Diagnosis* (New York: Russell Sage Foundation, 1917).

36. Cf. Robinson, p. 38.

37. The definitive account of the mental hygiene movement is Christine Mary Shea, "The Ideology of Mental Health and the Emergence of the Therapeutic Liberal State: The American Mental Hygiene Movement, 1900–1930," Ph.D. diss., University of Illinois at Champaign-Urbana, 1980.

38. Cited in Shea, p. 156.

39. Cited in Shea, pp. 160–61.

40. E. E. Southard, "The Mental Hygiene of Industry," *Industrial Management*, Feb. 1920, also published in *Mental Hygiene* 4 (Jan. 1920): 43–64, and reprinted as *Engineering Society Reprint* (New York: Engineering Society, 1920), pp. 16–17. Also see E. E. Southard, "Trade Unionism and Temperament," *Industrial Management* (Apr. 1920), also published in *Mental Hygiene* 4 (Apr. 1920): 281–300; E. E. Southard, "The Modern Specialist in Unrest," *Industrial Management* (June 1920), also published in *Mental Hygiene* 4 (July 1920): 550–63; Mary C. Jarrett, "The Mental Health of Industry," *Mental Hygiene* 4 (Oct. 1920): 867–84; Margaret J. Powers, "The Industrial Cost of the Psychopathic Employee," *Mental Hygiene* 4 (Oct. 1920): 932–80; C. Macfie Campbell, "Mental Hygiene in Industry," *Mental Hygiene* 5 (1921): 468–78; Boyd Fisher, "Has Mental Hygiene a Practical Use in Industry?" *Mental Hygiene* 5 (1921): 479–96; Stanley Cobb, "Applications of Psychiatry to Industrial Hygiene," *Journal of Industrial Hygiene* 1 (Nov. 1919): 343–47. The uses of industrial mental hygiene at the end of the decade are summarized in V. V. Anderson, *Psychiatry in Industry* (New York: Harper, 1929), and W. V. Bingham, "Achievements of Industrial Psychology," *Mental Hygiene* 14 (1930): 369–83. Cf. Loren Baritz, *Servants of Power* (New York: Wiley, 1960).

41. Shea, pp. 208–85.

42. E. E. Southard and Mary C. Jarrett, *The Kingdom of Evils* (New York: Macmillan, 1922), p. 40.

43. Arnold Gesell, "Significance of the Nursery School," *Childhood Education* 1 (1924): 18, cited in Shea, p. 256.

44. Lawrence K. Frank, *Society as the Patient* (1948), cited in Shea, p. 257.

45. This belief is widely held. Two examples, chosen arbitrarily, are Mary L. Gottesfeld and Mary E. Pharis, *Profiles in Social Work* (New York: Human Sciences Press, 1977). chap. 1; and Carolyn Saari, "On the Place of Reality in Social and Psychoanalytic Theory," *Clinical Social Work Journal* 11, no. 1 (1983): 7–21.

46. M. J. Karpf, *The Scientific Basis of Social Work* (New York: Columbia University Press, 1931). Cf. Murray Leviner and Adeline Levine, "The More Things Change: A Case History of Child Guidance Clinics," *Journal of Social Issues* 26, no. 3 (1978): 19–34.

47. Cited in A. T. Poffenberger, "Trends in Therapy: Specific Psychological Therapies," *American Journal of Orthopsychiatry* 9 (1939): 755–60. All citations are from the *American Journal of Orthopsychiatry, 1930*.

48. Bertha C. Reynolds, *An Uncharted Journey* (New York: Citadel Press, 1963), pp. 116–19.

49. M. J. Karpf, "The Relation between Sociology and Social Work," *Social Forces* 3, no. 3 (1925): 419–27.

50. Reynolds, pp. 124–29. Cf. Miriam Van Waters, "Philosophical Trends in Modern Social Work," *Proceedings of the National Conference of Social Work, 1930* (Chicago, 1931), pp. 3–19.

51. It is for this reason that Leslie Alexander's questioning of the quantitative evidence for the "psychiatric deluge" ("Social Work's Freudian Deluge: Myth or Reality?" *Social Service Review* 46 [1972]: 517–38) is irrelevant. The point is not that the average social worker was abreast of current psychiatric thinking but rather that social work leaders could use the psychiatric approach as a means to professional status. The dominance of a psychiatric perspective among the leadership of the profession by 1930 is widely confirmed by contemporary observers. See Chapter 3, note 5 for representative references.

52. Ehrenreich and English, chap. 3; Brown, chap. 2–4; Starr, op. cit.; Rosemary Stevens, *American Medicine and the Public Interest* (New Haven: Yale University Press, 1971), chap. 3; Morris J. Vogel and Charles E. Rosenberg, eds., *The Therapeutic Revolution: Essays in the Social History of American Medicine* (Philadelphia: University of Pennsylvania Press, 1979).

53. Mary Richmond, *What Is Social Case Work?* (New York: Russell Sage Foundation, 1922), pp. 98–99, 102.

54. Cited in Lawson G. Lowery, "Trends in Therapy: Evolution, Status, and Trends," *American Journal of Orthopsychiatry* 9 (1939): 669–76.

55. Porter R. Lee and Marian Kenworthy, *Mental Hygiene and Social Work* (New York: Commonwealth Fund, 1929), p. 152.

56. Mary C. Jarrett, "The Psychiatric Thread Running through All Social Case Work," *Proceedings of the National Conference of Social Work, 1919* (Chicago, 1920), pp. 587–92.

57. Gordon Hamilton, "Theory and Practice of Social Casework," cited in Kathleen Woodroofe, *From Charity to Social Work* (London: Routledge & Kegan Paul, 1962), p. 146.

58. Nathan Ackerman (1937), cited in Philip J. Guerin, "Family Therapy: The First Twenty-Five Years," in Philip J. Guerin, ed., *Family Therapy: Theory and Practice* (New York: Gardner Press, 1976), pp. 2–22.

59. Van Waters, op. cit.

60. Jessie Taft, "The Spirit of Social Work," *Family* 9, no. 4 (1928): 103–7.

61. Cited in Lubove, p. 95.

62. Lee and Kenworthy, p. 283; Robert W. Kelso, "The Private Practice of Social Work," *Survey* 59 (1928): 767–70; Raymond Clapp, "Who Uses Social Agencies?" *Survey* 60 (1928): 221. Cf. Richard A. Cloward and Irwin Epstein,

"Private Welfare's Disengagement from the Poor," in Meyer Zald, ed., *Social Welfare Institutions* (New York: Wiley, 1965), pp. 623–44.

63. Kelso, op. cit. Also cf. *Survey* 63 (1930): 583, and Sidney Leverstein, *Private Practice in Social Casework* (New York: Columbia University Press, 1964).

64. Charlotte Towle, "Changes in the Philosophy of Social Work," *Mental Hygiene* 14 (1930): 341–68.

CHAPTER 3. *The Construction of the Welfare State*

1. Neva R. Deardorff, "Social Work as a Profession," *Social Work Yearbook, 1929* (New York: Russell Sage Foundation, 1930), pp. 435–38.

2. National Association of Social Workers, *Statistics on Demographic and Social Welfare Trends* (Washington, D.C.: NASW, 1981); Irene Farnham Conrad, "Education for Social Work," *Social Work Yearbook, 1929* (New York: Russell Sage Foundation, 1930), pp. 148–54.

3. Lula Jean Elliott, *Social Work Ethics* (New York: American Association of Social Workers, 1931); Deardorff, op. cit. Also see *Survey* 61 (1929): 779 and *Survey* 62 (1929): 101.

4. Judith Torlander, *Settlement Houses and the Great Depression* (Detroit: Wayne State University Press, 1975); Judith Ann Trolander, "The Response of Settlements to the Great Depression," *Social Work* 18, no. 5 (1973): 92–102.

5. Paul U. Kellogg and Mary Ross, "Social Work at the Golden Gate," *Survey* 62 (1929): 515–21; S. C. Kohs, "We've Gone Psychiatric," *Survey* 64 (1930): 188–90; Kathleen Ormsby Larkin, "Psychiatric Social Work," *Social Work Yearbook, 1929* (New York: Russell Sage Foundation, 1930), pp. 341–44; Roy Lubove, *The Professional Altruist: The Emergence of Social Work as a Career, 1880–1920* (Cambridge: Harvard University Press, 1965), p. 109.

6. See, for example, Bertha C. Reynolds, "Can Case Closing Be Planned as a Part of Treatment?" *Family* 12 (1931): 135–41, and Bertha C. Reynolds, "Rethinking Social Casework II," *Social Work Today* 5, no. 8 (May 1938): 5–7.

7. See Walter M. West, "Social Work as a Profession," *Social Work Yearbook, 1933* (New York: Russell Sage Foundation, 1933), pp. 492–96; Grace Marcus, "Social Case Work," *Social Work Yearbook, 1935* (New York: Russell Sage Foundation, 1935), pp. 451–58.

8. American Association of Social Workers, *Social Case Work: Generic and Specific: A Report of the Milford Conference* (New York: AASW, 1931), pp. 11–12.

9. Marcus, op. cit.; Kenneth L. M. Pray, "Symposium: The Training of the Psychiatrist IV: Training in the Social Sciences," *American Journal of Orthopsychiatry* 1 (1931): 386–90; Lawson G. Lowery, "Trends in Therapy I: Evolution, Status, and Trends," *American Journal of Orthopsychiatry* 9 (1939): 669–706; Mildred C. Scoville, "An Inquiry into the Status of Psychiatric

Social Work," *American Journal of Orthopsychiatry* 1 (1931): 145–51; Jessie Taft, "Informal Discussion," following paper presented by Edith R. Spaulding, "The Training School for Psychiatric Social Work at Smith College," *Proceedings of the National Conference of Social Work, 1919* (Chicago, 1920), p. 611.

10. American Association of Social Workers, *Social Case Work: Generic and Specific*, p. 15.

11. Ibid.

12. Lawson G. Lowery, "Some Trends in the Development of Relationships between Psychiatry and General Social Case Work," *Mental Hygiene* 10 (1926): 277–84.

13. Ernest Boulding Harper, "Shifting Emphases in Case Work: The Sociological Viewpoint," *Social Forces* 9, no. 4 (1931): 507–14.

14. Earle Edward Eubank, "Toward Professional Social Work," *Survey* 54 (1925): 362–64.

15. West, p. 494; J. B. B., "The Challenge to Social Workers," *Survey* 45 (1920): 164–66.

16. Beulah Weldon, "Training for Social Work," *Survey* 58 (1927): 510–11; Robert W. Kelso, "The Private Practice of Social Work," *Survey* 59 (1928): 767–70; report on private practice in *Survey* 63 (1930): 583. More recent reflections of the same analysis include Arnulf Pins, *Who Chooses Social Work, When, and Why* (New York: Council on Social Work Education, 1963); A. Kadushin, "The Prestige of Social Work," *Social Work* 3, no. 2 (Apr. 1958): 37–48; and George Brager and John A. Michael, "The Sex Distribution in Social Work: Causes and Consequences," *Social Casework* 50 (1969): 595–601.

17. Lillian Brandt, "The 46th National Conference," *Survey* 42 (1919): 447–52; Geddes Smith, "Behemoth Walks Again," *Survey* 56 (1926): 359–63.

18. *Survey* 41 (1919): 437, 740–46; Clarke A. Chambers, *Seedtime of Reform: American Social Service and Social Action, 1918–33* (Ann Arbor: University of Michigan Press, 1963), pp. 96–97.

19. West, pp. 493–94.

20. Eduard C. Lindemann, "The Social Worker as Statesman," *Survey Graphic* 52 (1924): 222–24, cited in Gisela Konopka, *Eduard C. Lindemann and Social Work Philosophy* (Minneapolis: University of Minnesota Press, 1958), p. 123.

21. Jane Addams, "How Much Social Work Can a Community Afford: From the Ethical Point of View," *Proceedings of the National Conference of Social Work, 1926* (Chicago: 1926), pp. 108–13.

22. For a detailed discussion of efforts at social reform in the 1920s, see Chambers, op. cit.

23. Paul U. Kellogg and Mary Ross, "New Beacons in Boston," *Survey* 64 (1930): 341–47; Torlander, op. cit.

24. Kellogg and Ross, p. 341.

25. Robert L. Heilbroner, *The Economic Transformation of America* (New York: Harcourt Brace Jovanovich, 1977), pp. 173–77.

243

26. U.S. Department of Commerce, *Historical Statistics of the United States, Colonial Times to 1970* (Washington, D.C.: U.S. Government Printing Office, 1975).

27. Hoover is cited in Gene Smith, *The Shattered Dream* (New York: Morrow, 1970), p. 15, among many other sources.

28. U.S. Department of Commerce, *Historical Statistics,* op. cit.; Art Preis, *Labor's Giant Step* (New York: Pioneer, 1964), pp. 7–8, 41.

29. On the unemployed movement, see Frances Fox Piven and Richard A. Cloward, *Poor People's Movements* (New York: Pantheon, 1977), and Irving Bernstein, *The Lean Years: A History of the American Worker, 1920–1933* (Baltimore: Penguin, 1970); Roy Rosenzweig, "Radicals and the Jobless: The Musteites and the Unemployed Leagues, 1932–36," *Labor History* 16 (Winter 1975): 52–77; Roy Rosenzweig, "Organizing the Unemployed: The Early Years of the Great Depression," *Radical America* 10 (July–Aug. 1976): 37–62.

30. Chambers, pp. 224–25.

31. Cited in *New York Times,* Mar. 4, 1983.

32. Moley is cited in David W. Noble, David A. Horowitz, and Peter N. Carroll, *Twentieth Century Limited* (Boston: Houghton Mifflin, 1980), p. 224; Cutting is cited in Arthur A. Schlesinger, Jr., *The Coming of the New Deal* (Boston: Houghton Mifflin, 1959), p. 5.

33. Tugwell is cited in Edwin Rozwenc and Thomas Bender, *The Making of American Society,* vol. II, 2d ed. (New York: Knopf, 1978), p. 348.

34. Richard Hofstadter, "Franklin D. Roosevelt: The Patrician as Opportunist," in William E. Leuchtenberg, ed., *Franklin Delano Roosevelt: A Profile* (New York: Hill & Wang, 1967), pp. 96–134. Cf. Barton J. Bernstein, "The New Deal: The Conservative Achievements of Liberal Reform," in Barton J. Bernstein, ed., *Towards a New Past* (New York: Random House, 1968), pp. 263–88.

35. Hofstadter, p. 118.

36. See John Ehrenreich, "Adding Up the Unemployed," *Nation,* July 25–Aug. 1, 1981, p. 1.

37. On the labor movement of the 1930s, see Irving Bernstein, *The Turbulent Years: A History of the American Worker, 1933–1941* (Boston: Houghton Mifflin, 1971); Walter Galenson, *The CIO Challenge to the AF of L* (Cambridge: Harvard University Press, 1960); Philip Taft, *The AF of L from the Death of Gompers to the Merger* (New York: Octagon Books, 1970); Preis, op. cit.; Joel Seidman, *American Labor from Defense to Reconversion* (Chicago: University of Chicago Press, 1953); Richard O. Boyer and Herbert M. Morais, *Labor's Untold Story* (New York: United Electrical Workers, 1955). On Republic Steel's arsenal, labor spies, and so on, cf. Seidman, pp. 17–18; Boyer and Morais, pp. 278–81 and 312–13; Galenson, pp. 129–30.

38. Preis, pp. 41–42.

39. Olson and the La Follettes are cited in Rozwenc and Bender, pp. 358–59.

40. On Long see Hugh D. Graham, *Huey Long* (Englewood Cliffs, N.J.: Prentice-Hall, 1970); on Townsend, see Abraham Holtzman, *The Townsend Movement* (New York: Octagon Books, 1975).

41. Richard Hofstadter, *The Age of Reform* (New York: Vintage, 1960), p. 308.

42. Jacob Fisher, *The Response of Social Work to the Depression* (Boston: Hall, 1980), p. 120; Rozwenc and Bender, pp. 369–70; Henry L. Allen, "A Radical Critique of Federal Work and Manpower Programs, 1933–74," in Betty Reid Mandell, ed., *Welfare in America* (Englewood Cliffs, N.J.: Prentice-Hall, 1975), pp. 23–38; Raymond Wolters, *Negroes and the Great Depression* (Westport, Conn.: Greenwood Press, 1970).

CHAPTER 4. *The Crisis in Social Work, 1929–1945*

1. Cited by Jeanette G. Glassberg, "The Social Environment of Casework," *Family* 12 (June 1931): 108–10.

2. *Compass*, Dec. 1930, cited in "Editorial," *Family* 11 (Feb. 1931): 324.

3. *Compass* 14 (1) (Sept. 1932): 1–2.

4. Florence Hollis, "The Function of a Family Society," *Family* 12 (Oct. 1931): 186–91.

5. Grace L. Coyle, "Social Workers and Social Action," *Survey*, May 1937, reprinted in Fern Lowry, ed., *Readings in Social Casework* (New York: Columbia University Press, 1939), pp. 565–68.

6. *Compass* 13 (May 1932): 2.

7. June Purcell Guild, "Is Social Work Socially Immoral?" *Social Forces* 10, no. 1 (Oct. 1931): 49–53.

8. Gordon Hamilton, "Refocusing Family Casework," *Proceedings of the National Conference of Social Work, 1931*, reprinted in Lowry, pp. 81–98, and *Family* 12 (Oct. 1931): 174–83.

9. Cited by Jacob Fisher, *The Response of Social Work to the Depression* (Boston: Hall, 1980), p. 7.

10. Leroy A. Ramsdell, "The New Deal in Social Work," *Family* 14 (Oct. 1930): 191–92.

11. "A Letter to President Roosevelt," *Compass* 15 (May 1934): 1–2.

12. Gertrude Springer, "Rising to a New Challenge," *Survey* 70, no. 6 (June 1934): 179–80.

13. Mary Van Kleeck, "Our Illusions Concerning Government," *Proceedings of the National Conference of Social Work, 1934* (Chicago, 1934), pp. 284–303.

14. Mary Van Kleeck, "The Common Goals of Labor and Social Work," *Proceedings of the National Conference of Social Work, 1934* (Chicago, 1934), pp. 284–303.

15. Springer, p. 179.

16. William Hodson, "The Social Worker in the New Deal," *Proceedings of the National Conference of Social Work, 1934* (Chicago, 1934), pp. 3–12.

17. Springer, p. 180.

18. Frank Bruno, *Trends in Social Work* (New York: Columbia University Press, 1948), p. 300.

19. Cited in Rick Spano, *The Rank and File Movement in Social Work* (Washington, D.C.: University Press of America, 1982), p. 156.

20. Stuart A. Queen, "What Is Unemployment Doing to Family Social Work?" *Family* 12 (Feb. 1932): 299–301.

21. Hamilton, op. cit.

22. Walter West, "Social Work as a Profession," *Social Work Yearbook, 1933* (New York: Russell Sage Foundation, 1933), pp. 492–96; Russell H. Kurtz, "Unemployment Relief," *Social Work Yearbook, 1935* (New York: Russell Sage Foundation, 1935), pp. 519–28; Walter M. West, "Social Work as a Profession," *Social Work Yearbook, 1935* (New York: Russell Sage Foundation, 1935), pp. 479–86.

23. Rachel Childrey, "Professional Protection for the Social Worker," *Compass* 16 (June 1935): 13–18.

24. Dorothy C. Kahn, "Professional Standards in Social Work," *Compass* 16 (June 1935): 1–5.

25. West, 1935, pp. 479–86.

26. Stanley P. Davies, "The Professional Influence in Social Work," *Compass* 15 (June 1934): 7–9.

27. Helen I. Clark, "The Future of the Emergency Workers," *Compass* 14 (Oct. 1932): 3.

28. "A Plan for Provisional Membership," *Compass* 16 (Sept. 1934): 5–6; "Provisional Recognition in Social Work," *Compass* 16 (Oct. 1934): 7–8; "AASW Drops Associate Membership Requirement," *Social Work Today* 2, no. 3 (Jan. 1935): 6.

29. My account draws heavily on Spano, op. cit.; Fisher, op. cit.; Bertha C. Reynolds, *An Uncharted Journey* (New York: Citadel Press, 1963), chap. 10; Joseph H. Levy, "New Forms of Organization among Social Workers," *Social Work Today* 2, no. 1 (Oct. 1934): 10–12; and on the accounts of rank-and-file ideas and activity in the rank-and-file movement's journal, *Social Work Today* (1934–42).

30. *Compass* 19 (June 1938): suppl., p. 15; Spano, p. 215; Jacob Fisher, "Trade Unionism in Social Work," *Social Work Yearbook, 1939* (New York: Russell Sage Foundation, 1939), pp. 437–40.

31. New York Discussion Club, "The Case for the Practitioners Movement," *Compass* 15 (Oct. 1933): 4–5; cf. Levy, op. cit.; "A Glossary for Rank and Filers: 'AASW,' " *Social Work Today* 3, no. 2 (Nov. 1935): 19–20.

32. Fisher, *Reponse of Social Work,* p. 119. Fisher was the first editor of *Social Work Today.*

33. Eduard C. Lindemann, "The Future of Social Work," *Social Work Today* 1, no. 2 (July 1934): 14–15, cited in Spano, p. 82; "A Glossary for Rank and Filers: 'Professionalism,' " *Social Work Today* 3, no. 4 (Jan. 1936): 24.

34. "AASW Examines the Dawson Report," *Social Work Today* 2, no. 4 (Feb. 1935): 25–27; Reynolds, pp. 338–39.

35. Grace Marcus, "The Status of Social Casework Today," *Compass* 16, no. 9 (June 1935): 5–12.

36. Fisher, *Response of Social Work*, pp. 112–13; cf. Jacob Fisher, "The Rank and File Challenge," *Social Work Today* 2, no. 5 (April 1935): 5–8.

37. "More About Casework," *Social Work Today* 2, no. 4 (Feb. 1935): 130; also cf. Fisher, *Response of Social Work,*p. 120.

38. Dorothy C. Kahn, "Professional Standards in Social Work," *Compass* 16, no. 9 (June 1935): 1–5.

39. Grace Marcus, "The Status of Social Casework Today," *Compass* 16, no. 9 (June 1935): 5–12.

40. Porter Lee, "A Critical Period in Education for Social Work," *Bulletin of the New York School of Social Work*, Oct. 1934, reprinted in Porter Lee, *Social Work as Cause and Function* (New York: Columbia University Press, 1937), pp. 201–14; also see citations in Fisher, *Response of Social Work*, p. 168.

41. Spano, p. 156, citing *Social Work Today* 5, no. 4 (Jan. 1938): 5–7.

42. Bertha C. Reynolds, "Rethinking Social Casework," Part I: *Social Work Today* 5, no. 7 (April 1938): 5–7; Part II: *Social Work Today* 5, no. 8 (May 1938): 5–7, Part III: *Social Work Today* 5, no. 9 (June 1938): 5–8.

43. "Meeting Social Need: A Peaceful Program," *Social Work Today* 7, no. 1 (Jan. 1940): 5–6; Celia Antopolsky Neiman, "The Caseworker in a Changing World," *Social Work Today* 8, no. 3 (Dec. 1940): 21–24.

44. Virginia Robinson, "Is Unionization Compatible with Social Work?" *Compass* 18, no. 8 (May 1937): 5–9. Other erstwhile targets of the rank-and-file movement who wrote for *Social Work Today* after 1938 included Gordon Hamilton, Katherine Lenroot, and Florence Perkins.

45. Linton Swift, "Our Problems of Today in the Light of Our Past and Future" (presidential address, American Association of Social Workers), *Compass* 19, nos. 10 and 11 (July–Aug. 1938): 5–7.

46. See, for example, Earle Edward Eubank, "Some Contributions of Sociological Theory to Social Work," *Social Forces* 7, no. 4 (June 1929): 486–94; Ada E. Sheffield, "The 'Situation' as the Unit of Family Case Study," *Social Forces* 9, no. 4 (June 1931): 465–74; Gordon Hamilton, "The Underlying Philosophy of Social Casework," *Family* 23 (July 1941): 139; Ernest Bouldin Harper, "Shifting Emphases in Case Work: The Sociological Viewpoint," *Social Forces* 9, no. 4 (June 1931): 507–14.

47. Virginia Robinson, *A Changing Psychology in Social Case Work* (Chapel Hill: University of North Carolina Press, 1930).

48. Bertha C. Reynolds, "A Changing Psychology in Social Case Work" (review), *Family* 12 (June 1931): 135–42.

49. Mary L. Gottesfeld and Mary E. Pharis, *Profiles in Social Work* (New York: Human Services Press, 1977), p. 109.

50. The fully developed "functional school" position is described in Ruth

Smalley, "The Functional Approach to Casework Practice," in Robert W. Roberts and Robert H. Nee, eds., *Theories of Social Casework* (Chicago: University of Chicago Press, 1970), pp. 77–128; for the "diagnostic school" position see Florence Hollis, "The Psychosocial Approach to the Practice of Casework," in Roberts and Nee, pp. 33–75. Other useful summaries of the controversy, from several different perspectives, appear in *A Comparison of Diagnostic and Functional Casework Concepts* (New York: Family Service Association of America, 1950); Alan Keith-Lucas, "The Political Theory Implicit in Social Casework Theory," *American Political Science Review* 47 (Dec. 1953): 1076–91; Reynolds, *Uncharted Journey*, chaps. 9 and 10; Scott Briar and Henry Miller, *Problems and Issues in Social Casework* (New York: Columbia University Press, 1971), chaps. 1 and 3. Also see references in notes 51–60.

51. Jessie Taft, "The Relation of Function to Process in Social Case Work," *Journal of Social Work Process* 1 (Nov. 1937):3, reprinted in Virginia Robinson, ed., *Training for Skill in Social Case Work* (Philadelphia: University of Pennsylvania Press, 1942), pp. 100–16; Virginia Robinson, "The Meaning of Skill," in Robinson, *Training for Skill*, pp. 7–31; Jessie Taft, "The Function of the Personality Course in the Practice Unit," in Robinson, *Training for Skill*, pp. 55–74.

52. Robinson, *Training for Skill*, pp. 100–16.

53. Ibid., p. 101.

54. Ibid., pp. 101–2.

55. Ibid., p. 104.

56. Ibid., p. 108.

57. Ibid.

58. Ibid., pp. 61–62.

59. Ibid., p. 63.

60. Ibid., pp. 64–66.

61. For an alternative statement of this position, see Robinson, "Meaning of Skill."

62. Hamilton, "Underlying Philosophy." Also cf. Gordon Hamilton, "Basic Concepts in Social Casework," *Family* 18 (July 1937): 147–55.

63. Kenneth L. M. Pray, "The Agency's Role in Service," in Robinson, *Training for Skill*, pp. 117–26.

64. Hamilton, "Underlying Philosophy."

65. Ibid.; Gordon Hamilton, *Theory and Practice of Social Casework* (New York: Columbia University Press, 1940).

66. Helen Ross and Adelaide M. Johnson, "The Growing Science of Casework," *Journal of Social Casework* 27, no. 7 (Nov. 1946), pp. 273–78, reprinted in Cora Kasius, ed., *Principles and Techniques in Social Case Work* (New York: Family Service Association of America, 1950), pp. 48–57.

67. Lucille Austin, "Trends in Differential Treatment in Social Casework," *Journal of Social Casework* 29 (June 1948): 203–11.

68. Grace Marcus, *The Nature of Service in Public Assistance Administration*

(Washington, D.C.: Federal Security Agency, 1947), cited in Keith-Lucas, p. 1084.

69. Hollis, op. cit.

70. Lionel C. Lane, "The 'Aggressive' Approach to Preventive Casework with Children's Problems," *Social Casework* 33 (Feb. 1952): 61–66, cited in Keith-Lucas, op. cit.

71. Dorothy Hutchinson, "Reexamination of Some Aspects of Casework Practice in Adoption," *Child Welfare League of America Bulletin* 25 (Nov. 1946): 4–7, 14, cited in Keith-Lucas, op. cit.

72. Smalley, pp. 80–81.

73. Hollis, p. 57.

74. Florence Hollis, *Social Casework in Practice* (New York: Family Welfare Association of America, 1939), cited in Keith-Lucas, pp. 1085–86.

75. Gordon Hamilton, "Helping People: The Growth of a Profession" (1948), cited in Keith-Lucas, p. 1086, reprinted in Kasius, p. 89.

76. On the penetration of ego concepts into social work, see Helen Harris Perlman, "The Basic Structure of the Case-Work Process," *Social Service Review* 27 (Sept. 1953): 308–15 (which also notes the "parallel formulation" of the functional school); Cora Kasius, ed., *Social Casework in the Fifties* (New York: Family Service Association, 1962); Lucille N. Austin, "Trends in Differential Treatment in Social Casework," *Journal of Social Casework* 20, no. 6 (June 1948): 203–11; Grace F. Marcus, "Family Casework in 1948," *Family* 29, no. 7 (July 1948): 261–70 (who also notes the convergence of Freudian and Rankian ideas on the ego); Gordon Hamilton, "A Theory of Personality: Freud's Contribution to Social Work," in Howard J. Parad, ed., *Ego Psychology and Dynamic Casework* (New York: Family Service Association, 1958), pp. 11–37; Annette Garrett, "Modern Casework: The Contribution of Ego Psychology," in Parad, pp. 38–52; Isabelle L. Stamm, "Ego Psychology in the Emerging Theoretical Base of Casework," in Alfred J. Kahn, ed., *Issues in American Social Work* (New York: Columbia University Press, 1959), pp. 80–109; Bernice Simon, "Social Casework Theory: An Overview," in Roberts and Nee, pp. 353–94. On the convergence of Rogerian and existential psychology with functional school ideas, see Helen Harris Perlman, "The Problem-Solving Model in Social Casework," in Roberts and Nee, pp. 129–79; and interview with Florence Hollis in Gottesfeld and Pharis, p. 140.

77. For Rank's own ideas (the basis of the functional school, although by no means identical to it), see *Will Therapy* (New York: Norton, 1968).

78. For example, see Joel Kovel, *A Complete Guide to Therapy* (New York: Pantheon, 1976), p. 88 (although Kovel does, in passing, note Rank's influence on Carl Rogers and on social work).

79. For example, the dialectic of infantile separation and attachment, often now associated with the works of Margaret Mahler, is a major Rankian concern; while the centrality of the therapist–client relationship, the emphasis on strengthening client ego functions, the therapeutic use of "termina-

tion," and the use of time-limited (i.e., short- and medium-term) therapy, all central components of many current models of casework intervention, were major characteristics of the functional school.

CHAPTER 5. *Social Policy in the Affluent Society, 1945–1960*

1. Statistics in this chapter, unless otherwise noted, are from U.S. Department of Commerce, *Historical Statistics of the United States, Colonial Times to 1970* (Washington, D.C.: U.S. Government Printing Office, 1976); U.S. Department of Commerce, *Statistical Abstract of the United States* (Washington, D.C.: U.S. Government Printing Office, various dates); *Statistics on Demographic and Social Welfare Trends* (Washington, D.C.: National Association of Social Workers, 1980).

2. Joel Seidman, *American Labor From Defense to Reconversion* (Chicago: University of Chicago Press, 1953); Art Preis, *Labor's Giant Step* (New York: Pioneer, 1964), chap. 5.

3. On the Red Scare, see David Caute, *The Great Fear* (New York: Simon & Schuster, 1978).

4. The Red Scare in the unions is discussed in Caute, pp. 349–463. On the case of the United Electrical Workers, see James J. Matles and James Higgins, *Them and Us* (Englewood Cliffs, N.J.: Prentice-Hall, 1974) and Stanley Aronowitz, *False Promises* (New York: McGraw-Hill, 1973).

5. John Kenneth Galbraith, *The Affluent Society* (Boston: Houghton Mifflin, 1958), pp. 340–50. Cf. Lewis A. Coser, "The Sociology of Poverty," *Social Problems* 13, no. 2 (1965): 141.

6. Michael Harrington, *The Other America: Poverty in the United States* (New York: Macmillan, 1962).

7. Frances Fox Piven and Richard A. Cloward, *Regulating the Poor: The Functions of Public Welfare* (New York: Vintage, 1971), pp. 123–80.

8. Ibid., pp. 218–19.

9. On the impact of urban renewal, see Jewel Bellush and Murray Hansknecht, ed., *Urban Renewal: People, Politics, and Planning* (Garden City, N.Y.: Doubleday, 1967); James Q. Wilson, ed., *Urban Renewal: The Record and the Controversy* (Cambridge: M.I.T. Press, 1966); Robert C. Weaver, *The Urban Complex* (Garden City, N.Y.: Doubleday Anchor, 1966).

10. Kenneth R. Schneider, *Autokind vs. Mankind* (New York: Schocken, 1972); Ed Cray, *Chrome Colossus* (New York: McGraw-Hill, 1980), pp. 129–30, 345–46, 356–60; Marty Jezer, *The Dark Ages: Life in the United States 1945–1960* (Boston: South End Press, 1982), pp. 138–46.

11. Paul M. Sweezy, "Cars and Cities," *Monthly Review* 24, no. 11 (April 1973): 1–18.

12. Quoted in *The Cleveland Papers* (Cleveland, Ohio: Electric Illuminating Co., 1971).

13. Sheila Tobias and Lisa Anderson, "What Really Happened to Rosie

the Riveter?—Demobilization and the Female Labor Force, 1944–47," in Linda K. Ferber and Jane DeHart Mathews, eds., *Women's America* (New York: Oxford University Press, 1982).

14. Henry L. Allen, "A Radical Critique of Federal Work and Manpower Programs, 1933–74," in Betty Reid Mandell, ed., *Welfare in America* (Englewood Cliffs, N.J.: Prentice-Hall, 1975), p. 36.

15. For a discussion of the economic modernization of the South and its consequences, see Harold M. Baron, "The Demand for Black Labor," *Radical America* 5 (March–April 1971): 1–46; Piven and Cloward, pp. 200–45; Frances Fox Piven and Richard A. Cloward, *Poor People's Movements* (New York: Vintage, 1979), pp. 181–211; Karl E. Taueber and Alma F. Taueber, *Negroes in Cities* (New York: Atheneum, 1969); Jezer, pp. 154–75.

16. Piven and Cloward, *Regulating the Poor*, pp. 250–56; Piven and Cloward, *Poor People's Movements*, pp. 195–202, 213–18, 225–28.

17. Richard A. Cloward and Lloyd E. Ohlin, *Delinquency and Opportunity: A Theory of Delinquent Gangs* (New York: Free Press, 1960). Cloward and Ohlin also review much of the earlier literature.

18. Robert H. Felix, *Mental Illness: Progress and Prospects* (New York: Columbia University Press, 1967); Robert Castel, Françoise Castel, and Anne Lovell, *The Psychiatric Society* (New York: Columbia University Press, 1982), chaps. 3–5; Joel Kovel, "The American Mental Health Industry," in David Ingleby, ed., *Critical Psychiatry: The Politics of Mental Health* (New York: Pantheon, 1980), pp. 72–101. Kovel, in particular, discusses the reasons for the increase in real or apparent mental illness in the postwar years.

19. Felix, pp. 67–68.

20. C. Wright Mills, *The Sociological Imagination* (New York: Oxford University Press, 1959), esp. pp. 3–11.

21. Cf. Aronowitz, pp. 323–94.

22. See Howard Zinn, *SNCC: The New Abolitionists* (Boston: Beacon Press, 1965); Howell Raines, *My Soul Is Rested* (New York: Putnam, 1977); Clayborne Carson, *In Struggle: SNCC and the Black Awakening of the 1960s* (Cambridge, Mass.: Harvard University Press, 1981); Lester A. Sobel, ed., *Civil Rights, 1960–66* (New York: Facts on File, 1967); Anthony Lewis, *Portrait of a Decade* (New York: Random House, 1964); Piven and Cloward, *Poor People's Movements*, pp. 181–263.

23. Richard A. Cloward and Frances Fox Piven, "Rent Strike: Disrupting the Slum System," *New Republic*, Dec. 2, 1967, reprinted in Cloward and Piven, *The Politics of Turmoil* (New York: Pantheon, 1972); *Report of the National Advisory Commission on Civil Disorders* (New York: Bantam, 1968), pp. 35–36; C. Eric Lincoln, *The Black Muslims in America* (Boston: Beacon Press, 1963); E. U. Essien-Udom, *Black Nationalism* (New York: Dell, 1964); *The Autobiography of Malcolm X* (New York: Grove Press, 1966); Floyd B. Barbour, ed., *The Black Power Revolt* (Boston: Sargent, 1968); Stokely Carmichael and Charles V. Hamilton, *Black Power* (New York: Vintage, 1967); Lewis, op. cit.; Arthur Waskow, *From Race Riot to Sit-In* (Garden City, N.Y.:

Doubleday, 1966), pp. 239–46; Massimo Teodori, ed., *The New Left* (Indianapolis: Bobbs-Merrill, 1969), documents and references, pp. 128–49.

CHAPTER 6. *Kennedy, Johnson, and the Great Society*

1. Frances Fox Piven and Richard A. Cloward, *Poor People's Movements* (New York: Vintage, 1979), p. 244; Frances Fox Piven and Richard A. Cloward, *Regulating the Poor* (New York: Vintage, 1971), pp. 222–84; Edwin Rozwenc and Thomas Bender, *The Making of American Society* (New York: Knopf, 1978), vol. II, p. 555.

2. Piven and Cloward, *Poor People's Movements*, p. 244.

3. On the poverty program as a response to the civil rights movement, in addition to references in note 1, see John C. Donovan, *The Politics of Poverty* (New York: Pegasus, 1967), pp. 22–23, and Mitchell Sviridoff, "Contradictions in Community Action," *Psychiatry and Social Service Review* 2, no. 10 (Oct. 1968): 4–7.

4. James L. Sundquist, "Origins of the War on Poverty," in James L. Sundquist, ed., *On Fighting Poverty: Perspectives from Experience* (New York: Basic Books, 1969), pp. 6–33.

5. Oscar Lewis, *Children of Sanchez* (New York: Random House, 1961), Introduction.

6. Michael Harrington, *The Other America: Poverty in the United States* (New York: Macmillan, 1962).

7. Daniel Patrick Moynihan, "The Negro Family," reprinted in Lee Rainwater and William Yancey, eds., *The Moynihan Report and the Politics of Controversy* (Cambridge: M.I.T. Press, 1967).

8. A number of comments are in Rainwater and Yancey, op. cit. Also see Eleanor Burke Leacock, ed., *The Culture of Poverty: A Critique* (New York: Simon & Schuster, 1971); William A. Ryan, *Blaming the Victim* (New York: Vintage, 1976); Eliot Liebow, *Tally's Corner* (Boston: Little, Brown, 1967); Carol Stack, *All Our Kin* (New York: Harper, 1974); Hyman Rodman, "The Lower-Class Value Stretch," *Social Forces* 42, no. 2 (Dec. 1963): 205–15; Stephen M. Rose, *The Betrayal of the Poor* (Cambridge, Mass.: Schenkman, 1972), chap. 3; Herbert G. Gutman, *The Black Family in Slavery and Freedom, 1750–1925* (New York: Pantheon, 1976); Charles A. Valentine, *Culture and Poverty* (Chicago: University of Chicago Press, 1968). A recent reflection of the controversy, among black thinkers and organizations, is reported in the *New York Times*, May 3 and May 7, 1984.

9. On the way in which these theories were understood by the planners of the poverty program, see Peter Marris and Martin Rein, *Dilemmas of Social Reform: Poverty and Community Action in the United States* (New York: Atherton Press, 1967), pp. 37–44; Rose, pp. 82–122; Daniel Patrick Moynihan, "The Professors and the Poor," *Commentary* (1968), reprinted in Daniel Patrick Moynihan, *Maximum Feasible Misunderstanding: Community Action in the*

War on Poverty (New York: Free Press, 1969); John G. Wofford, "The Politics of Local Responsibility: Administration of the Community Action Program," pp. 70–102, Adam Yarmolinsky, "The Beginnings of OEO," pp. 34–51, Sanford A. Kravitz, "The Community Action Program—Past, Present, and Its Future?" pp. 52–69, in Sundquist, *On Fighting Poverty.*

10. Yarmolinsky, p. 36.

11. For a critical survey of the major programs, see Sar A. Levitan and Robert Taggart, *The Promise of Greatness* (Cambridge: Harvard University Press, 1976), and Sar A. Levitan, *The Great Society's Poor Law* (Baltimore: Johns Hopkins University Press, 1969).

12. Cited in Donovan, p. 40.

13. On the role of community protest in defining "maximum feasible participation," see Wofford, pp. 80–81; Marris and Rein, pp. 216–18; Kravitz, pp. 62–64. A much more critical view of "maximum feasible participation" (from the left) can be found in Joel Blau, "The Consent of the Served: Some Notes on the Literature of Citizen Participation," *Catalyst* 2, no. 1 (1980): 71–78.

14. Donovan, p. 35.

15. Piven and Cloward, *Regulating the Poor,* pp. 270–71.

16. Sargent Shriver, "Poverty in the United States—What Next?" *Social Welfare Forum, 1963* (New York: National Conference on Social Welfare, 1963), pp. 55–66.

17. On "sociotherapy," see articles by Wittenberg, Fishman and Solomon, Brager, and the editors' introduction in Frank Riessman, Jerome Cohen, and Arthur Pearl, eds., *Mental Health of the Poor* (New York: Free Press, 1964): and Martin Rein, "Social Work in Search of a Radical Profession," *Social Work* 15, no. 2 (April 1970): 13–28.

18. *Youth and the Ghetto* (New York: Harlem Youth Opportunities Unlimited, 1964), pp. 36, 371–72.

19. Cited in Marris and Rein, p. 49.

20. T. Kahn, "Unfinished Revolution" (pamphlet, 1960), cited in Jacob R. Fishman and Frederick Solomon, "Youth and Social Action: Perspectives on the Sit-In Movement," in Riessman, Cohen, and Pearl, pp. 400–11.

21. Fishman and Solomon, op. cit.

22. For other examples, see Henry Gottesfeld and Gerterlyn Dozier, "Changes in Feelings of Powerlessness in a Community Action Project," *Psychological Reports* 19 (1966): 978; Louis A. Zurcher, Jr., "The Poverty Board: Some Consequences of 'Maximum Feasible Participation,' " *Journal of Social Issues* 26, no. 3 (1970): 85–107; Charles Silberman, *Crisis in Black and White* (New York: Vintage, 1964), pp. 157–59. On similar impacts of participation in the women's liberation movement, see Carol Hamisch, "The Personal Is Political," in *Notes from the Second Year: Women's Liberation* (New York: n.p., 1970), A dissenting view is Barbara Susan, "About My Consciousness Raising," in Leslie B. Tanner, ed., *Voices from Women's Liberation* (New York: New American Library, 1970), pp. 238–43.

23. Shriver, p. 59.
24. For example, Marris and Rein, pp. 58–70.
25. Sviridoff, p. 4.
26. Charles F. Grosser and Edward V. Sparer, "Legal Services for the Poor: Social Work and Social Justice," *Social Work* 11, no. 1 (Jan. 1966): 81–87; Piven and Cloward, *Regulating the Poor,* pp. 306–9; National Advisory Council on Economic Opportunity, *Final Report* (Washington, D.C.: National Advisory Council, 1981), pp. 91–101; Levitan and Taggart, chap. 6.
27. Arthur Pearl and Frank Riessman, *New Careers for the Poor: The Non-Professional in Human Services* (New York: Free Press, 1965); George Brager, "The Indigenous Worker: A New Approach to the Social Work Technician," *Social Work* 10 no. 2 (Apr. 1965): 33–40; Felice Perlmutter and Dorothy Durham, "Using Teenagers to Supplement Casework Service," *Social Work* 10, no. 2 (Apr. 1965): 41–46; Frank Riessman, "The 'Helper' Therapy Principle," *Social Work* 10, no. 2 (Apr. 1965): 27–32; Bertram M. Beck, "Wanted Now: Social Work Associates," *Social Welfare Forum, 1963* (New York: National Conference on Social Welfare, 1963), pp. 195–205; Francine Sobey, *The Non-Professional Revolution in Mental Health* (New York: Columbia University Press, 1970); Charles Grosser, William E. Henry, and James G. Kelley, eds., *Non-Professionals in the Human Services* (San Francisco: Jossey-Bass, 1969), esp. B. M. Beck's "Non-Professional Social Work Personnel."
28. Barbara Ehrenreich and John Ehrenreich, *The American Health Empire* (New York: Random House, 1970), chap. 18; Seymour R. Kaplan and Melvin Roman, *The Organization and Delivery of Mental Health Services in the Ghetto: The Lincoln Hospital Experience* (New York: Praeger, 1973).
29. Wofford, p. 73.
30. Cited in James Lieby, *A History of Social Welfare and Social Work in the United States* (New York: Columbia University Press, 1978), p. 332. Also see Robert Castel, Françoise Castel, and Anne Lovell, *The Psychiatric Society* (New York: Columbia University Press, 1982), pp. 124–69; Ehrenreich and Ehrenreich, chap. 6; Health Policy Advisory Center, *Evaluation of Community Involvement in Community Mental Health Centers* (Rockwell, Md.: National Institute of Mental Health, 1970); Felice Perlmutter and Herbert A. Silverman, "Community Mental Health Centers: A Structural Anachronism," *Social Work* 17, no. 2 (Mar. 1972): 78–85.
31. Ehrenreich and Ehrenreich, chaps. 4 and 5; "Neighborhood Health Centers," *Health PAC Bulletin,* no. 42 (June 1972): 1; "NENA: Community Control in a Bind," *Health PAC Bulletin,* no. 42 (June 1972): 3–12.
32. Rose, pp. 123–60; Camille Lambert, Jr., and Leah R. Lambert, "Impact of Poverty Funds on Voluntary Agencies," *Social Work* 15, no. 2 (Apr. 1970): 53–61.
33. Marris and Rein, pp. 58–70.
34. Donovan, pp. 54–57; Wofford, pp. 98–99.
35. James L. Sundquist, "The End of the Experiment," in Sundquist, pp. 235–51.

36. Donovan, pp. 117–20.

37. National Advisory Council on Economic Opportunity, *Final Report,* p. 36; "Poverty Rate Rose to 15% in '82, Highest Level since Mid-1960s," *New York Times,* Aug. 8, 1983, p. A-1.

38. National Advisory Council on Economic Opportunity, *Final Report,* p. 38.

39. Nathan Glazer, "The Limits of Social Policy," *Commentary* 52, no. 3 (Sept. 1971): 51–58. The Moynihan "benign neglect" speech is reported in the *New York Times,* Mar. 1, 1970, p. A-1.

40. Frances Fox Piven and Richard A. Cloward, *The New Class War* (New York: Pantheon, 1982), p. 118.

41. Ibid. Also see Frank Ackerman, *Reaganomics: Rhetoric vs. Reality* (Boston: South End Press, 1982). For statements from Reagan advisers, see Martin Anderson, *Welfare* (Palo Alto, Calif.: Hoover Institution Press, 1978); George Gilder, *Wealth and Poverty* (New York: Basic Books, 1981); William Greider, "The Education of David Stockman," *Atlantic* 248 (Dec. 1981): 27–40.

CHAPTER 7. *A House Divided: The Second Crisis in Social Work, 1960–1980*

1. Bertha C. Reynolds, *An Uncharted Journey* (New York: Citadel Press, 1963), p. 277, and chaps. 17 and 19.

2. Mary Antoinette Cannon, "Guiding Motives in Social Work," in Cora Kasius, ed., *New Directions in Social Work* (New York: Harper, 1954), p. 27.

3. Julia Hall, "Status and Social Change," *Social Work* 9, no. 4 (Oct. 1963): 107–8.

4. Richard Cloward and Irwin Epstein, "Private Welfare's Disengagement from the Poor: The Case of Family Adjustment Agencies," in Meyer N. Zald, ed., *Social Welfare Institutions* (New York: Wiley, 1965), pp. 623–43.

5. Murray Levine and Adeline Levine, "The More Things Change: A Case History of Child Guidance Clinics," *Journal of Social Issues* 26, no. 3 (1970): 19–34.

6. Sidney Levenstein, *Private Practice in Social Casework* (New York: Columbia University Press, 1964).

7. Ibid; Shirley A. Reece, "Social Work Practice: An Exploratory Study," *Social Work* 6, no. 3 (July 1961): 59–67; Josephine Peek and Charlotte Plotkin, "Social Caseworkers in Private Practice," *Smith College Studies in Social Work* 21, no. 5 (June 1951): 165–97; Michael Cohen, "Some Characteristics of Social Workers in Private Practice," *Social Work* 11, no. 2 (Apr. 1966): 69–77; Max Siporin, "Private Practice of Social Work: Functional Role and Social Control," *Social Work* 6, no. 2 (Apr. 1961): 52–60; Sherman Merle, "Some Arguments against Private Practice," *Social Work* 7, no. 1 (Jan. 1962): 12–17; Carl M. Shafer, "The Family Agency and the Private Casework Practitioner," *Social Casework* 40, no. 10 (Dec. 1959): 531–38; Ruth Fizdale, "Formalizing the

Relationship between Private Practitioners and Social Agencies," *Social Casework* 40, no. 10 (Dec. 1959): 539–44; Sydney Koret, "The Social Worker in Private Practice," *Social Work* 3, no. 3 (July 1958): 11–17; letters in *Social Work* 7, no. 2 (Apr. 1962): 94–101; "Statement on Private Practice of Social Work," *N*[ational] *A*[ssociation of] *S*[ocial] *W*[ork] *News* 4, no. 3 (May 1959): 2–3.

8. Fernando G. Torgenson, "Differentiating and Defining Casework and Psychotherapy," *Social Work* 7, no. 2 (Apr. 1962): 35–35. On the penetration of ego psychology into social work theory and practice, see Chapter 4, note 76.

9. Ernest Greenwood, "Attributes of a Profession," *Social Work* 2, no. 3 (July 1957): 45–55.

10. Eveline Burns, "Social Action and the Professional Social Worker," *Compass* 29, no. 4 (May 1942): 37; Helen Harris Perlman, cited in Helen Harris Perlman, "Social Work Method: A Review of the Past Decade," *Social Work* 10, no. 4 (Oct. 1965), supp.: 166–78; Hyman J. Weiner, "Towards Techniques for Social Change," *Social Work* 6, no. 2 (Apr. 1961): 26–35; Charles Frankel, "Obstacles to Action for Human Welfare," *Social Welfare Forum, 1961* (New York: National Conference on Social Welfare, 1961), pp. 271–82. Also cf. Alvin L. Schorr, "The Retreat to the Technician," *Social Work* 4, no. 1 (January 1959): 29–33; Herbert Bisno, "How Social Will Social Work Be?" *Social Work* 1, no. 2 (Apr. 1956): 12–18; Lloyd Ohlin, "Conformity in American Society Today," *Social Work* 3, no. 2 (April 1958): 58–66; Alan D. Wade, "Social Work and Political Action," *Social Work* 8, no. 4 (Oct. 1963): 3–10; Nathan Cohen, "Social Conscience and Social Work," *Social Welfare Forum, 1963* (New York: National Conference on Social Welfare, 1963), pp. 128–42; Benjamin E. Youngdahl, "Social Work at a Cross-roads," *Social Work Journal* 34, no. 3 (July 1953): 11.

11. Marion K. Sanders, "Social Work: A Profession Chasing Its Tail," *Harpers*, March 1957, pp. 56–62.

12. Peter Marris and Martin Rein, *Dilemmas of Social Reform: Poverty and Community Action in the United States* (New York: Atherton Press, 1967), pp. 14–32; George Brager, "Organizing the Unaffiliated in a Low-Income Area," *Social Work* 8, no. 2 (Apr. 1963): 34–40; George A. Brager and Francis F. Purcell, eds., *Community Action Against Poverty: Readings from the Mobilization Experience* (New Haven: College and University Press, 1967).

13. Samuel Mencher, "Two Nations or One-Third of a Nation," *Social Work* 8, no. 1 (Jan. 1963): 111–12.

14. R[obert] M[orris], "Editor's Page," *Social Work* 9, no. 1 (Jan. 1964): 2 and *Social Work* 9, no. 2 (Apr. 1964): 2.

15. Stephen M. Rose, *The Betrayal of the Poor* (Cambridge, Mass.: Schenkman, 1972), pp. 123–60; R[obert] M[orris], "Editor's Page," *Social Work* 10, no. 1 (Jan. 1965): 2; Social Workers for Community Projects, "NASW—Quick or Slow," *Social Work* 10, no. 2 (Apr. 1965): 126–27: W. Joseph Hefferman, Jr., "Political Action and Social Work Executives," *Social Work* 9, no. 2 (Apr. 1964): 18–23; Sargent Shriver, "Poverty in the United States—What Next?"

Social Welfare Forum, 1965 (New York: National Conference on Social Welfare, 1965), pp. 55–66; Charles F. Grosser, *New Directions in Community Organizing* (New York: Praeger, 1973), pp. 19–20, 107–8.

16. Richard A. Cloward and Frances Fox Piven, "Birth of a Movement," *Nation*, May 8, 1967, reprinted in Cloward and Piven, *The Politics of Turmoil* (New York: Pantheon, 1972), pp. 127–40; Grosser, pp. 92–93.

17. Naomi Harward, "Peace Corps: The Modern Hull House or a Threat to Professionalism?" *Social Work* 8, no. 4 (Oct. 1963): 11–17.

18. Interview with Florence Hollis, in Mary L. Gottesfeld and Mary E. Pharis, *Profiles in Social Work* (New York: Human Services Press, 1977), pp. 132–33.

19. A[lvin] L. S[chorr], "Editor's Page," *Social Work* 12, no. 3 (July 1967): 2; cf. James H. Dodson, "Professionalism, Not Membership," *Social Work* 12, no. 4 (Oct. 1967): 120–21.

20. Shriver, p. 58.

21. R[obert] M[orris], "Editor's Page," *Social Work* 11, no. 1 (Jan. 1966): 2.

22. Helen Rehr, "Problems for a Professional in a Strike Situation," *Social Work* 5, no. 2 (Apr. 1960): 22–28; letters, *Social Work* 5, no. 3 (July 1960): 110–16; Grosser, pp. 93–95; Milton Tambor, "The Social Worker as Worker: A Union Perspective," *Administration in Social Work* 3, no. 3 (1979): 289–300; Leslie B. Alexander and Milton D. Speizman, "The Union Movement in Voluntary Social Work," *Social Welfare Forum 1979* (New York: National Conference on Social Welfare, 1979), pp. 179–87; Elma Phillipson Cole, "Unions in Social Work," in National Association of Social Workers, *Encyclopedia of Social Work* 16 (1973), pp. 1507–11; Judith Transue, "Collective Bargaining on Whose Terms?" *Catalyst* 2, no. 1 (1980): 25–37.

23. Joseph E. Paul, "Recipients Aroused: The New Welfare Rights Movement," *Social Work* 12, no. 2 (Apr. 1967): 101–6; Cloward and Piven, "Birth of a Movement"; Frances Fox Piven and Richard A. Cloward, *Regulating the Poor* (New York: Vintage, 1971), pp. 320–40; Frances Fox Piven and Richard A. Cloward, *Poor People's Movements* (New York: Vintage, 1979), pp. 264–362; Grosser, pp. 86–96; T. George Silcott, "Social Welfare Priorities—A Minority View," *Social Welfare Forum, 1970* (New York: National Conference on Social Welfare, 1970), pp. 137–46. The critical Piven and Cloward paper was subsequently published as "A Strategy to End Poverty," *Nation*, May 2, 1966, pp. 510–17.

24. Grosser, p. 91.

25. Ibid. pp. 92–93.

26. George Brager, "Conflict on Campus," *Social Work* 12, no. 2 (Apr. 1967): 120–21; A[lvin] L. S[chorr], "Editor's Page," *Social Work* 14, no. 3 (July 1969): 2; John L. Erlich and John E. Tropman, "The Politics of Participation: Student Power," *Social Work* 14, no. 4 (Oct. 1969): 64–72; Arnulf M. Pins, "Changes in Social Work Education and Their Implications for Practice," *Social Work* 16, no. 2 (Apr. 1971): 5–15.

27. Erlich and Tropman, p. 68.

28. Charles L. Sanders, "Growth of the Association of Black Social Workers," *Social Casework* 51, no. 5 (May 1970): 277–84; Wayne Vasey, "The San Francisco Story," *Social Welfare Forum, 1968* (New York: National Conference on Social Welfare, 1968), pp. 156–63; John C. Kidneigh, "The New York Conference Story," *Social Welfare Forum, 1969* (New York: National Conference on Social Welfare, 1969), pp. 178–87; Howard E. Pruntz, "The New York Story—A Participant's Viewpoint," *Social Welfare Forum, 1969* (New York: National Conference on Social Welfare, 1969), pp. 185–92; Dan W. Dodson, "Institutionalized Racism in Social Welfare Agencies," *Social Welfare Forum, 1970* (New York: National Conference on Social Welfare, 1970), pp. 88–98; Howard E. Pruntz, "Chicago Scene II: Report from a Participant," *Social Welfare Forum, 1970* (New York: National Conference on Social Welfare, 1970), pp. 156–60. A sampling of issues raised early on by the new black presence in social work can be found in James A. Goodman, ed., *The Dynamics of Racism in Social Work Practice* (Washington, D.C.: National Association of Social Workers, 1973). Also see Joan Cole and Marc Pilisuk, "Differences in the Provision of Mental Health Services by Race," *American Journal of Orthopsychiatry* 46, no. 3 (July 1976): 510–25, and references in Chapter 8, note 22.

29. Pruntz, p. 192.

30. Alan Haber, "Issues Beyond Consensus," paper presented at the National Council for New Careers Organizing Conference, Detroit, 1968; Barbara Haber and Alan Haber, "Getting By with a Little Help from Our Friends," in Priscilla Long, ed., *The New Left* (Boston: Sargent, 1969), pp. 289–309; Erlich and Tropman, op. cit.; Ronald Gross and Paul Osterman, eds., *The New Professionals* (New York: Simon & Schuster, 1972); *Radicals in the Professions* (Ann Arbor, Mich.: Radical Education Project, 1967); *Radicals in the Professions Newsletter,* published by Radical Education Project, Ann Arbor, Mich., 1967–69; Barbara Ehrenreich and John Ehrenreich, *The American Health Empire* (New York: Random House, 1970), chap. 17.

31. Cloward and Epstein, op. cit., reviews these studies. Cf. Richard A. Mackey, "Professionalization and the Poor," *Social Work* 9, no. 4 (Oct. 1964): 108–10; Harry C. Bredemeier, "The Socially Handicapped and the Agencies: A Market Analysis," in Frank Riessman, Jerome Cohen, and Arthur Pearl, eds., *Mental Health of the Poor* (New York: Free Press, 1964), pp. 88–109; Greenleigh Associates, *Facts, Fallacies, and Futures: A Study of the Aid for Dependent Children Program of Cook County, Illinois* (New York: Greenleigh Associates, 1960), pp. 86–88.

32. The major studies through 1971 are reviewed in Joel Fischer, "Is Casework Effective? A Review," *Social Work* 18, no. 1 (Jan. 1973): 5–20. Contemporary responses to these studies include A[lvin] L. S[chorr], "Mirror, Mirror, on the Wall," *Social Work* 10, no. 3 (July 1965): 112–13; letters, *Social Work* 10, no. 4 (Oct. 1965): 136–38; Scott Briar, "The Casework Predicament," Social *Work* 13, no. 1 (Jan. 1968): 5–11; letters, *Social Work* 18, no. 2 (March 1973): 124–27; no. 3 (May 1973): 104–9; no. 2 (July 1973): 3–4, 104–10. Later reviews covering more recent studies of casework effectiveness are

Katherine Wood, "Casework Effectiveness: A New Look at the Research Evidence," *Social Work* 23 (Nov. 1978): 437–58; and William J. Reid and Patricia Hanrahan, "Recent Evaluations of Social Work: Grounds for Optimisim," *Social Work* 27, no. 4 (July 1982): 328–40. The latter, especially, is more optimistic as to the effectiveness of casework. For a more basic criticism of the methodological assumptions underlying such studies, see Ludwig L. Geismar and Katherine M. Wood, "Evaluating Practice: Science as Faith," *Social Casework* 63 (May 1982): 271; Roy Ruckdeschel and Buford E. Farris, "Science: Critical Faith or Dogmatic Ritual?" *Social Casework* 63 (May 1982):274; Frederick R. Hine, David Werman, and Dale Simpson, "Effectiveness of Psychotherapy: Problems of Research on Complex Phenomena," *American Journal of Psychiatry* 139 (Feb. 1982): 205; David Ingleby, "Understanding Mental Illness," in David Ingleby, ed., *Critical Psychiatry: The Politics of Mental Health* (New York: Pantheon, 1980), pp. 23–71.

33. Martin Rein, "Social Work in Search of a Radical Profession," *Social Work* 15, no. 2 (April 1970): 13–28; Jeffrey Galper, *Social Work Practice: A Radical Perspective* (Englewood Cliffs, N.J.: Prentice-Hall, 1980); Roy Bailey and Mike Brake, eds., *Radical Social Work* (New York: Pantheon, 1975).

34. See Chapter 6, notes 17–20.

35. George Brager, "Institutional Change: Perimeters of the Possible," *Social Work* 12, no. 1 (Jan. 1967): 59–69; George A. Brager, "Advocacy and Political Behavior," *Social Work* 13, no. 2 (Apr. 1968): 5–15; Briar, op. cit.; Charles Grosser, "Community Development Programs Serving the Urban Poor," *Social Work* 10, no. 3 (July 1965): 15–21; Henry Miller, "Value Dilemmas in Social Casework," *Social Work* 13, no. 1 (Jan. 1968): 27–33; Paul Terrell, "The Social Worker as Radical: The Role of Advocacy," *New Perspective: The Berkeley Journal of Social Welfare* 1 (Spring 1967): 83–88; Daniel Thursz, "Social Action as a Professional Responsibility," *Social Work* 11, no. 3 (July 1966): 12–21; Ad Hoc Committee on Advocacy, "The Social Worker as Advocate: Champion of Social Victims," *Social Work* 14, no. 2 (Apr. 1969): 16–22; David Wineman and Adrienne James, "The Advocacy Challenge to Schools of Social Work," *Social Work* 14, no. 2 (Apr. 1969): 23–32; Mary J. McCormick, "Social Advocacy: A New Dimension in Social Work," *Social Casework* 51 (Jan. 1970): 3–11.

36. Rein, p. 20.

37. Grosser, "Community Development Programs Serving the Urban Poor," pp. 18–19.

38. Andrew Billingsley, "Bureaucratic and Professional Orientation Patterns in Social Casework," *Social Service Review* 38 (Dec. 1964): 404–7; Barbara K. Varley, "Are Social Workers Dedicated to Service?" *Social Work* 11, no. 2 (Apr. 1966): 84–91.

39. Henry Miller, "Social Work in the Black Ghetto: The New Colonialism," *Social Work* 14, no. 3 (July 1969):65–76.

40. Briar, p. 5.

41. A[lvin] L. S[chorr], "Editor's Page," *Social Work* 11, no. 3 (July 1966): 2.

42. George Brager and John A. Michael, "The Sex Distribution in Social

Work: Causes and Consequences," *Social Casework* 50 (Dec. 1969): 595–601; WAR (Women of the American Revolution), "Letter to Our Sisters," in Robin Morgan, ed., *Sisterhood Is Powerful* (New York: Vintage, 1970), pp. 524–26; Aaron Rosenblatt, Eileen M. Turner, Adalene R. Patterson, and Clare K. Rolloson, "Predominance of Male Authors in Social Work Publications," *Social Casework* 51 (July 1970): 421–30; Barbara Stevens, "The Psychotherapist and Women's Liberation," *Social Work* 16, no. 3 (July 1971): 12–18; C. B. Scotch, "Sex Status in Social Work: Grist for Women's Liberation," *Social Work* 16, no. 3 (July 1971): 5–11; Janet Saltzman Chafetz, "Women in Social Work," *Social Work* 17, no. 5 (Sept. 1972): 12–18; Leatrice Hauptman, Janet Bruin, Virginia Burns, and Florence Field, "Women's Issues in Social Welfare," *Social Welfare Forum*, 1972, pp. 213–26; Jeanne M. Giovanni and Margaret E. Purvine, "The Myth of the Social Work Matriarchy," *Social Welfare Forum*, 1973, pp. 166–95; Mary S. Hanlan, "Women in Social Work Administration: Current Role Strains," *Administration in Social Work* 1, no. 3 (Fall 1977): 259–66; Felice Davidson Perlmutter and Leslie B. Alexander, "Racism and Sexism in Social Work Practice," *Administration in Social Work* 1, no. 4 (Winter 1977): 433–42. Mimi Abramovitz, "Social Work and Women's Liberation: A Mixed Reponse," *Catalyst* 1, no. 3 (1978): 91–104; Jacquelyn A. Sutton, "Sex Discrimination among Social Workers," *Social Work* 27, no. 3 (May 1982): 211–17; E. Howell and M. Bayes, eds., *Women and Mental Health* (New York: Basic Books, 1981).

43. Naomi Weisstein, "Psychology Constructs the Female," in Vivian Gornick and Barbara K. Moran, eds., *Women in Sexist Society* (New York: Basic Books, 1971); Phyllis Chesler, *Women and Madness* (Garden City, N.Y.: Doubleday, 1972); Inge K. Broverman, Donald M. Broverman, and Frank E. Clarkson, "Sex-Role Stereotypes and Clinical Judgments of Mental Health," *Journal of Consulting and Clinical Psychology* 34 (1970): 1–7. Additional references can be found in Abramovitz, noted 4–8.

44. Pruntz, op cit.; Helen Harris Perlman, "Casework and the 'Diminished Man,'" *Social Casework* 51, no. 4 (Apr. 1970): 216–24.

45. Robert Knickmeyer, "A Marxist Approach to Social Work," *Social Work* 17, no. 4 (July 1972): 58–65; Helen Shonick, "The Crisis in Social Work," *Social Work* 17, no. 4 (July 1972): 102–4; Harry Specht, "The Deprofessionalization of Social Work," *Social Work* 17, no. 2 (Mar. 1972): 3–15; A[lvin] L. S[chorr], "The Real Thing," *Social Work* 16, no. 3 (July 1971): 2; letters, *Social Work* 16, no. 3 (July 1971) and 17, no. 5 (Sept. 1972); special issue on ethnicity, *Social Work* 17, no. 3 (May 1972); James E. Craigen, "The Case for Activism in Social Work," *Social Welfare Forum, 1972* (New York: National Conference on Social Welfare, 1972), pp. 153–61; Piven and Cloward, *Regulating the Poor,* p. 338.

46. Charles D. Cowgen and Charles R. Atherton, "Social Control: A Rationale for Social Welfare," *Social Work* 19, no. 4 (1974): 456–62.

47. Mary E. Pharis, "Societies for Clinical Social Work," *Social Work* 18, no. 3 (May 1973): 99–103.

48. On the BSW issue, see Arthur J. Katz, "The View from 8th Avenue,"

Social Work Education Reporter 30, no. 2 (May 1982): 4. On job pressures see David Wagner and Marcia B. Cohen, "Social Workers, Class, and Professionalism," *Catalyst* 1, no. 1 (1978): 25–55. On the conferences on the knowledge base of clinical social work, see "Special Issue on Conceptual Frameworks," *Social Work* 22, no. 5 (Sept. 1977), and "Conceptual Frameworks II: Second Special Issue on Conceptual Frameworks," *Social Work* 26, no. 1 (Jan. 1981).

CHAPTER 8. *The Next Phase*

1. Jerald Shapiro, "Commitment to Disenfranchised Clients," in A. Rosenblatt and D. Waldfogel, eds., *Handbook of Clinical Social Work* (San Francisco: Jossey-Bass, 1983), p. 888.

2. Carol H. Meyer, *Social Work Practice: A Response to the Urban Crisis* (New York: Free Press, 1970), pp. 106–8.

3. Harold L. Wilensky and Charles N. Lebeaux, *Industrial Society and Social Welfare* (New York: Russell Sage Foundation, 1958).

4. Diane Pearce, "The Feminization of Poverty: Women, Work, and Welfare," *Urban and Social Change Review* 11 (Feb. 1978): 28–36. Cf. National Advisory Council on Economic Opportunity, *Final Report* (Washington, D.C.: U.S. Government Printing Office, 1981), pp. 7–32; Barbara Ehrenreich and Karin Stallard, "The Nouveau Poor," *ms.* 11, no. 1–2 (July–Aug. 1982): 217; Karin Stallard, Barbara Ehrenreich, and Holly Sklar, *Poverty in the American Dream: Women and Children First* (Boston: Institute for New Communications and South End Press, 1983).

5. National Advisory Council on Economic Opportunity, *Final Report.*

6. Ibid.

7. Frank Ackerman, *Reaganomics: Rhetoric vs. Reality* (Boston: South End Press, 1982); Barry Bluestone and Bennett Harrison, *The Deindustrialization of America* (New York: Basic Books, 1982); Tom Christoffel, "The Permanent Job Shortage," in Tom Christoffel, David Finkelhor, and Dan Gilbarg, eds., *Against the American Myth* (New York: Holt, Rinehart and Winston, 1970), pp. 259–75.

8. Unless otherwise noted, statistics in this chapter are from U.S. Department of Commerce, *Historical Statistics of the United States, Colonial Times to 1970* (Washington, D.C.: U.S. Government Printing Office, 1975), and U.S. Department of Commerce, *Statistical Abstract of the United States* (Washington, D.C.: U.S. Government Printing Office, various dates).

9. John Ehrenreich, "Adding Up the Unemployed," *Nation,* July 25–Aug. 1, 1981, p. 1.

10. Barbara Ehrenreich and John Ehrenreich, *The American Health Empire* (New York: Random House, 1970), chaps. 7 and 8.

11. Frances Fox Piven and Richard A. Cloward, *Regulating the Poor* (New York: Vintage, 1971), esp. pp. 341–48.

12. Neil Gilbert, "The Transformation of Social Services," *Social Service Review* 51 (1977): 625–41.

13. Ibid.; Charles L. Schultz, *The Public Use of Private Interest* (Washington, D.C.: Brookings Institution, 1977); Paul Terrell, "Private Alternatives to Public Human Services Administration," *Social Service Review* 53 (Mar. 1979): 56–74; Arnold S. Relman, "The New Medical-Industrial Complex," *New England Journal of Medicine* 303 (1980): 963–70; Suzanne Sankar, "Contracting Out: Attrition of State Employees," in Union of Radical Political Economists, *Crisis in the Public Sector* (New York: Monthly Review Press, n.d.), pp. 275–80; Richard K. Ghere, "Effects of Service Delivery Variations on Administration of Municipal Human Services: The Contract Approach vs. Agency Implementation," *Administration in Social Work* 5, no. 1 (Spring 1981): 65–78; Ann Withorn, *The Circle Game: Services for the Poor in Massachusetts, 1966–78* (Amherst, Mass.: University of Massachusetts Press, 1982); Louanne Kennedy, "Hospitals in Chains: The Transformation of American Hospitals," *Health PAC Bulletin* 12 (no. 7) (1981): 9; Louanne Kennedy, "Voluntary Compulsions: The Transformation of American Hospitals II," *Health PAC Bulletin* 12, (no. 8) (1982): 11; Paul Starr, *The Social Transformation of American Medicine* (New York: Basic Books, 1982), pp. 420–49; Sheila B. Kammerman, "The New Mixed Economy of Welfare: Public and Private," *Social Work* 28 (Jan.–Feb. 1983): 5–10; "Hospitals for Profit," *Dollars and Sense,* no. 89 (Sept. 1983): 6–8; "Report Says Hospital Chains Rely on High Fees for Profits," *New York Times,* Aug. 11, 1983, p. A-14.

14. *New York Times,* July 19, 1983.

15. Robert Castel, Françoise Castel, and Anne Lovell, *The Psychiatric Society* (New York: Columbia University Press, 1982), p. 96.

16. Sankar, op. cit.

17. Ehrenreich and Ehrenreich, chaps. 3–6, 14, 15; Ghere, op. cit.

18. For the argument that poverty is no longer a major problem, see Martin Anderson, *Welfare* (Palo Alto, Calif.: Hoover Institution Press, 1978). Critiques of this position are in Michael Harrington, *Decade of Decision* (New York: Simon & Schuster, 1980), pp. 222–55, and National Advisory Council on Economic Opportunity, *Final Report,* pp. 33–54. On mental health services and the poor, see Shapiro, op. cit., and Raymond P. Lorion, "Mental Health and the Disadvantaged," *Social Policy* 8, no. 1 (May/June 1977): 17–27.

19. *New York Times,* Aug. 3, 1983, p. A-1.

20. *New York Times,* July 24, 1983, p. E-22.

21. Stallard, Ehrenreich, and Sklar, op. cit.

22. A useful review of these issues for the case of the white professional and the black client is Alex Gitterman and Alice Schaeffer, "The White Professional and the Black Client," *Social Casework* 53 (May 1972): 280–91. Also see George P. Banks, "The Effects of Race on One-to-One Helping Interviews," *Social Service Review* 45, no. 2 (June 1971): 137–44; Alfred Kadushin, "The Racial Factor in the Interview," *Social Work* 17, no. 3 (May

1972): 88–98; "Special Issue: Social Work and People of Color," *Social Work* 27, no. 1 (Jan. 1982); special issue on social work with Puerto Ricans, *Social Casework* 55 (Feb. 1974); Armando Morales, "Social Work with Third World People," *Social Work* 26, no. 1 (Jan. 1981): 45–51; James A. Goodman, ed., *The Dynamics of Racism in Social Work Practice* (Washington, D.C.: National Association of Social Workers, 1973); Barbara Bryant Solomon, "Value Issues in Working with Minority Clients," in Aaron Rosenblatt and Diana Waldvogel, eds., *Handbook of Clinical Social Work* (San Francisco: Jossey-Bass, 1983); Sonia Badillo Ghali, "Culture Sensitivity and the Puerto Rican Client," *Social Casework* 58 (Oct. 1977): 459–68; Braulio Montalvo, "Home-School Conflict and the Puerto Rican Child," *Social Casework* 55 (Feb. 1974): 100–10.

23. Paul Ylvisaker, "Working Session on Centralization and Decentralization," *Daedalus* 96 (Summer 1967): 682, cited in Meyer, p. 96. King is cited in Piven and Cloward, p. 246.

24. Cf. among others, Arthur Maglin, "Social Values and Psychotherapy," *Catalyst* 1, no. 3 (1978): 69–79; Stephen M. Rose, *The Betrayal of the Poor* (Cambridge, Mass.: Schenkman, 1972); Carol Gilligan, *In a Different Voice* (Cambridge: Harvard University Press, 1982); Karl Figlio, "Sinister Medicine: A Critique of Left Approaches to Medicine," *Radical Science Journal* no. 9 (1979): 14–68; Marc Renaud, "On the Structural Constraints to State Intervention in Health," *International Journal of Health Services* 5, no. 4 (1975): 559–72.

25. For these and similar formulations, see Gordon Hamilton, *Theory and Practice of Social Casework* (New York: Columbia University Press, 1940); Florence Hollis, *Casework: A Psychosocial Theory* (New York: Random House, 1964); Carel B. Germain, ed., *Social Work Practice: People and Environments.* (New York: Columbia University Press, 1979).

26. On race and self-identity, see Leon Chestang, "Character Development in a Hostile Environment," *Occasional Paper No. 3*, University of Chicago School of Social Service Administration, Nov. 1972; Ronald L. Taylor, "Psychosocial Development among Black Children and Youth: A Reexamination," *American Journal of Orthopsychiatry* 46 (Jan. 1976): 4–19; Barbara E. Shannon, "The Impact of Racism on Personality Development," *Social Casework* 54 (Nov. 1973): 519–25; Madison Foster and Lorraine R. Perry, "Self-Valuation among Blacks," *Social Work* 27, no. 1 (Jan. 1982): 60–67; Dorcas Bowles, "The Development of the Ethnic Self-Representation Unit," mimeographed (Smith College School for Social Work, 1982). On class and self-identity, see Jonathan Cobb and Richard Sennett, *The Hidden Injuries of Class* (New York: Vintage, 1972); Lillian Rubin, *Worlds of Pain* (New York: Basic Books, 1976); Sandy Carter, "Class Conflict: The Hidden Dimension," in Pat Walker, ed., *Between Labor and Capital* (Boston: South End Press, 1979). On gender and self-identity, see Nancy Chodorow, *The Reproduction of Mothering* (Berkeley: University of California Press, 1978); Carol Gilligan, *In a Different Voice* (Cambridge: Harvard University Press, 1982).

27. Cf. Abraham Kardiner, *Psychological Frontiers of Society* (New York:

Columbia University Press, 1946); John W. Whiting and Irving Child, *Childhood Training and Personality* (New Haven, Conn.: Yale University Press, 1953).

28. Jane Addams, *Twenty Years at Hull House* (New York: Signet 1960), chap. 16; Wini Breines, *Community and Organization in the New Left, 1952–1968: The Great Refusal* (New York: Praeger, 1982), esp. chaps. 3 and 4.

Index

Ackerman, Nathan, 74–75
Addams, Jane, 34–35, 39, 40, 63, 82–83, 233; mentioned, 9, 60, 62, 67, 203
Affirmative Action Order, 163, 183, 184
Agricultural Adjustment Administration (AAA), 89–90, 95
American Association of Social Workers (AASW), 58, 78, 102–4, 108–14
American Federation of Labor (AFL), 25, 87, 93–94
American Medical Association, 48, 97
Association of Black Social Workers, 199
Atherton, Charles R., 207
Austin, Lucille, 133; mentioned, 125
automobiles, 50, 145–46

Baer, George, 24
Baldwin, Roger, 82
Beers, Clifford, 65–66
Bell, Daniel, 152
Bernstein, Irving, 85
blacks: civil rights movement of, 155–57, 161–64; as clients of white social workers, 199, 201; and education, 150; family structure of, 165–66, 202–3; and Great Society programs, 221; improvement in conditions of, 181; migration to cities of, 22–23, 46–47, 145–46, 149–50, 181; and the New Deal, 100; in the 1980s, 222; and 1960s social reform, 209; politicization of, 46–47, 149–51, 152, 163, 215; in post-WWII labor force, 148–49;

and poverty, 165–66; and racism, 41, 46; as social workers, 193, 198–200; unemployment among, 149; after WWI, 46–47
Bonus Marchers, 88
Brager, George, 172–73, 204
Briar, Scott, 203
Brown v. *Board of Education*, 156
Bruno, Frank, 106–7
Burns, Eveline, 189
business, 14, 140; and blacks, 150; during the Depression, 98, 105; in the latter nineteenth century, 22–23; and the New Deal, 91; and 1960s antipoverty programs, 171; and the Reagan administration, 185–86; and reform, 37

Candler, Asa, 24
Cannon, Mary Antoinette, 187
capitalism: and consumerism, 53, 67; efforts to stabilize, 19–20, 28, 30–31, 33–34, 42, 43–44, 54–55; in the Progressive Era, 36–38, 42; and social work, 54, 76, 105; turn-of-century crisis of, 27, 32; and women, 34
Carnegie, Andrew, 23, 25; mentioned, 36
Carnegie Foundation, 30, 58
Carter, Jimmy, 184
casework: beginnings of, 60, 63–65; Bertha Reynolds's discussion of, 118–19; diagnostic school of, 131–35; functional school of, 124–31, 133–38;

Index

Index

Truman, Harry, 140, 155
Tugwell, Rex, 90–91, 106; mentioned, 104

unemployment: among blacks, 149; in the Depression, 86, 87–88, 91–92, 99, 100, 104; effect of government spending on, 92; fear of after WWII, 146–47; and the federal government since the Depression, 96, 140; and the Kennedy administration, 161; and the New Deal, 97, 99, 220–21; in the 1980s, 215–18; in the 1950s, 142; in the 1920s, 48; vs. nonemployment, 216–17; and WWII, 139
unemployment compensation, 97, 99, 155
unions: attacks on in the 1920s, 48, 52; during the Depression, 87, 93–94, 95–96; and immigrants, 21, 87; and McCarthyism, 141; and the New Deal, 95–96, 221; in the 1950s and 1960s, 155; objects of, 224–25; and post-WWI Red Scare, 48; of social workers, 111–14, 117, 120, 187, 193–95, 208, 230; during WWI, 44; during WWII, 139–40
upper classes, 24, 55–56, 68, 75
urbanization, 20–21

Vanderbilt, William, 23
Van Kleeck, Mary, 104–5, 106, 117; mentioned, 34
Van Waters, Miriam, 10, 75
veterans, 69–70, 88, 140, 144, 146–47
Veterans Administration, 144
Vietnam War, 99, 178, 180, 182, 221
VISTA (Volunteers in Service to America), 169
Voting Rights Act, 163, 181

Wagner, Robert, 179
Wagner Act, 95–96, 97
War Labor Board, 44
War on Poverty, 10, 163, 167–82, 193; reasons for failures of, 176–80; successes of, 180–82; theoretical basis for, 227. *See also* Economic Opportunity Act; Great Society
Weaver, James B., 26
Weiner, Hyman J., 189

Weldon, Beulah, 81–82
welfare capitalism, 52
welfare rights movement, 191–92, 195–97
welfare state, 38, 42, 95–101, 131, 224; decline of during Reagan administration, 211–13; expansion of under Johnson, 163, 182; expansion of under Kennedy, 161, 182; origins of, 195–98; after WWII, 143
West, Walter, 109
Whyte, William F., 152
Wilensky, Harold, 211
Wilson, Sloan, 152
Wilson, Woodrow, 37, 38; mentioned, 36, 90
Wines, Frederick H., 61
Wobblies, 25–26
Wofford, John G., 177–78
women: and capitalism, 34; and Great Society programs, 221; increasing political independence of, 215; job-market discrimination against, 164, 214, 223–24; in the labor force, 51, 146–47; low status of, 56–57; and the New Deal, 101; in the 1980s, 222–23; and poverty, 213–14, 222–23; in the Progressive Era, 34–35, 40; in social work, 35, 55, 61, 81, 200–201, 203–5; and unions, 87
women's liberation movement, 173, 182, 183–84, 199, 203–5
working class: attempts to control, 30–34, 39–40, 42; and blacks, 151; child rearing in, 68; failure of to challenge capitalism, 32–33, 146; and industrialization, 32; in the 1920s, 52; politicization of during the Depression, 94, 96, 97; at the turn of the century, 23–26
Work Projects Administration (WPA), 96; mentioned, 99, 106
World War I, 44, 46, 51–52
World War II, 139–40

Yarmolinsky, Adam, 167
Yerkes, Robert M., 123
Yezierska, Anzia, 39
Ylvisaker, Paul, 224
Young Lords, 173
youth, in the mid-1950s, 152–53

Library of Congress Cataloging in Publication Data

Ehrenreich, John, 1943–
    The altruistic imagination.

    Bibliography: p.
    Includes index.
    1. Social service—United States—History.   2. United States—Social
policy—History.   I. Title.
HV91.E38   1985   361.3'0973   84-45807
ISBN 0-8014-1764-3 (alk. paper)